A Timely Look Back at the Era That Shaped Our World

Thousands of years of recorded history show that the main way in which human societies have been organized is as empires. Today, the evidence of recent European overseas empire's lasting effects is all around us: from international frontiers and fusion cuisine to multiplying apologies for colonial misdeeds. *European Overseas Empire, 1879–1999: A Short History* explores the major events in this critical period that continue to inform and affect our world today.

New access to archives and a renewed interest in the most recent era of European overseas empire building and the decolonization that followed have produced a wealth of fascinating information that has recharged perennial debates and shed new light on topics previously considered settled. At the same time, current events are once again beginning to echo the past, bringing historical perspective into the spotlight to guide our actions going forward. This book examines our collective past, providing new insight and fresh perspectives as it:

- Traces current events to their roots in the European overseas imperialism of the 19th and 20th centuries
- Challenges the notion of political, cultural, social, and economic exchanges of the era as being primarily "Europe-outward"
- Examines the complexity and contingency of colonial rule, and the range of outcomes for the various territories involved
- Explores the power dynamics of overseas empires, and their legacies that continue to shape the world today

Matthew G. Stanard is Associate Professor and Department Chair of History at Berry College. He is the author of *Selling the Congo: A History of European Pro-Empire Propaganda and the Making of Belgian Imperialism* (2011) and coauthor of *European Empires and the People: Popular Responses to Imperialism in France, Britain, the Netherlands, Belgium, Germany, and Italy* (2011).

WILEY SHORT HISTORIES
General Editor: Catherine Epstein

This series provides concise, lively introductions to key topics in history. Designed to encourage critical thinking and an engagement in debate, the books demonstrate the dynamic process through which history is constructed, in both popular imagination and scholarship. The volumes are written in an accessible style, offering the ideal entry point to the field.

Published
A History of the Cuban Revolution, 2nd edition
Aviva Chomsky

Vietnam: Explaining America's Lost War, 2nd edition
Gary R. Hess

A History of Modern Europe: From 1815 to the Present
Albert S. Lindemann

Perspectives on Modern South Asia: A Reader in Culture, History, and Representation
Kamala Visweswaran

Nazi Germany: Confronting the Myths
Catherine Epstein

World War I: A Short History
Tammy M. Proctor

European Overseas Empire, 1879–1999: A Short History
Matthew G. Stanard

European Overseas Empire, 1879–1999

A Short History

Matthew G. Stanard

WILEY Blackwell

This edition first published 2018
© 2018 John Wiley & Sons, Inc.

All rights reserved. No part of this publication may be reproduced, stored in a retrieval system, or transmitted, in any form or by any means, electronic, mechanical, photocopying, recording or otherwise, except as permitted by law. Advice on how to obtain permission to reuse material from this title is available at http://www.wiley.com/go/permissions.

The right of Matthew G. Stanard to be identified as the author of this work has been asserted in accordance with law.

Registered Office
John Wiley & Sons, Inc., 111 River Street, Hoboken, NJ 07030, USA
John Wiley & Sons Ltd, The Atrium, Southern Gate, Chichester, West Sussex, PO19 8SQ, UK

Editorial Office
101 Station Landing, Medford, MA 02155, USA

For details of our global editorial offices, customer services, and more information about Wiley products visit us at www.wiley.com.

Wiley also publishes its books in a variety of electronic formats and by print-on-demand. Some content that appears in standard print versions of this book may not be available in other formats.

Limit of Liability/Disclaimer of Warranty
While the publisher and authors have used their best efforts in preparing this work, they make no representations or warranties with respect to the accuracy or completeness of the contents of this work and specifically disclaim all warranties, including without limitation any implied warranties of merchantability or fitness for a particular purpose. No warranty may be created or extended by sales representatives, written sales materials or promotional statements for this work. The fact that an organization, website, or product is referred to in this work as a citation and/or potential source of further information does not mean that the publisher and authors endorse the information or services the organization, website, or product may provide or recommendations it may make. This work is sold with the understanding that the publisher is not engaged in rendering professional services. The advice and strategies contained herein may not be suitable for your situation. You should consult with a specialist where appropriate. Further, readers should be aware that websites listed in this work may have changed or disappeared between when this work was written and when it is read. Neither the publisher nor authors shall be liable for any loss of profit or any other commercial damages, including but not limited to special, incidental, consequential, or other damages.

Library of Congress Catalog Number: 2017049159

Hardback: 9781119130109
Paperback: 9781119130116

Cover Design: Wiley
Cover Images: (Front cover) SierraLeoneHofstra3.1.tiff by Sjoerd Hofstra, 1898–1983 [Collection Hofstra, African Studies Centre, Leiden (The Netherlands)] is licensed under CC BY-SA; (Back cover) © OnstOn/iStockphoto

Set in 10/12.5pt Bembo by SPi Global, Pondicherry, India

Printed in Singapore by C.O.S. Printers Pte Ltd

Contents

List of Illustrations	vii
Acknowledgements	ix
List of Selected Abbreviations	xi
Introduction	1
1 The Nineteenth-Century Context	11
2 The Civilizing Mission and the Race for Empire, 1879–1902	33
3 Resistance and Consolidation, 1902–1912	67
4 Empires at War, 1912–1922	87
5 The Colonial Era, 1922–1931	109
6 World War II, 1931–1945	131
7 Unfinished and Finished Empires, 1945–1958	153
8 Decolonization's Second Wave, 1958–1975	181
9 Empire After Imperialism: 1975–1999 and Beyond	201
Index	223

List of Illustrations

Maps

Map 1.1	Real control? The French occupation of Algeria, 1830–1956	29
Map 2.1	European claims in Africa: ca. 1879 and 1914	45
Map 4.1	Colonial troop movements during World War I	97

Figures

Figure 1.1	Vasily Vereshchagin, *Blowing from Guns in British India* (1880s)	22
Figure 3.1	Édouard Manduau, *La Civilisation au Congo* (1884)	72
Figure 3.2	Hanoi's Pont Doumer, around 1912	77
Figure 4.1	*Spahis* from Morocco in Ribecourt, France, around 1915–1920	97
Figure 4.2	Grave of Nedjimi Bouzid Ben Tayeb in Saint-Charles de Potyze Military Cemetery	98
Figure 5.1	Gandhi with Jawaharlal Nehru during a meeting of the All India Congress, July 1946	112
Figure 5.2	Omar Mukhtar under arrest in Benghazi, Libya, September 1931	126
Figure 7.1	Vietnamese refugees leaving a French ship for USS *Montague*, August 1954	161
Figure 8.1	Nelson Mandela burning his pass in front of press photographers, 1960	195
Figure 9.1	Statue of Leopold II in Brussels, Belgium, with wreaths, December 2009	218

Acknowledgements

It is a pleasure to recognize those who have helped bring this book to fruition. A first thank you goes to Catherine Epstein for suggesting the book to me and for her valuable input, and to Peter Coveney for getting the project underway. It was a pleasure to work with Haze Humbert and her team at Wiley-Blackwell. Thanks is due also to the anonymous readers who provided feedback on the original book proposal and those others who read and commented on a draft manuscript.

I still gain much inspiration from my graduate school advisor, the late Bill Cohen, as well as the many others who guided me while at Indiana University-Bloomington, including Jim Diehl, Phyllis Martin, George Alter, Carl Ipsen, George Brooks, David Pace, Jim Madison, and Dror Wahrman. At Bloomington, I had the good fortune to meet the prolific Jason Lantzer, and his encouragement and advice has been invaluable for years now. For inspiration, support, and friendship, I thank Mike Campbell, Nigel Dalziel, Zana Aziza Etambala, Rick Fogarty, Vincent Grégoire, Jim Le Sueur, John MacKenzie, Chad Parker, Jody Prestia, Berny Sèbe, Martin Thomas, Patricia Van Schuylenbergh, Guy Vanthemsche, Jean-Luc Vellut, Jason Vuic, and Kara Dixon Vuic. I benefited greatly from the camaraderie and intellectual stimulation of a National History Center Decolonization Seminar in Washington, D.C., an experience that fed into this project in significant ways. My thanks to Wm. Roger Louis, Philippa Levine, John Darwin, Jason Parker, Pillarisetti Sudhir, and all my fellow 2011 Decolonization Seminar participants.

Several people had a more direct hand in the production of this book, including my student research assistant Beth Anne DeKeizer, who provided important feedback. A book such as this would be impossible to write were it not for the numerous incredibly rich works of history on which it is based. The reader will find in the footnotes and chapter bibliographies many key studies that were

Acknowledgements

particularly valuable in the preparation of this book. I must also highlight the assistance of Larry Marvin and Jason Vuic, both of whom generously read an early draft of the manuscript, and whose input was invaluable. Jacqueline Harvey did a fantastic job copy-editing the final manuscript. Of course, any shortcomings or mistakes in the book are my responsibility alone.

My home institution of Berry College has been unfailingly supportive. Dean Tom Kennedy has provided generous funding and encouragement over the years. A number of Berry College Faculty Development Grants and Summer Stipends have underwritten my research and writing, including a 2016 Summer Research Stipend that allowed me to set aside the entire summer for writing. I owe a particularly fond debt of gratitude to my cherished colleagues Jon Atkins, Larry Marvin, Christy Snider, and Jen Hoyt, whose support is constant, and with whom it is simultaneously humbling and delightful to work.

Thank you to my parents and to my brothers and their beautiful families for their endless cheer and support. My Spanish family not only tolerated me while writing this book, they sustained me. As to my wife Noemi and my sons Marlon and Ivan, words fail to express my love and my gratitude. I thank them for their constant support.

List of Selected Abbreviations

AEF	Afrique Équatoriale Française (French Equatorial Africa)
ANC	African National Congress
ANZAC	Australia and New Zealand Auxiliary Corps
AOF	Afrique Occidentale Française (French West Africa)
CAF	Central African Federation
CFS	État Indépendant du Congo (Congo Free State)
EIC	(British) East India Company
FLN	Front de Libération Nationale (National Liberation Front)
FRELIMO	Frente de Libertação de Moçambique (Mozambique Liberation Front)
IBEAC	Imperial British East Africa Company
OAS	Organisation Armée Secrète (Secret Army Organization)
PAC	Pan-Africanist Congress
PPA	Parti Populaire Algérien (Algerian Popular Party)
RDA	Rassemblement Démocratique Africain (African Democratic Rally)
VOC	Vereenigde Oostindische Compagnie (United East India Company)

Introduction

Many books have been written about nineteenth- and twentieth-century European overseas imperialism, and some may argue that that there are more pressing historical subjects, such as the history of globalization, of terrorism, or of global warming and the environment. In today's world of nation-states and non-state actors like the United Nations, non-governmental organizations, and Daesh (so-called Islamic State, or ISIS), empire might seem to some like ancient history. In the year this author was born, 1973, there remained just one European colonial empire of any significance, namely that of the Portuguese in Angola, Portuguese Guinea, and Mozambique, and it was limping toward its ignominious end. Why another book on imperialism?

Surveying thousands of years of recorded history reveals that empire in its various guises has been the primary way in which human societies have been organized, for better and for worse. Although our twenty-first-century world is one of nation-states, we should not let our familiarity with nation-states lead us to conclude that they were "natural" or inevitable, meaning that we need to explore how they came about. Another reason to take up empire as a subject of study is because we can neither understand how things have changed over the past 200 years, nor fully grasp contemporary history and current events, without having some understanding of recent European imperialism and its consequences. There is evidence everywhere of how colonialism and decolonization profoundly reshaped the world: in the debate over the United Kingdom leaving the European Union (popularly known as "Brexit"); in international frontiers; in Daesh propaganda; in cuisine; in ongoing tensions between India and Pakistan, or China and Japan; in the multiplying government apologies for colonial

European Overseas Empire, 1879–1999: A Short History, First Edition. Matthew G. Stanard.
© 2018 John Wiley & Sons, Inc. Published 2018 by John Wiley & Sons, Inc.

misdeeds; and so forth. Not only did European imperialism affect places that were colonized; it also reshaped Europe, and was intertwined with other world-changing historical developments, including industrialization, globalization, both world wars, and the creation of the United Nations.

There are other important reasons that make this a good time to turn to the study of imperialism, one being the recent renewed scholarly interest in the history of empire, which has led to a slew of fascinating work reshaping our understanding of the past. There have also been exciting recent discoveries. A certain time period, sometimes decades, is often required before researchers are granted access to archives, which remain the main source of evidence for historians. Many such restrictions are now lapsing, giving researchers access to documents that improve our historical understanding.

In some ways, greater distance from the colonial era allows us to better grasp its history and its actors on their own terms. It may seem paradoxical that being further distant from past events enables us to better understand them. But the politics of imperialism and decolonization often colored past histories. Early studies debated why a new wave of empire began in the late nineteenth century in the first place. Many of them identifed European industrial and financial capitalism as a cause, an interpretation that was given new life by the Cold War competition between capitalism and communism. The persistence of European colonial rule shaped historical studies in the first half of the twentieth century: they often focused on colonial administration, military conquest, and Europe's "expansion" by means of overseas political control, infrastructure development, Christian missionaries, and the spread of European technology, culture, and languages. The history of empire waned as emphasis shifted during the decolonization era to the study of resistance and the precolonial origins of African and Asian nations, which legitimized newly independent states. The history of empire has come roaring back since the mid-1990s as scholars have adopted new approaches and uncovered subtler aspects of empire, including gender, race, culture, and colonial knowledge. Younger generations of historians – few directly implicated in this history – are exploring the legal history of empire, colonial policing, empire's effects on Europe and its cultures, migration, colonies and the two world wars, and the United States and empire. Decolonization, only recently a "current event," has now become a field of history in its own right. All this said, even if greater distance in time allows us to study imperialism more dispassionately, as students of history we must remain attuned to present-day biases and our personal predispositions.

The years 1879 and 1999 bookend the story told here. The late 1870s witnessed a hastening of overseas expansionism that led to an era of European global dominance and the decline of other powers, most notably the Turkish Ottoman empire and the Manchu Qing empire. This book examines European overseas conquests and formal colonial rule through the first half of the 1900s,

Introduction

into the era of decolonization, and then through independence following World War II. The year 1999, the book's chronological end point, saw Portugal formally relinquish Macau to China after nearly four and a half centuries of Portuguese rule. Today there remains only a very small number of tiny areas subject to any kind of colonial status, even if the legacies of the colonial era live on innumerable ways.

A Word about Words

What is "empire" exactly? What is a colony? Are imperialism and colonialism the same thing? Is there a difference between decolonization and independence? It is worthwhile defining at the outset several terms that recur throughout the book.

Definitions depend on whom you ask, and when, as well as where you are from and the languages you speak. To many in the United States, terms like "colonial history" or the "colonial era" evoke an American history, namely the years from the first European settlements in North America down to the Revolutionary War. Ask someone from India, Senegal, or Indonesia about the "colonial era," and you are likely to get three different responses, none having much to do with the United States. In France, the term *l'impérialisme français* generally refers to empire building in Europe, primarily under Napoleon Bonaparte. *L'empire colonial* refers to France's overseas empire, from its "old" colonies in the Caribbean, the Americas, and south Asia to those of the nineteenth and twentieth centuries in Africa, the Indian Ocean, southeast Asia, and Oceania. In a US history context the term "empire" can refer to British rule in North America, US overseas rule in Hawai'i and the Philippines, informal US influence in Latin America, or the even more nebulous but no less real global power wielded by the United States after World War II, especially after 1989. Such examples can be multiplied. Complicating the matter is the fact that all these terms refer to human concepts whose meanings have changed over time. "Colony" as the Puritans of the Mayflower would have known the concept differs from how Queen Victoria would have understood it, just as both differ from how a historian would understand the term today.

The term "empire" dates back millennia, to at least the Romans, whose rulers – first under the republic, then under the empire after around 27 BCE – exercised *imperium*, or "the power to get things done," including command over non-Romans and their lands. An empire is a form of political control where one people commands other states, peoples, or lands, and where there is a power differential such that the state or people in control enjoys greater authority, prestige, rights, or other advantages than subject peoples. Scholars often use the term "metropole" to refer to the country or state exercising power over foreign peoples and lands, which avoids gender-loaded terms such as "mother country" or "fatherland." As we shall see, the division between metropole and colony was not as clear as we might have first thought.

From the word "empire" come the terms "imperialism" and "imperialistic." Use of the term "imperialism" in any modern sense dates back only to the mid-nineteenth century, when British critics of Emperor Napoleon III of France accused him of engaging in "imperialism," a seemingly strange accusation today considering that Britain ruled a huge empire at the time. What these critics meant was that Napoleon was engaging in aggressive, militaristic, and nationalistic tactics to extend France's influence abroad. By the end of the century, detractors of empire in Britain itself used the term to attack British overseas rule. "Imperialism" refers to the practice of conquering abroad to create and rule an empire. "Imperialistic," an adjective, makes reference to an attitude or mindset that is in favor of imperialism.

"Colonialism" is oftentimes used interchangeably with the term "imperialism" – and will be at times in this book – even though the former often has a more specific connotation deriving from the word "colony," which itself has multiple meanings. One kind of colony comprises a group of people that leaves one place to settle in a distant land, and who then remain free of formal control of their country of origin. Ancient Greeks who departed the area around the Aegean Sea to establish settlements around the Mediterranean are an example of this, as is, more recently, the "colony" of Italians who settled in New York City from the late 1800s. A colony can also be such a settlement that remains controlled by the land from which the colonists originated. By 241 BCE, the Roman Republic had established its first province in Sicily, for instance. More recent examples are Virginia and Australia, founded as British colonies in 1607 and 1788, respectively. A third type of colony is a territory conquered by a foreign power and placed in a subservient relationship within that power's empire, but that, for whatever reason, is not settled by large numbers of people from the metropole. A good example is Italian Somaliland, a territory on the Horn of Africa of some one million souls by the 1920s, very few of whom were Italian: a 1931 census revealed 1,631 Italians living there, some 0.16 percent of the population. A "colonist" is someone from a colonizing power who settles in a foreign or colonized land, a "colonizer" someone who engages in conquest and foreign rule, and the "colonized" those people subject to colonization, that is, indigenous people (natives) ruled over by foreigners and oftentimes dispossessed of their lands.

To "colonize" (noun: "colonization") usually refers to setting up a colony, that is, taking and populating lands. "Colonialism," by contrast, often refers either to colonization or more generally to engaging in the practice of empire. This book emphasizes a major distinction, namely between "colonies" controlled by a metropole yet overwhelmingly populated by indigenous peoples, and "settler

Introduction

colonies," lands where colonists took land for settlement. Good examples of the latter are Korea under Japanese rule from 1910 to 1945, during which time tens of thousands of Japanese settlers snapped up arable land, and French Algeria, where hundreds of thousands of Europeans had settled by the 1950s.

Other important terms include the "New Imperialism," the "new imperial history," "late colonialism," and the "late colonial state." Some referred to the wave of late nineteenth-century empire building as the New Imperialism, to distinguish it from the earlier era of European overseas empire building dating back to the sixteenth century, which followed Christopher Columbus's voyages. Lately, scholars have taken to using the term "new imperial history" to refer to recent work that integrates the history of Europe with that of Europe's overseas imperialism, which were traditionally treated as distinct subjects. Some use the term "late colonialism" to refer to European empire across the nineteenth and twentieth centuries, to distinguish it from the seaborne empires dating back to the era of Columbus. Others refer to the "late colonial state" when talking about empire during the post-World War II era. In this book, concerned as it is with the period from the late nineteenth through the twentieth century, the terms "late colonialism," "late imperialism," and "late colonial" make reference to the last few decades of formal empire, roughly the post-World War II period.

Then there are the terms "decolonization," "transfer of power," "independence," and "neocolonialism," which refer to the end of empire and its aftermath. As scholar Stuart Ward has shown, the term decolonization is of recent vintage, referring to the retreat of empire in the twentieth century. Neocolonialism refers to the continuation or reimposition of imperial relations between a more powerful state – perhaps an erstwhile metropole – and a former colony that has achieved political independence but not autonomy in all realms. The Belgian approach toward the Belgian Congo's independence in 1960 provides a good illustration. When in the late 1950s Congolese began to agitate for change, Belgian officials embraced rapid decolonization because they believed the Congo was so unprepared for independence that it would remain dependent upon them for their expertise. Then, as Belgians negotiated independence in 1960, they undermined the soon to be independent Congolese state diplomatically, financially, and economically. Belgian leaders were willing to accede to Congo's wish for formal independence, but they were also determined to remain the real masters there. All this said, some observers of international relations have misappropriated the term "neocolonialism" to refer to any unbalanced power relations within or between states – not dissimilar to the overuse of the term "fascist" – with the inevitable result of watering down its meaning. This book will hew to a strict definition of neocolonialism.

Introduction

People have similarly appropriated the term "postcolonial" to the point that it is a word that risks meaning everything and nothing. In a narrow sense, "postcolonial" refers to something that follows the colonial era chronologically. Thus events in Nigeria following political independence from Britain in 1960 can be considered postcolonial. But postcolonialism also makes reference to an interpretive stance toward history, literature, and other disciplines that views the world from below, from the position of the (formerly) colonized. Much postcolonial study focuses less on tangible manifestations of power and more on culture, influences, representations, and knowledge. As almost everything is connected in some fashion or another to imperialism, the ambit for postcolonial studies is practically limitless.

Empires in History

Looking at a world map today makes clear that we live in a world of nation-states, something that is now taken for granted. Over some seven decades, the United Nations has grown from 50 to nearly 200 member states. So great is our attachment to the nation-state that world leaders fight tooth and nail to preserve "failed" nation-states, including Iraq, Libya, Syria, and Somalia. We have difficulty dealing with major non-state actors, for example international drug cartels, Daesh, or large multinational corporations.

But when one looks at a world map from a century ago, at the time of World War I, it is evident that the world was one of empires. Rather than being an anomaly, the world of the early twentieth century adhered more to the norm because, as noted, empire has been the predominant way in which people have been organized throughout history. One can detect aspects of imperialism when studying the first human settlements and civilizations in ancient Mesopotamia. When the eighteenth-century BCE ruler Hammurabi promulgated his code across the lands between the Tigris and Euphrates rivers, he was reinforcing his authority over the varied peoples he ruled, including Sumerians, Kassites, and Assyrians.

For millennia, central and southwest Eurasia was the epicenter of empire building. Persians, a subject people under Assyrian and then New Babylonian rule, rose under King Cyrus (r. 559–530 BCE) to capture Babylon and topple the New Babylonian empire in 539 BCE. By the time of the emperor Darius (r. 522–486 BCE), the Persian empire was the largest the world had ever seen. The Greek Macedonian ruler Alexander (r. 336–332 BCE) went after the same territories. His rapid, almost continuous campaigning overwhelmed Anatolia, the eastern Mediterranean, Egypt, Syria, and Persia. Only a threatened mutiny by his officers prevented him from invading India. Although this produced "the Hellenistic World" and the spread of Greek culture, southwest Asia's influence

Introduction

was suggested by how much the Persians inspired Alexander and the Greeks. In some ways, Alexander annexed Greece and Macedonia to the Persian world rather than the reverse.

Rome rose to preeminence in the Mediterranean following the Punic Wars between Rome and Carthage (264–146 BCE). The Pax Romana of the first to second century CE represented a new scale of imperial power, Rome exercising sovereignty over peoples from what is today the English–Scottish border to present-day Iraq. The Roman empire consisted of a western, more rural, Latin half centered on Rome and an eastern, Greek-speaking half centered, by the early 300s, on Constantinople. No less impressive were contemporary east Asian empires. King Jeng (259–210 BCE) of the Qin state launched a war of unification in 230 BCE to bring all of China under his rule. Following his success, he became the emperor Qin Shihuangdi in 221 BCE. The short-lived Qin dynasty was succeeded by the Han dynasty, which further unified and then expanded China's territory.

Arab Muslims took the perennially contested region of southwest Asia beginning in the eighth century, and the Umayyad Caliphate eventually extended even further, from the Indus River in the east through southwest Asia across north Africa and north to the Pyrenees. Other Arab Muslims deposed the Umayyads in 750, setting up the long-lived Abbasid Caliphate. In the east, subsequent Chinese dynasties such as the Tang extended China's reach from Vietnam all the way to the Himalayan state of Tibet.

Both the Abbasid Caliphate and China later came under the sway of the Mongols, who created the largest empire in world history. By the thirteenth century, Mongol control spanned most of Eurasia, and the Mongols launched attacks as far afield as present-day Hungary, Poland, Japan, and Baghdad. Kublai Khan (1215–1294), the grandson of Genghis Khan, became the Great Khan, basing his rule in China, where he founded the foreign, Mongol Yuan dynasty (1271–1368). As Mongol power declined, however, locals took advantage and native Han Chinese overthrew the Mongols by 1368, establishing the Ming dynasty. Russian princes of Muscovy overturned their vassal status to the Mongols beginning in the fifteenth century. Timur the Lame, or Tamerlane (d. 1405), of Turkish–Mongol descent, tried to recreate the Ilkhanate of Persia in southwest Asia as a first step toward restoring the Mongol empire. His whirlwind campaigns laid waste to cities and massacred innumerable souls in southwest Asia. His successors never ruled anything like what he had hoped, and his efforts represented the last gasp of the great Eurasian empire builders as much empire building shifted to the seas.

Still, other land-based empires did come into being. Contemporaneous with Mongol rule was the powerful and wealthy west African Mali empire, founded by Sundiata (r. 1230–1255). It is said that, as he passed through Cairo making the hajj to Mecca in 1324–1325, the Mali emperor Mansa Musa gave away so much gold that he crashed the city's gold market. In the Americas, the Mexica people on Lake Tenochtitlan built up a wealthy state capable of subduing its neighbors. Their elaborate tributary empire reached its zenith under emperors Itzcóatl (r. 1428–1440) and Moctezuma I (r. 1440–1469). Central Asian Turks, who had lived along the Abbasid Caliphate's borders and converted to Islam sometime around the tenth century, invaded "Rûm," or the remnants of it: Rome's eastern half, which had survived as the Byzantine empire. The Turkish conquest of Byzantine lands and the 1453 capture of Constantinople put the Muslim Ottoman empire on the map.

After Tamerlane, small yet powerful states emerged alongside regional empires and great, globe-spanning maritime imperial formations that profited less from acquisition of land and control over people than from trade and commercial ties. Christopher Columbus's 1492 voyage opened up a set of exchanges between world areas that, for all intents and purposes, had never been in contact before, leading to a new era of colonialism. As it developed, the Spanish empire functioned as an international enterprise, with ships financed and manned by non-Spaniards, bullion moved from the Americas through the Philippines to China, and massive interest payments on Spanish debt financed by American gold forfeited to Italian and French bankers.

By the early eighteenth century, Europeans claimed extensive holdings throughout the Americas, with the Portuguese in Brazil, the Spanish in South and Central America, the French and British in the Caribbean and North America, and the Dutch in the Caribbean. Most important were Brazilian and Caribbean lands that produced sugar, a prized commodity that produced huge profits. Sugar cane cultivation also was labor-intensive. A decline in the indigenous populations of the Americas led Europeans to turn to Africa for labor, resulting in the creation of trading posts along the African coasts. By the 1780s, at the height of the Atlantic slave trade, on average 88,000 souls a year were enslaved by Africans and Europeans, the latter shipping them like cargo to the Americas.

As the Spanish and Portuguese and later the British, French, and Dutch expanded in the sixteenth and seventeenth centuries, they only joined in empire building. The Ming dynasty (1368–1644) represented a new height of power and prosperity in China, which continued after another foreign group, the Manchu, overthrew the Ming to establish the Qing dynasty (1644–1912). By the seventeenth century Muscovy's princes had established Romanov rule across a growing Eurasian empire. Ottoman Turks continued their rule over a multiethnic empire centered on Anatolia and straddling three continents, and to their east was the Shi'a Muslim Safavid empire, centered on present-day Iran. Foreign (Sunni) Muslim rulers lorded over most of the northern, predominantly Hindu Indian subcontinent beginning with Babur (r. 1526–1530). The Mughal empire's wealth and power was reflected in massive projects like the Taj Mahal, built

Introduction

during Shah Jahan's reign (1628–1658). Such wealth and power sustained Mughal rule in India into the eighteenth century.

Thus the imperialism at the heart of this book – late nineteenth- and twentieth-century European overseas colonialism – followed on millennia of empire building. It was also contemporaneous with empire building *within* Europe: by the English in the British Isles, and on the Continent by Napoleon, the Habsburgs, Germany during the two world wars, and Russia's Romanovs. Although anti-imperialism was inherent to the Marxist–Leninist ideology espoused by the Bolsheviks after 1917, the Soviets in many ways replicated their tsarist imperialist predecessors. Relying on an extensive network of secret police, the Soviet state represented another centralized, expansionistic Russian-dominated regime ruling over innumerable non-Russians. There was also a US empire, a rare case of a former colony become a colonizing power.

Themes of the Book

Any short history of a subject as wide ranging as recent overseas colonialism cannot cover everything. This book is not encyclopedic. Certain subjects are addressed only in passing, for instance England's rule over Ireland, Wales, and Scotland; Jewish colonization in Palestine; and US informal imperialism in Latin America. A short study must also choose certain emphases for reasons of space and cohesion.

This book develops three major themes, the first of which is *exchange*. Recent overseas imperialism set in motion myriad interchanges between numerous peoples with profound cultural, political, economic, social, and other effects across the globe. For long the direction of these exchanges was believed to have been predominantly Europe-outward. As this book will show, exchanges moved in myriad directions: from European metropoles outward, from colonized lands "back" to Europe, and between empires.

The second of this book's three themes is the *complexity and contingency* of colonial rule. Imperialism was never a straightforward story of the projection of Europe outward to rule the globe, followed by a period of "retreat" in the form of decolonization. European rule was often highly contingent upon agreements or "buy-in" from local peoples. In some places, colonialism was utterly devastating, upending existing realities. Yet in many places in the "colonized world," people continued to live their lives and to build their futures with little regard for European claims to authority. European states never fully controlled the many territories they claimed, and their empires were always in a process of becoming, never finished. People reacted variously to colonialism, and neither the colonizer nor the colonized constituted undifferentiated monolithic blocs.

Introduction

A third theme that emerges in the pages that follow is *power*. Who controlled what resources and had what rights are perennial questions of critical historical importance. This book is based on important work of recent years that has revealed the many powers of resistance and agency of colonized peoples across the globe. At the same time, this book never loses sight of the fact that nineteenth- and twentieth-century overseas empire was at its core an astonishing projection of European power across the globe, the ramifications of which we continue to live with today.

Citations

Page Source
5   "decolonization." Stuart Ward, "The European Provenance of Decolonisation", *Past & Present* 230, no. 1 (2016), 227–260.

Bibliography

Aldrich, Robert, and Kirsten McKenzie, eds. *The Routledge History of Western Empires*. Abingdon, UK: Routledge, 2013.

Burbank, Jane, and Frederick Cooper. *Empires in World History: Power and the Politics of Difference*. Princeton: Princeton University Press, 2010.

Cooper, Frederick. *Colonialism in Question: Theory, Knowledge, History*. Berkeley: University of California Press, 2005.

Crosby, Alfred W. *Ecological Imperialism: The Biological Expansion of Europe, 900–1900*. Cambridge: Cambridge University Press, 1986.

Darwin, John. *After Tamerlane: The Global History of Empire Since 1405*. New York: Bloomsbury Press, 2008.

Diamond, Jared. *Guns, Germs, and Steel: The Fates of Human Societies*. New York: W. W. Norton, 1997.

Hobsbawm, E. J. *The Age of Empire, 1875–1914*. New York: Vintage, 1987.

Jones, E. L. *The European Miracle: Environments, Economies, and Geopolitics in the History of Europe and Asia*. 2nd ed. Cambridge: Cambridge University Press, 1987.

Maier, Charles S. *Among Empires: American Ascendancy and Its Predecessors*. Cambridge, MA: Harvard University Press, 2006.

1
The Nineteenth-Century Context

> *The conquest of the earth, which mostly means the taking it away from those who have a different complexion or slightly flatter noses than ourselves, is not a pretty thing when you look into it too much.*
>
> Joseph Conrad, Heart of Darkness (1902)

Makana Nxele began to speak of visions in the spring of 1819. Nxele was Xhosa, a people living around the Great Fish River in southern Africa who were suffering from intrusions from neighboring peoples. Invaders included white settlers, including "Boers" of Dutch origin and Britons, who for years had encroached on Xhosa lands, seized their cattle, and disrupted their lives in myriad other ways. Nxele was a convert to Christianity who claimed to be a prophet and a younger son of Jesus Christ. He said that the Xhosa had to rise up, fight, and drive the whites out. People listened, and many joined up. In April, Nxele led an attack on a British outpost in Grahamstown. The British put down the uprising, captured Nxele, and imprisoned him on Robben Island, the same island on which South Africa's apartheid regime would imprison Nelson Mandela in the 1960s. (Although Mandela survived Robben Island, Nxele did not: he drowned during an escape attempt in December 1819.)

In 1856 another Xhosa, a girl named Nongqawuse, preached a series of prophetic visions. Nongqawuse foretold that the morning sun would set and that the ancestors would arise and drive the whites into the sea, thus saving the Xhosa. First, though, the Xhosa had to prove their faith by destroying their crops and slaughtering all livestock; only if they did so would the prophecy come true, on the eighth day. Nongqawuse's uncle Mhlakaza was among those who embraced her

European Overseas Empire, 1879–1999: A Short History, First Edition. Matthew G. Stanard.
© 2018 John Wiley & Sons, Inc. Published 2018 by John Wiley & Sons, Inc.

vision, and he won over the Xhosa ruler, Sarhili. Like Mhlakaza before him, Sarhili destroyed his cattle and crops, and then persuaded a number of his advisers and subordinates to do the same. Others bought into Nongqawuse's vision, so desperate were they to rid themselves of the whites.

Whites were not the only problem: the Xhosa also felt pressure from the Zulu, a successful and expansionistic people to their east. Zulu success dated back to Dingiswayo, a king among the Nguni people who had transformed his society, doing away with traditional "bush schools" that required cohorts of boys of the same age – "age grades" – to sequester themselves from society, undergo education, and be circumcised. Instead of removing productive young men from society for an extended period, Dingiswayo organized age grades into military units, and these young men became full members of society through military service. This transformed the Nguni into a fighting force. Dingiswayo's successor, Shaka, made his Zulu clan dominant among the Nguni. Shaka Zulu put the Zulu on a permanent war footing, instituted more combat training and years-long segregation of men in military groups, and introduced the assegai, a short stabbing spear used as a sword at close quarters. Shaka also introduced new tactics, including the "cow horn" formation, combining a central group with swift-moving wings to attack an opponent's flanks and rear. Innovation translated into Zulu dominance over large areas of southeastern Africa and, when others adapted or adopted Zulu tactics, warfare became more destructive. The result was the Mfecane or "time of troubles," during which Shaka himself was assassinated, in 1828.

By the time of Shaka's successor, Dingane (r. 1828–1840), the Mfecane had spread widely, reaching the Xhosa people. Heeding Nongqawuse's visions, Xhosa slaughtered thousands of head of cattle and destroyed crops. Then came the eighth day. "Nothing happened. The sun did not set, no dead person came back to life, and not one of the things that had been predicted came to pass." Instead there was starvation, devastation, and death. By 1857 the Xhosa were no longer capable of putting up any resistance to expanding European colonization.

How could anyone have such faith, to the point of destroying all their crops and cattle? One can analyze such apocalyptic visions and those who believed them from anthropological, psychological, religious, gender, or other perspectives. The historical explanation is straightforward: the Xhosa were under intense pressure as a result of Zulu and European expansionism. The same was true of other indigenous peoples, from Khoi, San, Nama, and Herero in southwestern Africa, to Bantu-speaking peoples such as the Sotho, Ndebele, and Shona. A series of droughts coupled with population growth compounded such problems. The Xhosa were unable to compete, in particular in the face of European technological superiority.

As the experience of the Xhosa suggests, many actors and factors shaped global history in the nineteenth century, including local conflicts, movements of people, competition for resources, climate, the environment, religious beliefs, and military tactics. As this chapter will emphasize, it was local concerns and actions that drove much change for much of the world and for most of the century. Europe remained for most people a distant peninsula on the western end of Eurasia. That Europe was not dominant is revealed in how its overseas efforts were motivated by the need to procure things that Europeans needed more of, such as land or goods that they could not make like fine silks; this meant that Europe was dependent on much of the rest of the world.

Growing free trade, the independence of most of Spain's and Portugal's American colonies, and the power of non-Europeans made a renewed wave of empire building seem unlikely. Then a series of developments, beginning in the 1850s, signaled that change was taking place. Parts of Europe and the United States were industrializing, and both world areas emerged stronger following the American Civil War and the unifications of Germany and of Italy. Failed reforms in the Ottoman empire, Russia's defeat in the 1853–1856 Crimean War, and the 1850–1864 Taiping Rebellion in China signaled the profound challenges these large land-based empires faced. Still, the renewed wave of overseas imperialism that soon followed was never a simple story of a more powerful Europe expanding outward in some well-planned colonial takeover, and we should not project back into the past the dominance that western Europe, the United States, and Russia exercised over much of the world by 1900. This power was neither inevitable, nor was it in any way complete.

New and Unlikely Empires

Around the mid-nineteenth century, another wave of European overseas empire building seemed improbable, for a number of reasons. The abolitionist movement had suggested a turning away from the subjugation of foreign peoples, and Enlightenment ideals of a shared humanity had spread widely throughout the Atlantic world. Britain outlawed the slave trade, beginning in 1807, imposed this on others through its naval supremacy, and outlawed slavery itself in 1833. France followed in 1848. In other places slavery was on the way out. When in 1860 the Dutch banned slavery in Batavia – the main European settlement and trading outpost in the Dutch East Indies – it already had diminished to near insignificance. Despite its continued profitability, the United States (1865), Cuba (1886), and Brazil (1888) also finally abolished slavery, although the Indian Ocean slave trade endured.

Other signs suggested that overseas empire building had largely run its course. France lost almost all its foreign possessions at the end of the Seven Years War (1756–1763), and Britain relinquished 13 North American colonies two decades later. Independence for Haiti, across Central and South America, and in some other parts of the Caribbean followed in the first quarter of the nineteenth century. Large, landed empires had more staying power, including the Ottoman empire (spanning southeastern Europe, southwest Asia, north Africa, and the Arabian peninsula), Russia's massive expanse, and to a much lesser extent India under the declining Mughals. Britain's 1793 Macartney Embassy revealed Qing China's strength. The British envoy George Macartney arrived in China hoping to open ports to trade, but the Qianlong Emperor rejected his requests, telling Macartney:

> Strange and costly objects do not interest me ... Our dynasty's majestic virtue has penetrated unto every country under Heaven, and Kings of all nations have offered their costly tribute by land and sea. As your Ambassador can see for himself, we possess all things. I set no value on objects strange or ingenious, and have no use for your country's manufactures.

China had little time for what it saw as a small, backward island people halfway around the world. Macartney left empty-handed.

Developments nevertheless signaled a potential renewal of overseas expansionism. With the French Revolution and the abolitionist impulse to eliminate slavery came a more activist, outward-looking mindset, and Europeans began to see themselves as uniquely positioned to civilize benighted peoples everywhere. Although most colonies in the Americas had achieved independence by the 1830s, colonists from the Americas to Australia and New Zealand had created huge "neo-Europes" where settlers dominated natives – those who had not succumbed to disease – and where flora and fauna imported from Europe flourished, displacing indigenous animals and plants. This, and intensifying British rule in India, began to revolutionize international relations, economics, and culture, initiating a reordering of the global balance of power. Europe and North America enjoyed tremendous advantages such as natural resources like coal, whose use spurred innovations like the steam engine. Europe benefited from rising populations; new types and varieties of crops and imported foodstuffs; growing trade and transportation; legal institutions that protected property; and comparatively independent financial institutions. Europeans also were good at warfare. The uniqueness of Europe was not its strong states or patriotic identities, but rather the convergence of these "with economic dynamism, well-honed weapons of war making, and fierce rivalries between medium-sized polities." Viewed this way, Qing, Ottoman, and Mughal success at imposing peace over large empires contributed to their decline. Even if Europeans could not match the commercial capabilities of the Indians, Ottomans, and Chinese, competition and war within Europe's multistate system meant growing competitiveness and expansionism by the mid-nineteenth century. By that point, Europeans were more expansionistic than ever before and more so than any other people at the time, with the exception of land-hungry, western-bound US colonists. On top of it all, the growth of "civil society" in Europe lent its societies staying power. Then, in just two decades, from 1850 to 1870, world-changing events contributed to growing European advantage: war and revolt in China, a revolution in Japan, a civil war in the United States, and industrialization and national unification in Europe.

China's Qing Dynasty

The Qing were a foreign, Manchu dynasty in power since 1644, controlling far-flung territories and peoples with their military and a large, educated bureaucracy infused with Confucian principles emphasizing civilized behavior, ritual, family, and loyalty. Like Ming emperors before them, Qing rulers believed that they were at the center of the world. China was the "Middle Kingdom," fringed by peripheries including Korea, Japan, mainland southeast Asia, Mongolia, and other so-called barbarian lands at or beyond its borders. Success and isolationism discouraged innovation and invention. The imperial examination system, based on Confucian literature and values, fostered conservatism. Change occurred but always within a framework of tradition.

Mental inflexibility manifested itself in lackluster responses to internal and external threats. First was a massive domestic revolt, a result of growing population and rural poverty. Like Makala Nxele of the Xhosa, the failed Chinese civil servant and Christian convert Hong Xiuquan, who claimed to be the brother of Jesus of Nazareth, claimed bizarre religious visions and encouraged his followers to rebel against the Qing. Hong's Taiping Rebellion (1850–1864) was a massive uprising that cost millions of lives – 26 Chinese perished during the rebellion for each soldier who died in the contemporaneous American Civil War, the deadliest conflict in US history.

A second threat came from abroad as industrializing Europe pressured China to open its markets to trade. The Chinese remained uninterested in Western goods like cheap cotton textiles, which were inferior to domestic silks. Because they kept importing Chinese manufactures, European states faced yawning trade deficits. Britain's solution was to sell opium from India to China, provoking opposition from Chinese officials. When a Cantonese governor seized a stockpile of opium in 1839, British forces attacked the Chinese. As a result of its insularity, China had no navy to counter Britain's steamships. When a small British fleet sailed up the Yangtze River in 1842 and threatened China at the junction of the Yangtze and the Grand Canal, the Chinese sued for peace. The resulting treaty forced China to open up some of its markets.

Other conflicts over opium and trade followed between Britain and France on the one hand and China on the other. A second "opium war" (1856–1860) led to another defeat, and China never regained the upper hand. Chinese elites viewed such events as minor setbacks. Qing rule survived, after all. But, whereas a century earlier China had been one of the world's great powers, the Qing limped into the late nineteenth century. By the century's end, Chinese leaders were depending on European advisers to direct government reforms and on foreign merchants to conduct trade. The tables had been turned: China, for centuries an imperial power, was now a victim of imperialism.

Japan: From Isolation to Industrialization

Reactions to Chinese decline and Western expansionism varied across east Asia. Japan, long peripheral to and influenced by the Middle Kingdom, took a path that could not have been more different. Like China, Japan had closed itself off to the outside world, but even more so, following a policy of isolationism begun under Toyotomi Hideyoshi (d. 1598) that intensified during the Tokugawa shogunate (1603–1857). Tokugawa Japan expelled Christian missionaries, then all foreigners; prohibited overseas travel; and restricted trade, first to commerce only with the Portuguese, then only with the Dutch, and then only on a limited basis. Eventually Japanese restricted trade to exchanges with a handful of Dutch ships on one tiny island at Nagasaki, and then only once a year. Isolationism did not mean stagnation or backwardness: domestic trade, literature, art, and culture flourished. There also was political change: feudalism declined, replaced by a centralized dyarchy with an emperor who reigned and a shogun who ruled.

Seeking coaling stations, access to markets, and provisioning of ships, French, Russian, US, and other sailing vessels approached Japan only to be rebuffed. In 1853 the US commodore Matthew Perry entered Edo Bay, near Edo (Tokyo), and obliged the Japanese to open trade under threat of the use of force. Like their Chinese counterparts, Japanese elites wanted to maintain control over their destiny, but by contrast a small group of powerful Japanese men chose to adopt Western techniques to strengthen the country, to learn from the West, not imitate it. This was *kaikoku joi*, "open the country to expel the barbarians." Fearing that the shogun was not moving fast enough, they launched the 1868 Meiji Restoration, deposed the shogun, and "restored" the emperor to power; in reality, a small group of ministers were in control.

Japan embarked on a crash course of adaptation and industrialization. Whereas industrialization in the West was initially slow and driven by private investment and enterprise, in Japan it was largely state driven, and fast. The human toll was staggering. There were no worker protections. Industrialists prized children for their small size and servility, and silk factory owners enticed poor parents to send their daughters to them for the wages. Yet, measured by increases in productivity, economic growth, and heavy industrial production – of iron, steel, electricity, and machinery – Japan's industrialization was successful, confirmed by military victories over China in 1894–1895 and over Russia in 1904–1905.

Civil War in North America

At the moment Commodore Perry threatened to fire on Edo, and while the Qing battled Hong Xiquan's Taiping Rebellion, across the Pacific readers thrilled to the story of Harriet Beecher Stowe's *Uncle Tom's Cabin* (1852), a novel that humanized for white readers people living in their own country yet subjected to an inhumane fate. It addressed the central question of the nineteenth-century United States: would slavery survive?

The United States was born of contradictions. Its war of independence against Britain (1775–1783) was a fight for freedom, yet the republic that emerged enshrined bondage into its founding constitution. Victorious in a war against a colonial overlord, the United States turned around and played the game of colonial horse trading by buying the Louisiana territory from France in 1802, nearly doubling the country's size. In 1823 the United States declared the Monroe Doctrine to warn European states not to meddle in the Americas, yet the United States itself intervened in Latin America, creating an informal empire. A result of a war against empire, the United States became a colonizing power in its own right, devouring land in a westward march, and defeating and expelling natives and taking their land, oftentimes replacing them with imported African slaves. Conquest westward continued with an aggressive and successful war against another former colony, Mexico, in 1847–1848. Ironically, success provoked catastrophe because the United States could not peacefully resolve whether newly acquired territories would be free or slave. The North's victory in the Civil War not only proscribed slavery; it also produced a more centralized government, growing industrialism in the north, backwardness in an agricultural south, increased nationalism, and continued westward expansion.

Unification and Industrialization in Europe

The status quo was also upturned in mid-century Europe. There, the Revolutions of 1848 rocked the Continent, symbolized by the flight of Austrian first minister and arch-conservative Klemens von Metternich into exile. It was Metternich who had orchestrated the restoration of the pre-1789 *ancien régime* after Napoleon's downfall in 1815. Even if conservatives ultimately regained power after the 1848 Revolutions, leaders more amenable to change had emerged by the 1850s. "March at the head of the ideas of your century, and they will sustain you," said Napoleon Bonaparte's nephew, French emperor Napoleon III, "march against them and they will overthrow you." Or, as Prussia's conservative chancellor, Otto von Bismarck, put it: "If there has to be a revolution, we would rather make it than suffer it." And change was happening: subjects were becoming citizens because of public education, growing literacy, the development of a public sphere, and the spread of political ideologies including liberalism and socialism. The percentage of the voting population increased slowly, although women remained disenfranchised.

Unlike China or the Ottoman empire, Europe was composed of an international system of competitive states. In a similar way to post-Civil War (re)union in the United States, Europe witnessed consolidation and change. Italy unified, making a young state of an "old" nation. Prussia unified Germany through a series of wars from 1864 to 1871, and Prussians dominated the new German empire. Prussia's 1866 defeat of the Habsburgs sparked reforms creating the joint the Austro-Hungarian monarchy, and its 1870–1871 defeat of France led to Napoleon III's abdication and the inauguration of France's Third Republic. The French worried about a large, unified, and industrializing Germany, and their loss of the provinces of Alsace–Lorraine to Germany after the war created bitterness. Many French men and women turned an eye toward overseas empire as compensation and as a source of prestige and power. Britain had escaped the Revolutions of 1848, underwent political reform, including the extension of the franchise, even if, as late as 1890, still only 16.3 percent of Britons could vote.

Of critical importance was Europe's shift from slow, halting demographic growth to a period of rapid population increase. An agricultural revolution including new foods and rising productivity on old and newly cleared lands led to an attenuation of subsistence crises and better nutrition. A decline in some diseases and better sanitation led to lower mortality and longer life expectancy. England's population almost quadrupled from 1800 to 1900, Germany's more than doubled, while overall Europe grew from 205 to 414 million people, not counting 55 million emigrants who left between 1870 and 1914, emigrating mainly to Australia, the United States, Canada, and Argentina. Population pressures induced a search for territories for settlement.

The slave trade, the trade in sugar and other tropical products, and the export of manufactured goods led to an accumulation of wealth in Europe. Maritime trade was risky but highly profitable. Europeans also enjoyed a huge increase in "human capital." Exploration and trade resulted in growing knowledge of shipbuilding, seafaring technology, and business techniques, as epitomized by the British East India Company (EIC) and the Dutch Vereenigde Oostindische Compagnie (VOC, United East India Company), new kinds of organizations that were better able to manage large amounts of risks.

Most significantly, Europeans moved from agriculture into industry, mechanized production, and substituted fossil fuels for animal and natural power. This change was underway in England by the late eighteenth century, France and Belgium by 1830, German lands by the 1850s, northern Italy and parts of Russia toward the nineteenth century's end, and pockets elsewhere, such as northeastern Spain or around Vienna, the Habsburg capital. Accelerated industrialization at century's end emphasized steel, electricity, chemicals, communication, and transportation, boosting economic growth and the standard of living. The United States' Transcontinental Railroad was completed in 1869, the same year that Egypt's French-built Suez Canal opened. London's Underground began operating in 1863, the New York and Paris metros around 1900. Other advances included the telegraph (1840s), submarine cables (1850s), the telephone (1870s), postal service, and refrigerated ships. "In the 1830s an exchange of letters between Britain and India could take two years; by 1870, with the opening of the Suez Canal, a letter could reach Bombay in only one month." Gold discoveries in California (1849) and Australia (1851) increased the money supply, fueling economic growth. Military technological advances included more accurate guns, breech-loading rifles, and automatic weapons. As early as the 1830s, British naval engineers adapted steam power to military uses and built large, ironclad ships equipped with powerful guns, capable both of ignoring winds and currents and of traveling faster than any sailing vessel. A good example is the British gunboat *Nemesis*, which in 1842 chugged up the Yangtze River to bring the First Opium War to a close by threatening China from within. Europe and the United States rapidly outpaced the rest of the world in terms of economic expansion, industrial output, population growth, and new technologies.

The Ottoman Empire

While Chinese elites grappled with reform, and while the Meiji Restoration propelled Japanese industrialization, Ottoman elites wrestled with how to counter a more dynamic and expansionistic Europe. After reaching a height of power and territorial control in the seventeenth century, the Ottoman empire had entered a period of stasis, even decline. By the early 1800s it faced growing problems in an age of industrialization, nationalism, and more rapid communications. Trade routes that Europeans had opened with the Americas and Asia bypassed the Ottomans' strategic position at the juncture of Europe, Asia, and north Africa. Cheap, mass-produced European manufactured goods undercut Ottoman access to markets. Although the Ottomans rivaled the Habsburgs in central Europe, Turkish naval decline dated back to defeat at the 1571 Battle of Lepanto. Competition between European states fostered efficiency, innovation, and invention; centralization in the Ottoman empire stifled them. Because the

Ottoman empire consisted of a Turkish center, non-Muslim peoples in southeastern Europe, Kurds and Armenians in Asia Minor, and Arab populations in the Near (or Middle) East and north Africa, nationalism was a threat. Some territories achieved independence, including Greece (1830), and Romania and Serbia (by the 1860s). France seized Algeria in 1830. Many referred to the Turkish empire as the "sick man of Europe."

Decline led to a variety of responses, although Ottoman leaders, like their Chinese counterparts in China, were caught in a double bind. When they borrowed from foreign countries to pay for reforms, they lost control over their finances. Whereas some elites thought the pace of reforms was too slow, others thought it was too fast. In 1839 Reshid Mustafa Pasha, top minister under Sultan Abdul Mejid (r. 1839–61) launched the Tanzimat, or "reorganization." The reforms allowed for the greater involvement of non-Muslims in creating and implementing law, and showed that the Ottomans were serious about specific problems. However, the reforms were ineffective and were seen as too little too late by Christians in the empire, and as too much too fast by conservative opponents. The Ottomans also sent a number of educated people to Europe, especially to France because of its reputation as an advanced society. They returned not only with technical know-how but also Western-inspired ideas, and some argued that the most necessary reforms were political ones including limits on the sultan's power, a constitution, and the creation of a parliament. A new, European-educated bureaucracy was ineffective because of its separation from the general population, and financing reforms led to massive indebtedness. Finally, the sultan, worried about challenges to his rule resulting from increased borrowing from Europe – intellectual and otherwise – turned away from reform.

In 1876 reformers succeeded in deposing the sultan and imposing a constitution on his successor, Abdul Hamid II. Within two years, however, Abdul Hamid II consolidated his position and suspended the constitution, ruling as an autocrat. The government declared bankruptcy in the late 1870s. Bulgaria gained its independence after Russia defeated the Ottomans in a war in 1878. The condition of the sick man of Europe worsened.

The Crimean War

The third great Eurasian empire of the 1800s – alongside Qing China and the Ottoman empire – was the Russian empire, whose lands extended from eastern Europe to China and across Siberia to Alaska, which Russia sold to the United States in 1867. Russia's massive expanse resulted from its history of almost continuous expansion from its base in Muscovy. Russian princes had thrown off Mongol rule and then expanded, most notably under Peter the Great (1682–1725) and Catherine the Great (1762–1796).

Russia's defeat at the hands of France and Britain in the Crimean War (1853–1856) was a wake-up call. Britain and France, fighting thousands of miles from home, defeated Russia's armies on their home territory in the Crimea. This sparked Tsar Alexander II's "Great Reforms," which freed the empire's serfs and granted them full citizenship rights; created local political councils; fashioned a more independent judiciary; did away with much censorship of the press; and reformed the military along Western lines. Reforms did not touch the tsar's autocratic rule. Like their Ottoman counterparts, the Romanovs jealously guarded their authority and continued to reign and rule as absolute monarchs. By the 1870s, state-directed investment led to industrialization, including a huge transcontinental railway system. As a result, by 1900 Russia was one of the greatest industrial powers and could boast the world's largest army.

The Sepoy Uprising in India

Although they had been victorious in the Crimean War, Britons were scandalized by the large number of casualties. (As in the American Civil War, most soldiers had died not from battlefield wounds but from disease.) Then, just the year after the Crimean War ended, the British faced a major uprising in India, where the private chartered EIC had taken a dominant position vis-à-vis the failing Mughal rulers. The Indian Rebellion of 1857–1858, or "Sepoy Uprising," was not the first opposition the EIC had faced, for there had been small-scale revolts in the 1840s and 1850s. Although some consider the rebellion the "first Indian war of independence" – even though there was not a second one – in essence it was an anticolonial revolt.

In 1857 regiments of Indian soldiers serving under British control, called "sepoys," received new rifles that fired bullets wrapped in paper cartridges waxed with animal fat to protect them from moisture. During loading, when instructed to tear the paper off with their teeth, Hindu sepoys refused because they feared the grease was beef fat; Muslims declined because they had heard that it was made from pork fat. Although the British changed the procedures for packing and opening cartridges, the damage had been done. In May, a number of units revolted, killed their British officers, and declared the restoration of Mughal rule. About a fourth of India's territories joined in. Fighters overpowered the British garrison at Cawnpore, taking 60 soldiers, 180 civilians, and 375 women and children. They killed all the men – though many had surrendered – and, after holding Cawnpore for two weeks, they murdered all the women and children. When news of the massacre reached British authorities in India and then Britain itself, the reaction was overwhelming, stoking fears, especially a deep-seated dread of Indian violence against white women. Using superior communications and quick transportation, the British assembled and used a large force to

The Nineteenth-Century Context

Figure 1.1 Black and white reproduction of Vasily Vereshchagin, *Blowing from Guns in British India* (1880s). *Source*: Wikimedia Commons, https://commons.wikimedia.org/wiki/File:1857_%22Blowing_from_Guns_in_British_India%22.jpg.

crush the rebellion, which they accomplished by the spring of 1858. The British summarily executed many rebels, even tying some to cannons and blowing them to pieces (Figure 1.1). Others were caught, tried, and hanged.

The Sepoy Uprising resulted in more intensive British rule. The EIC lost its India monopoly and the state took over, installing Viscount Canning as the first viceroy responsible to the British government, inaugurating the British Raj (from the Urdu word *rāj*, or "rule"). In 1877 Queen Victoria became empress of India. There followed infrastructure investment in railways, land reorganization, and cash crop production of tea, opium, and coffee for export. Officials imposed a more uniform set of laws across the entire colony and more direct means of gathering taxes instead of depending upon traditional regional tax administrators. The administration remained small in terms of the number of Europeans: as late as 1900, the British colonial service consisted of 4,000 British bureaucrats supported by 250,000 Indian civil servants. But it kept growing.

Although the rebellion's outcome would suggest that colonial control was about military power, raw materials, administration, and infrastructure, its consequences reveal that colonial rule was also about knowledge, culture, and control over information. Events like Cawnpore led many Anglo-Indians, and people in Britain itself, to lose their respect for Indian culture, and India became for them something to westernize and change. British officials established a civil service examination, which exposed Indians to Western administrative ideas. Because the colonial administration did not discriminate against Indians on the basis of caste or skin color, this brought Indians together into a common setting. Islam and Hinduism engaged with Christianity, reshaping their presence in people's lives. As the British navigated Hindu and Muslim legal systems and classified "traditional" laws to systematize their administration, "traditions" became fixed. As the British codified the legal system, caste became more rigid. The British also took action to stop certain practices, most notoriously *sati*, where a widow would immolate herself in her husband's funeral pyre; in Bengal alone, this occurred 7,941 times between 1813 and 1825. British authorities forbade *sati* as early as 1829, but it took years to enforce a partially effective ban. Because *sati* was a sign of upper-caste status, as caste became more rigid the practice even spread. In sum, knowledge and culture were fundamental to the apparatus of power.

India became the "crown jewel" of the British empire, a formidable resource that exercised an outsized influence on British foreign and colonial policy and induced strategic colonial expansion to protect it. India was a huge market for British exports. EIC rule had undermined domestic manufacturing and driven people from cities to the countryside. By supplanting traditional authorities, the Raj decreased demand by local rulers for manufactured goods for patronage purposes, undermining domestic demand and making India reliant on imported manufactured goods, in particular textiles. A growing rural population made India a source of raw materials like tea and of manpower. Even after the mutiny, when the number of British troops increased to lower the ratio of Indian to British troops, the Indian Army remained overwhelmingly manned by indigenous soldiers: by 1881, there were 125,000 Indians to only 69,600 British. Many in Britain, which was a naval power, thought that India's large army – and its ability to increase its size almost without limit – allowed Britain to compete with land powers like Russia and Germany. Indian soldiers became crucial to the British empire elsewhere and were regularly dispatched across the world. Best of all, the colony was self-financing because the military, administration, and infrastructure were paid for by taxes on Indians. It did not cost the British taxpayer a penny.

Diversity in Africa

There were no counterparts in Africa to the Qing, Ottomans, and Romanovs; instead local rulers were in control. One major state was Egypt. Ostensibly part of the Ottoman empire, Egypt was largely self-ruling, in part because of growing Turkish weakness and Egyptian rulers' efforts to increase their autonomy. From 1803 to 1849, an innovative and assertive leader, Muhammad Ali, born of

Albanian parents in Ottoman Macedonia, served as viceroy. Ali was intent on modernizing Egypt, to bring it kicking and screaming into the nineteenth century. He restructured the army along European lines, reformed Egypt's higher education system, and developed cotton agriculture to meet growing European demand resulting from industrialization.

Muhammad Ali's successors extended Egyptian rule, moving southward up the Nile to take control of and to expand the Sudanese slave trade and ivory trade. Muhammad Ali's third son, Ismail Pasha (ruled 1863–1879), expanded cotton cultivation to take advantage of the interruption of US exports during that country's civil war. He sent a mercenary force up the Nile into Sudan to take more land, reaching as far as Lake Victoria. Egypt reformed with the assistance of European credit, armaments, and advisers, including explorer Samuel Baker who in 1869 occupied Egypt's "Equatorial Province" and his replacement after 1873, General Charles "Chinese" Gordon, whose nickname dated to his role in the Second Opium War. The 1869 opening of the Suez Canal turned Egypt into a nodal point for trade and communications between Europe and Asia. Continued modernization efforts directed toward the economy, the military, and schooling led to a massive debt increase, especially as cotton prices dropped after the American Civil War.

During the same era, jihads wracked parts of west Africa. Umar Tal (al-hajj Umar) began preaching in the Senegal River area in the early 1850s, after having visited Mecca and joined the Tijaniyya reformist brotherhood. When locals of the traditional Qadiriyya brotherhood largely rejected him, he launched a jihad along the upper Senegal and upper Niger rivers, before being killed by his own people, the Fulani, in 1864.

East Africa was marked by Portuguese decline and Arab-Swahili ascendance. The Portuguese had been active on east Africa's periphery since the 1500s, trading for ivory and slaves, but by the late 1700s their influence had waned. Portugal's attempts to move further inland and to link its Angolan and Mozambiquan territories had failed because of powerful indigenous resistance. Portugal had thus remained more focused on its possessions in the Americas (Brazil) and in the Far East. Nonetheless, Portuguese trade had spurred the development of interior commercial centers along key east African trade routes. From the late eighteenth century, a mix of Arabs and indigenous east African Swahili speakers flourished along the coast. Arab-Swahili merchants controlled and developed trade into the interior, exploiting and adapting to indigenous African commercial realities, while building major trading centers in the process.

Nyamwezi was one crucial east African trade center, which developed in support of goods transportation. Because Angola to the west was so affected by the slave trade, when interior peoples traded goods to the coasts, they tended to look eastward. Nyamwezi also benefited from trade from further north, especially from the densely populated kingdoms around Lake Victoria. Buganda was one such small but wealthy and centralized state in east Africa's interlacustrine region. When

British explorers first arrived there in 1862, they were astonished by the power of the Kabaka or "leader" of the Buganda kingdom, Mutesa I (ruled 1856–1884).

Thus, unlike the Portuguese, Arab-Swahili traders exerted control well into the interior. Sultan Seyyid Said, based at Muscat, Oman, exploited east African trade routes to their fullest, increasing the volume and value of shipments by increasing the number of porters and providing more credit for purchases. Seyyid Said developed two large interior trade centers at Tabor and Ujiji, and in 1840 moved his capital from Muscat to Zanzibar. After he died in 1856, however, his successors were unable to fend off British influence, which was growing in the Indian Ocean.

In the absence of any large, organized power, why was Europe's presence in Africa limited to coastal trading posts? First, local African rulers were powerful. Georg Schweinfurth's travelogue *The Heart of Africa* (1874), for instance, described the incredible riches and power of King Munza of the Mangbetu in north-central Africa. Well-established African traders kept Europeans out. Legitimate trade had grown after Britain banned the slave trade, and Europeans wanted to trade for resources, something reflected in the names they gave places like Côte d'Ivoire (Ivory Coast), the Gold Coast, and the Oil Rivers in what became Nigeria, along which valuable palm oil was traded to the coast. Europeans wished to get at the sources of such goods, but African middlemen outsmarted them, relegating them to the coast, as described in one 1861 French account: "I have heard the negroes called stupid, but my experience shows them to be anything but that. They are very shrewd traders indeed; and no captain or merchant who is a new hand on the coast will escape being victimized by their cunning in driving a bargain." Topography was also important. Most of the continent rises up sharply from the coasts, and waterfalls and steep rises kept European boats from traveling inland. Disease was another factor. "During the whole of the nineteenth century, the most important problem for Europeans in West Africa was simply that of keeping alive." During a voyage to Niger sponsored by the British government in 1841–1842, 44 of the 159 who went died from disease within the first two months, and 55 died in all before the ship returned to England.

"Europe" and Overseas Empire

We know now, of course, that European overseas empire ultimately reshaped much of the world. But it is debatable whether in the 1800s a "Europe" even existed that could extend its influence outward, and to what degree European states were coherent unities capable of "projecting" themselves. As a historical example, consider the Spanish empire. Many know that King Ferdinand and Queen Isabella financed explorations and then conquistadors like Hernán Cortés and Francisco Pizarro, leading to discoveries, conquests, and riches in the Americas. After a few hundred conquistadors captured the Philippines, Spain ruled a globe-spanning empire, transforming American silver and gold into power in Europe. Spain's clout reached a zenith under Charles V, who inherited Habsburg lands in Austria and Burgundy from his father and Castile, Aragon, Sicily, Naples, and the Spanish American empire from his mother. Even if European hegemony proved elusive, and if during the early 1800s Spain's many American colonies gained their independence, Spain continued as a global, albeit declining, imperial power through the nineteenth century. This only ended with Spain's defeat in the 1898 Spanish–American War, when the United States took control of the Philippines, Cuba, and Puerto Rico.

The problem with this story is that there was no "Spanish" empire. Rather than this history being a story of a European nation-state (Spain) projecting itself outward to the world, it was in truth an international endeavor. Christopher Columbus, for instance, was from Genoa. Ferdinand Magellan was from Portugal. Friar Junípero Serra, a founder of San Diego, was born in 1713 in Majorca, then part of the Crown of Aragon. Key individuals pursued their own interests, not those of the "Spanish" crown. Cortés was disobeying orders when he left for Mexico in 1519, and later he, like conquistadors elsewhere, relied on local allies. For the 1521 siege of Tenochtitlan that brought down the Aztec empire, Cortés's force of 86 horsemen, 118 musketeers and crossbowmen, 700 foot soldiers, and 400 sailors fought alongside some 50,000 Tlaxcalans and 75,000 other indigenous soldiers. Famous sixteenth-century "Spanish" victories in Europe such as the Battle of Pavia (1525) or the Battle of Lepanto (1571) were won by international coalitions including not only Castilians but sometimes Germans, English, Italians, Hungarians, and others. Once up and running, the empire benefited non-Spanish interests. Between 1500 and 1600 approximately 150,000 kilograms of gold and 7.4 million kilograms of silver arrived in Spain from the Americas, but non-Spanish ships and crews transported much of it, and it made its way to Italian, French, and other bankers from whom Charles V had borrowed vast sums in his bid for European hegemony. "What use is it," one Castilian writer wrote in the 1650s, "to bring over so many millions worth of merchandise, silver and gold in the galleons, at so much cost and risk, if it comes only for the French and Genoese?"

What is more, "Spain" did not even exist as a nation-state in the 1500s. Ferdinand II of Aragon and Isabella of Castile united most of the Iberian peninsula under their joint rule, but they and their successors ruled not a nation-state called Spain but a mosaic of kingdoms including Galicia, Asturias, Navarre, Leon, Castile, Aragon, Valencia, Granada, and others. This is reflected in modern-day Spain's many languages, which include Catalan, Basque, Galician, and Castilian (Spanish), among others. Emperor Charles V was not the king of Spain but rather the duke of Burgundy, king of Aragon and Castile, king of Naples and Sicily, archduke of Austria, and Holy Roman Emperor, among other titles. The term "king of Spain" did not come into regular use until the 1800s.

The Nineteenth-Century Context

Analogous situations obtained elsewhere in Europe well into the nineteenth century. French was not the first language of most people in France until the end of the nineteenth century. Germany's and Italy's unifications were not complete until 1871. Following Italian unification, Massimo d'Azeglio famously said, "Italy is made. It remains to make Italians." Overseas expansion actually helped consolidate European nation-states, and thus, as Europeans expanded and reshaped the world beyond, so did the rest of the world reshape Europe.

Europe's overseas colonies

All this said, European states did claim significant possessions overseas by the early nineteenth century. Even if maritime empire building seemed to some a thing of the past, many Europeans maintained their superiority and were more than willing to rule over people who, as Joseph Conrad states in this chapter's epigraph, were of a "different complexion" or had "slightly flatter noses" than themselves. The Caribbean remained very much a European sea, with Britain, France, the Netherlands, and Spain controlling numerous profitable sugar-growing islands, the most important being Cuba. Britain ruled over British Honduras in Central America, and there was Dutch Guiana, French Guiana, and British Guiana in northern South America. The British EIC ruled much of India, and Irish, Scottish, and English settlers (convicts or otherwise) continued to take land in New Zealand and Australia. In the latter, a decline in the Aboriginal population similar to the vast sixteenth-century depopulation in the Americas occurred after first contact with Europeans in the late eighteenth century. The Dutch had controlled coastal points in the Dutch East Indies for centuries by the nineteenth century, and the VOC dominated the area's trade. Spain claimed the Philippines, and the Portuguese remained active in Brazil and on the African and east Asian coasts. During Napoleon III's reign, France expanded in Algeria, and also in Senegal where the country had a longstanding foothold and where Governor Louis Faidherbe's forces moved up along the Senegal River. Faidherbe's success made his *tirailleurs sénégalais* – French-officered Senegalese troops – famous, a byword for all west African colonial troops. The French also conquered territories between 1858 and 1862 in southern Vietnam (Cochinchina) – in the Mekong Delta area and in north Vietnam – as they sought access to mythically vast Chinese markets.

As Makala Nxele's and Nongqawuse's stories showed, there was a major European presence in southern Africa. This dated back to the 1652 establishment of a Dutch outpost at the Cape of Good Hope as a way station from Europe to the East Indies for the VOC. Despite VOC intentions, Dutch settlers spread out, inviting conflict with Khoi, Xhosa, and others. In 1815, at the end of the Napoleonic Wars, the British took control of the Cape Colony, seeing it as strategic for India. In the 1830s many Dutch settlers – now called "Boers" – departed the Cape to escape from British control. British abolitionism struck Boers as oppressive and ridiculous, as to them Europeans were obviously superior to Africans. Thousands moved inland in what came to be called "the Great Trek," provoking conflict with native Africans in a violent struggle for land and resources.

Boer and later British successes seizing land in southern Africa underscores the technological advantages Europeans possessed. A pattern emerged from the Mfecane and the Great Trek that dominated the years after the 1830s: both Africans and Boers sought land to accommodate growing numbers of people. In the end, the Boers, being technologically more advanced, defeated the Africans. Conflicts on or beyond the Cape Colony frontier were always over land, and the outcome of each encounter left Africans with further losses, less able to maintain herds, grow crops, collect fuel for fires, or build infrastructure.

The establishment of independent settlements became a source of Boer pride. In 1852 Boers founded the independent state of Transvaal, and in 1854 the Orange Free State. The British extended a protectorate over what was called Bechuanaland to the north of the Cape Colony, and the Briton Cecil Rhodes worked to establish a colony even further north, in what became Rhodesia. The discovery of diamonds in 1867 at Kimberly, bordering on Orange Free State, heightened interest in the region. In 1877 the British invaded and occupied Transvaal.

The question of control

Europeans rarely exercised complete authority over the lands they claimed, and for long their control was limited to sea routes, coastal areas, key communications points, and trading posts. The Spanish Philippines and French Algeria are illustrative examples.

Despite neatly colored maps showing the Philippines as "Spanish" from the 1500s, Spain never fully controlled them. The Spanish first learned of the islands from Magellan's 1519 circumnavigation of the globe, but approached them only in 1565, establishing control over an area near present-day Manila. By 1600 Spain occupied coastal regions of the central and northern islands, and its control grew haltingly; it never controlled the Philippines' second largest island, Mindanao, in the south. Moreover, it took months, sometimes years for messages to be carried back and forth across the world's oceans, leading one Spanish viceroy to remark that, "If death came from Madrid, we should all live to a very old age."

One often reads in history texts that France conquered Algeria in 1830, or that by the time of the 1954–1962 French–Algerian War the colony had been French "for more than a hundred years." Neither is true. French forces attacked Algiers in May 1830. The kingdom's monarch, Charles X, hoped it would boost his flagging popularity. (It did not. He lost the throne in the July Revolution the same year.) By the year's end France had negotiated a protectorate over Algeria's coast, leaving interior regions beyond its reach, including vast and sparsely populated

The Nineteenth-Century Context

desert areas to the south. Beginning in 1834, the Arab Muslim leader Abd el-Kader then rebelled against the French; he did not surrender until 1847. By that point France had extended its control further inland out of perceived military necessity. It then absorbed Algeria by creating the three *départements* of Oran, Alger, and Constantine and having European settlers there send representatives to the capital, Paris. Still, sporadic armed resistance continued into the 1860s, and when France tried to extend its presence further, Cheikh Mohamed El-Mokrani led a revolt in 1871 that garnered the support of perhaps a third or more of the indigenous population. Mokrani lost his life, and France prevailed by 1872. In short, France's claims remained tenuous many decades after its initial attack on Algiers, and the country would not exercise control over Algeria's vast south until well into the twentieth century (Map 1.1).

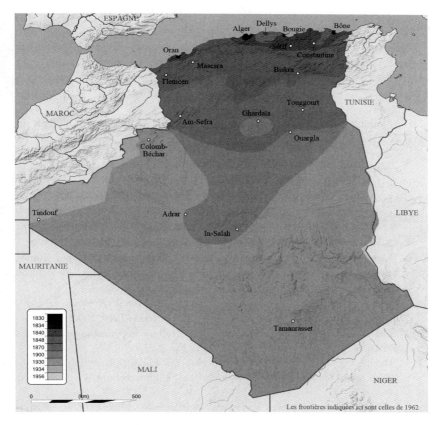

Map 1.1 Real control? The French occupation of Algeria, 1830–1956. *Source*: Sémhur, Wikimedia Commons, https://ca.wikipedia.org/wiki/Fitxer:French_Algeria_evolution_1830-1962_map-fr.svg.

Conclusion

Through most of the 1800s, Europe's overseas expansion was halting and its control over new colonial territories limited. Power remained largely in indigenous hands, and local actors continued to drive most developments. Nonetheless, substantive changes had occurred by the late 1870s. In Europe and the United States, industrialization had accelerated, and the size and power of the state had grown. One state on the forefront, Britain, applied growing strength to a more intensified colonialism in India after suppressing a rebellion there. Russia's Great Reforms, the failure of the Tanzimat, and China's Taiping Rebellion revealed faltering empires. Even if the renewed era of overseas empire building that followed was never a story of inexorable European expansion – Japan's success showed this – by the late 1870s, several European states were positioned to maneuver globally, and they had the capital, tools, and motivations to do so.

Citations

Page	Source
12	"Nothing happened." William Gqoba, "The Cause of the Cattle-Killing at the Nongqause Period," translated by A. C. Jordan, in *Towards an African Literature: The Emergence of Literary Form in Xhosa* (Berkeley: University of California Press, 1973), quoted in *African Voices of the Global Past: 1500 to the Present*, edited by Trevor R. Getz (Boulder, CO: Westview Press, 2014), 55.
14	"Strange and costly..." Quoted in Arnold J. Toynbee, *A Study of History*, abridgement of vols. 1–6, by D. C. Somervell (New York: Oxford University Press, 1946), 37.
14	"economic dynamism." C. A. Bayly, *The Birth of the Modern World 1780–1914: Global Connections and Comparison* (Malden, MA: Blackwell, 2004), 71.
17–8	"March at the head..." and "march against..." Both quoted in Robert Tombs, "Politics," in *The Nineteenth Century: Europe 1789–1914*, edited by T. C. W. Blanning (Oxford: Oxford University Press, 2000), 41.
19	"In the 1830s..." Barbara D. Metcalf and Thomas R. Metcalf, *A Concise History of Modern India*, 2nd ed. (Cambridge: Cambridge University Press, 2006), 99.
25	"I have heard the negroes..." Paul Belloni du Chaillu, *Explorations and Adventures in Equatorial Africa* (New York: Harper & Bros., 1861), 37.
25	"During the whole of the nineteenth century..." Philip D. Curtin, *The Image of Africa: British Ideas and Action, 1780–1850*, vol. 1 (University of Wisconsin Press, 1964), 177.
26	"What use is it..." Quoted in Henry Kamen, *Spain, 1469–1714: A Society of Conflict*, 4th ed. (London: Routledge, 2014), 281–282.

Bibliography

Anderson, Benedict. *Imagined Communities: Reflections on the Origin and Spread of Nationalism.* London: Verso, 1983.

Bayly, C. A. *The Birth of the Modern World: Global Connections and Comparisons.* Malden, MA: Blackwell, 2004.

Frank, Andre Gunder. *ReORIENT: Global Economy in the Asian Age.* Berkeley: University of California Press, 1998.

Kamen, Henry. *Imagining Spain: Historical Myth and National Identity.* New Haven: Yale University Press, 2008.

Karsh, Efraim, and Inari Karsh. *Empires of the Sand: The Struggle for Mastery in the Middle East, 1789–1923.* Cambridge, MA: Harvard University Press, 1999.

Porter, Andrew, ed. *The Oxford History of the British Empire.* Vol. 3: *The Nineteenth Century.* Oxford: Oxford University Press, 1999.

2

The Civilizing Mission and the Race for Empire, 1879–1902

Take up the White Man's burden –
Send forth the best ye breed –
Go bind your sons to exile
To serve your captives' need;
To wait in heavy harness,
On fluttered folk and wild –
Your new-caught, sullen peoples,
   Half-devil and half-child.

Rudyard Kipling, *"The White Man's Burden"* (1899)

"The White Man's Burden," a poem by the Englishman Rudyard Kipling (1865–1936), written around the time of the 1898 Spanish–American War, exhorted Americans to embrace the *mission civilisatrice* or "civilizing mission." Born in British India, Kipling was molded by empire. Castigated today for his pro-imperialism, he was probably the most widely read author in the English language during his lifetime, and he won the Nobel Prize in Literature in 1907. Those like Kipling who believed in the "civilizing mission" held that people of European descent were members of a superior race who should spread their civilization to the rest of the world, a view justifying European political, economic, and military control over other peoples and their lands and resources. While it is today closely associated with overseas imperialism, the *mission civilisatrice* was not exclusive to it: many Russians living in far-flung outposts of the Romanov empire saw themselves as bringing civilization to benighted peoples of the Eurasian Steppe. Many whites believed in the superiority of middle-class

---

European Overseas Empire, 1879–1999: A Short History, First Edition. Matthew G. Stanard.
© 2018 John Wiley & Sons, Inc. Published 2018 by John Wiley & Sons, Inc.

European civilization, and this motivated explorers, missionaries, civil servants, colonial company employees, and others to leave home for remote destinations such as the south Asian or African tropics.

Demonstrating the broad appeal of the civilizing mission is the story of one woman, born the same year as Kipling and, like him, of British descent. Almost all who left the comfortable confines of home to venture among the "uncivilized masses" were men, making this woman an exception that proved the rule. She was the daughter of a plantation owner who had moved his family to a small town in a remote subtropical area when she was an infant. By her twenties she was venturing into the wilderness where she encountered poor brutes scratching out an existence from the land, isolated and largely untouched by the industrial world. They lived in lean-tos. Most were unable to read any European language. They were unfamiliar with the basics of Christianity.

Like many missionaries, this woman opened a school centered on teachings and stories from the Bible. One school became two, then four. Her father gave her land in support of her work, and she acquired more on her own. Like many who embarked on the civilizing mission, although she was not from the area, she remained where she worked, unmarried, dedicating her life to others. She outlived Kipling by just a few years, passing away in 1942. She had directed her schools for more than four decades.

What makes this story somewhat unique is that this apostle of Western, Christian culture did not embark on the civilizing mission in a tropical region of Africa, south Asia, or Latin America, but among "whites" in the US state of Georgia. This woman was Martha Berry, founder of Berry College, the institution where this author works. Her story demonstrates how deep the *mission civilisatrice* had taken root throughout Europe and the United States and how many people shared the idea of "uplifting" natives in what were to them remote corners of the earth.

Ms. Berry founded the Berry Schools in 1902. By that year, European states, joined by the United States and Japan, had carved out massive new colonial empires that reshaped the globe. What drove this momentous shift in world history? Contemporaries took up this question, and it became a major historical problem that students of history have debated ever since. This chapter answers this question by zeroing in on competing explanations as to the underlying cause or causes of this new era of empire.

Before addressing the question as to what drove the New Imperialism, it is worthwhile examining the story of how this new era of overseas conquest unfolded, and it is with that story that the chapter begins. European colonialism, underway by around 1879, accelerated from 1885, following a conference in Berlin that launched a "scramble" for overseas territories. Competition between European states put innumerable people on the move, increasing migration. Even if peoples beyond Europe continued to shape their own destinies, they were increasingly forced to contend with European wealth, industrial power, advanced technologies, and aggression, oftentimes forcing them to choose between resistance, accommodation, or collaboration. At stake was power: who would control which territories and resources, and who would rule whom. Europeans, who were in the ascendant, were anything but omnipotent, nor were their empires inevitable. Many states remained independent, and Japan even became an imperial power in its own right.

A Scramble for Colonial Territories

A new era of European overseas colonialism dawned in the late 1870s. Russia defeated the Ottomans in the Russo-Turkish War of 1877–1878, and the subsequent Treaty of Berlin (1878) gave Austria–Hungary authority over Bosnia–Herzegovina and freed now independent Montenegro, Serbia, Romania, and Bulgaria from Ottoman control. France took advantage of Turkish weakness with the 1881 Bardo Treaty, which declared a French protectorate over Tunisia, located east of Algeria and nominally under Ottoman control. The Italians protested: as the Italian island of Lampedusa is closer to Tunisia than to Sicily, and considering that in 1881 there were some 11,000 Italians in Tunisia compared to only 700 French, they believed that Tunisia lay within their sphere of influence.

The Bardo Treaty of 1881 precipitated a British countermove in Egypt, which, like Tunisia, was nominally subject to the Ottomans. Mounting debt owed to France and Britain had led to greater foreign involvement, and those two states continued to jockey for influence in Egypt as they had for decades. A failed attempt in 1879 to remove foreign influence led to the re-establishment of dual Franco-British control, which the British leveraged into a full-scale takeover in 1882 under Agent-General Evelyn Baring, later Lord Cromer. Cromer, like many of his contemporaries, did not believe that the Egyptians had the "character" necessary to run their own affairs. The British were supremely self-assured, convinced that they were delivering sound finance and administration for the Egyptians' own good and unaware of how their actions served their own narrow financial interests and their desire to control the Suez Canal's connection to India.

British self-confidence manifested itself as expansionism in southern Africa. The 1867 discovery of diamonds at Kimberley made the British see the area as crucial to the Cape Colony's well-being. The British invasion and occupation of the Boer republic of Transvaal in 1877 was followed by an incursion into Zululand in 1879, where the Zulu were victorious at the Battle of Isandhlwana. Shocked, the British sent a larger force, defeated the Zulu, broke up their nation, exiled their leader, Cetshwayo, and incorporated Zululand into Britain's Natal colony (1887). The once independent Transvaal rebelled, leading to another defeat for the British at the 1881 Battle of Majuba Hill, and the re-establishment of Transvaal's independence. Such defeats reveal that European success was hardly preordained.

The Civilizing Mission and the Race for Empire, 1879–1902

In Asia, the Dutch increased on-the-ground control in the East Indies to forestall French or British meddling, continuing a war against Aceh in Sumatra. Although the Dutch had backed away from overseas holdings elsewhere, for example on west Africa's coast, and had lost possessions like the Cape Colony (to the British), their growing assertiveness in the East Indies belied their expansionistic tendencies. Whereas around the mid-1800s Dutch control was limited to Java and other pockets, by the early 1900s it was to encompass nearly the entire archipelago, ushering in an era of intensified rule.

French involvement grew in mainland southeast Asia, a region where Catholic missionaries had been active for many years. As the French expanded into Annam, the Mekong Delta, the Red River Delta, and northeast Vietnam, individuals on the ground propelled conquest. Indochina's governor-general (and future French president) Paul Doumer tried to seize more territory, despite contrary orders from Paris. Conflict along colonial "turbulent frontiers" created by such European incursions then justified further expansion. France's claims brought it to China's southern border, precipitating a Sino-French War (1884–1885) and a French victory at Fuzhou extending and solidifying the French presence. France's defeat of Siam in 1892 was followed by the extension of a protectorate over Laos, creating French Indochina: Vietnam (Cochinchina, Annam, Tonkin), Laos, and Cambodia, the latter of which had been a French protectorate since 1867. Although missionaries had paved the way, the goal was less spreading Christianity than it was accessing Chinese markets and achieving national glory by creating France's own "crown jewel" of empire. Although the 1885 Treaty of Tianjin included provisions forcing China to open its markets, in reality it was more government officials than investors leading the way, the latter seeing better investment opportunities in Europe, whereas politicians, explorers, and imperial enthusiasts valued prestige over profit.

Already in greater control of India following the Sepoy Uprising, Britain went to war against Burma in 1885, the third in half a century. Britain's victory by 1886 forestalled further French incursions into mainland southeast Asia. The European appetite for territorial expansion reached new heights, with seizures of islands in Oceania and the continued colonization of Australia and New Zealand.

The 1884–1885 Berlin Conference

Growing overseas competition led Chancellor Otto von Bismarck – the driving personality in Germany, the Continent's leading power after 1870 – to convene a conference on west Africa in Berlin in 1884. No non-Europeans were invited. Ironically, Bismarck was uninterested in colonies at the time, his priority being Germany's position in Europe. When a colonial enthusiast presented him with a map of Africa in 1888, Bismarck pointed to one of Europe, saying, "Your map of Africa is quite nice, but my map of Africa lies here in Europe. Here is Russia.

The Civilizing Mission and the Race for Empire, 1879–1902

And here is France, and we are in the middle: that is my map of Africa." Bismarck wanted to ensure that no overseas conflicts spilled over into a European conflict. The conference did not divide up Africa and Asia; rather it set the ground rules for establishing "effective occupation," for example by getting local chiefs to sign treaties recognizing foreign sovereignty. Once everyone knew the rules, though, the "Scramble for Africa" began.

In truth, the scramble was already underway. Explorer Carl Peters, founder of the Gesellschaft für Deutsche Kolonisation (Society for German Colonization), returned to Germany from east Africa, treaties in hand, just as the Berlin Conference was wrapping up in the spring of 1885. He had persuaded chiefs and others to sign treaties recognizing German sovereignty, and he went on to head the German East Africa Company that set out to conquer, settle, and make profitable German possessions in east Africa. Peters faced competition from the Imperial British East Africa Company (IBEAC), a chartered company headed by Frederick Lugard. Earlier reports by Welsh American explorer Henry Morton Stanley about Kabaka Mutesa I's realm had elicited a huge reaction in England, and the Protestant Church Missionary Society sent missionaries to Buganda. Missionaries of the Catholic White Fathers followed, in response to Mutesa I's willingness to entertain them. Mutesa's death in 1884 precipitated a civil conflict between Catholics, Protestants, and Muslims. When European missionaries were killed in 1890, the IBEAC moved in, defeated an indigenous army, and established control over densely populated Buganda. In 1895–1896 the British government took over from the IBEAC.

Events in Buganda underscored not only how missionaries sometimes provoked greater involvement but also the importance of strategic considerations. Europeans sometimes saw it necessary to seize territories in order to protect existing interests. In the case of Britain, the felt need to control the Suez Canal and the route to India justified involvement in Egypt, the Sudan, and Buganda even further south. Even if a power did not want a territory, it would not want a rival to acquire it and potentially benefit as a result. Control of waterways and steamship coaling stations was also critical. This was a key argument of US Navy officer Alfred Thayer Mahan's widely read 1890 book, *The Influence of Sea Power on History*. (German Kaiser Wilhelm II is said to have kept a copy on his bedside table.) For many contemporaries, Britain's global sway and its navy (the world's largest) only confirmed Mahan's theory about sea power. Indeed, by the 1870s Britain was a global imperial power without need of new territories, and official policy proscribed seizing additional territories in tropical Africa. Yet strategic considerations caused this to happen.

As the IBEAC conquered Buganda for Britain, so did private companies do the dirty work of conquest for Germany in east Africa. In 1888 Arab-Swahili people revolted against foreign incursions and offensive German practices, for example bringing dogs into mosques. The IBEAC and the German East Africa Company suppressed the uprising together. In 1889, faced with mounting costs and the potential for further revolts, the German East Africa Company ceded its holdings to the government, creating the colony of German East Africa.

Whereas the British and Germans employed chartered companies, it was the French state that led the way in west Africa, where French forces did not meet as much resistance as they might have expected. Al-hajj Umar had in the 1860s created an empire around the Senegal and Niger rivers, but his rule was so brutal that he and his son and successor, Ahmadu Seku, were unpopular. (Al-hajj Umar was killed by his own people.) As French colonial troops moved southward from Algeria and Tunisia to meet forces advancing from the west African coasts, they allowed themselves to believe that they arrived as liberators, not as conquerors. The resistance of Samori Touré, who had created the state of Futa Jallon of the Mande people, reflected the true situation as he fought and defied the French for some twenty years.

The Royal Niger Company, under the command of Frederick Lugard — who had been active earlier in east Africa — campaigned in west Africa, moving northward and inland along the Oil Rivers from 1894 to 1906. Lugard's forces conquered the Fula and Hausa peoples who controlled territory to the north bordering the Sahel. Although British missionaries who arrived at this time made little headway in Northern Nigeria, where Islam was well established, they had more success in the south.

As in Indochina and India, conquests in Africa were spurred on by the man on the spot, that is colonial administrators or military officers far removed from their home country. The powerful Asante of west Africa believed that their Golden Stool held their power and represented the people and soul and good fortune of the nation. Frederick Hodgson, a British representative to the Asante with the title of governor was ignorant of the Golden Stool's importance. At a meeting of Asante chiefs in January 1900, he demanded, "Where is the Gold Stool? Why am I not sitting on the Golden Stool at this moment? I am the representative of the paramount power; why have you relegated me to this chair?" The Asante resisted this crude challenge (one did not sit on the Golden Stool), and Hodgson ordered his soldiers to find and seize it. As one eyewitness put it,

> The white man asked the children where the Golden Stool was kept ... The white man said he would beat the children if they did not bring their fathers from the bush. The children told the white man not to call their fathers. If he wanted to beat them, he should do it. The children knew the white men were coming for the Golden Stool. The children did not fear beating. The white soldiers began to bully and beat the children.

The search provoked a full-scale revolt led by the Asante queen mother, Yaa Asantewaa, and a siege of the governor in Kumase. It took a British expeditionary force to defeat the queen mother, and in 1901 the British annexed the defeated Asante.

The Civilizing Mission and the Race for Empire, 1879–1902

Elsewhere the scramble continued. German private companies and government officials staked claims in southwest Africa, Cameroon, and Togoland in west Africa. Without consulting any Africans, Britain and Germany signed the 1890 Anglo-German Treaty settling the boundaries of British Nigeria, Cameroon, and Togoland, among other provisions. Portugal transformed control of coastal zones in southern Africa into the colonies of Angola and Mozambique. War in Mozambique against the Gaza state in the 1890s culminated in the defeat and capture of the leader Ngungunyane, whom the Portuguese exiled to the Azores. Portugal's dominion was always tenuous nonetheless, and it never controlled more than perhaps 10 percent of territories it claimed. (The country's other overseas claims included small coastal enclaves or ports in south and east Asia, the Azores, Madeira, and Portuguese Guinea in west Africa, where its settlements dated back to the fifteenth century.) Also in southern Africa, the 1886 discovery of gold on the Witwatersrand led to another gold rush. The British imperialist, businessman, and South African politician Cecil Rhodes chartered the British South Africa Company (BSAC), deviously extracting mining rights from King Lobengula of the Ndebele people. Rhodes and his agents were only the latest in a long series of Europeans who tricked or cajoled local authorities into signing "blank treaties" that surrendered all kinds of resources and authority to Europeans. After defeating the Ndebele and Shona in the early 1890s, the BSAC established the colonies of Northern and Southern Rhodesia.

Like that of Rhodes, the impact of the Belgian king Leopold II in central Africa was outsized, underscoring the role of the individual in history. By financing explorations and through a series of diplomatic maneuvers, Leopold parlayed signed treaties into recognition by European powers of his personal sovereignty over the Congo River basin area, and he proclaimed the État Indépendant du Congo (Congo Free State, CFS) in 1885. Leopold II needed administrators, engineers, explorers, doctors, as well as officers, to staff an armed force known as the Force Publique. The CFS was in many ways an international colony, recruiting men from many parts of Europe, for example Italian doctors and Scandinavian military officers. After depleting his private savings, Leopold turned to the exploitation of natural rubber, ivory, and African labor to finance the colony, leading to a brutal regime of forced work. For a price, he turned over massive tracts of land to concessionary companies, which were allowed to exploit those territories in exchange for a share of their profits.

What followed were atrocities including coerced labor, hostage taking, imprisonment, forced starvation, mutilation, and whipping. The American Edgar Canisius, who worked for the CFS in 1896, reported, "I have occasionally seen even 100 lashes administered, the instrument used being the 'chicotte,' a heavy whip of hippopotamus hide." Forced laborers were often given a metal tag to wear on a chain around their necks – this "tagged" them – at which point they "became mere slaves to the company, for rubber-making occupied all their time, the victim having to search far and wide for the giant vines from which the sap is extracted. They were not even fed by their taskmasters." Just like the French, British, Germans, Dutch, and Portuguese elsewhere, the Force Publique waged military campaigns, especially from 1890 to 1894 against Arab-Swahili traders in eastern Congo. Leopold claimed that his goal was ending the Arab slave trade, but in reality he was after territory.

The year CFS forces concluded their antislavery campaigns, war broke out between Japan and China, and Japan's victory the following year confirmed China's weakness and the success of Meiji industrialization. The 1895 Treaty of Shimonoseki wrested Korea from a centuries-long vassal state relationship with China, and Japan swooped in. Japan's increased east Asian presence put it in competition with Russia, Britain, Germany, France, and the United States, the latter advocating an "open door" policy as outside powers carved out spheres of influence across China.

The year following the first Sino-Japanese War saw another war break out, this one in northeastern Africa. By the mid-1890s, Ethiopia's Menelik II was enlarging his realm, bringing him into proximity of other expansionist powers like the Italians, who had eked out a territory along the Red Sea coast — Eritrea — and who were trying to expand their influence inland. Ethiopia ceded the Italians a limited presence in the Treaty of Ucciali (Wuchale). Whereas the Italians read their version of the treaty as saying that Ethiopia was an Italian protectorate, the Ethiopians' Amharic version read otherwise. The Italians armed Ethiopia so that Menelik could consolidate his power, but then Menelik turned to the French to construct a railway from French Djibouti to his capital at Addis Ababa. The Italians used this move as a pretext for war. Ethiopia's decisive victory at the 1896 Battle of Adowa humiliated Italy, thereby confirming the power of European nationalism. More importantly, Adowa secured Ethiopia's independence as a major African state, and it later joined the ranks of legitimate nation-states when it became a member of the League of Nations after World War I.

The race to Fashoda

Inter-imperial relations reached a boiling point in 1898 at Fashoda, today a remote village in South Sudan, where French and British soldiers faced off in a tense stalemate in the summer heat. The French army captain Jean-Baptiste Marchand and some 140 officers and soldiers confronted a larger British force led by Horatio Kitchener. Both groups had been tasked to reach and claim Fashoda, an abandoned post on the White Nile in one of the last African regions unclaimed by Europeans. When news of the face-off reached Europe, the French and British publics lit up with nationalistic fervor. War loomed as the world looked on.

Marchand and Kitchener kept their cool and the French backed down, since Marchand faced a larger British force and Paris sought to avoid war. It was a surprising decision considering the grueling 14-month-long journey the French had endured. The dream was to link up France's west African territories with

French Somaliland on the Horn of Africa to control the north–south Sahara trade and to prevent any linking of British possessions from the Cape to Cairo. Marchand and his men had departed the Atlantic coast, made their way up the Congo and then Ubangi rivers, through the Bahr al-Ghazal to the White Nile, and finally Fashoda. It took months and entailed dragging necessities like a steamer (disassembled) and, naturally, crates of wine.

Kitchener's larger contingent had raced south up the Nile. At the beginning of September it engaged the forces of Muhammad Ahmad, a Sudanese leader who had proclaimed himself Mahdi – an Islamic messianic redeemer who, it was believed, would return one day – and who had created a Mahdist state in Sudan in defiance of Egypt. Kitchener's men defeated the Mahdi's forces decisively at the Battle of Omdurman. This represented a change in Britain's approach. It had been unwilling to intervene against the Mahdist state because of the cost. But because Egypt owed it so much money and Britain wanted repayment, because of Belgian and Italian designs on the region, and because of the Suez Canal's strategic importance, the British decided to have Egypt reassert control in the Sudan. Thus did a combined Anglo-Egyptian force march up the Nile and engage the Mahdi's forces near Khartoum. Armed with machine guns and steam ships with breech-loading cannons, it overwhelmed the Sudanese, by some estimates killing some 20,000 Mahdist soldiers. The Anglo-Egyptian force suffered a few dozen casualties. It then continued south, reaching Fashoda not long after Marchand.

Omdurman and Fashoda reveal several things, the first being Europeans' power to act at incredible distances, and locals' limited ability to stop them. Today, more than a century later, areas such as the Upper Nile and the Upper Ubangi remain remote. Even if local leaders continued to pursue their own expansionistic agendas, leaders in Paris and London and men on the spot believed that their real rivals were other Europeans, not native peoples. Fashoda also reveals the power of mass politics, rapid communication, and European nationalism. The publics in France and Britain followed the news from Sudan with passion inflamed by nationalism, and popular sentiment strongly constrained decision-makers' room for maneuver. France backed down, reinforcing the impression that, although France had once again become a great imperial power, it was operating in what was a British world. Shortly afterward, the British and French agreed on spheres of influence in Africa, and six years later signed an *entente cordiale*, or "friendly agreement," to regulate their colonial affairs, which brought them closer together.

Migration and Forced Labor

Although it coincided with an era of heightened European migration, the New Imperialism did not lead to mass migration to Africa or Asia, emigrants preferring the United States, Canada, South America, or Australia. Colonialism did put many indigenous people on the move, for instance in the CFS, where atrocities led people to flee. Jules Jacques was an official there from 1895 to 1898, tasked with harvesting rubber and further exploration. After the inhabitants of Inongo cut down rubber vines, Jacques wrote to the local European post chief:

> We have to beat them into complete subjection or into complete extermination ... Warn the people of Inongo a very last time and carry out your plan to take them to the woods as quickly as possible ... gather them in the village with a good club and address yourself to the proprietor of the first shack: here is a basket, go and fill it with rubber ... If you have not returned within ten days with a basket of 5 kilos of rubber, I will burn down the shacks. And you will burn it as promised ... Warn them that if they chop down one more rubber vine I will exterminate them to the last one.

Unsurprisingly, many Africans fled.

In southern Africa, Boer land hunger drove Africans off their lands. For many, movement and relocation were nothing new. Migration of entire homesteads among the Basotho, for instance, went back to the reign of King Moshoeshoe (d. 1870). It was not until the 1870s, however, that large-scale migration of adult men began. The nascent diamond mining industry needed labor, which worked in favor of people like the Basotho, whose chiefs directed male migration, one of their primary aims being to attain guns. When mining wages declined, Basotho returned home or sought employment elsewhere. It was only later, after gold's discovery and the rise of rural impoverishment that many Basotho were forced to become labor migrants, earning cash at the mines and then returning home.

Some got caught in a system of indentured labor for resource extraction. Although Europeans abolished slavery from almost all colonies by mid-century, they oftentimes replaced it with indentured labor, for example in the Caribbean. They also continued the longstanding practice of condemning criminals to penal colonies and using them as convict labor, for instance in British Australia, French Guiana, or Portuguese Angola. The brother of Mohamed El-Mokrani, who led an 1871 uprising in Algeria and was killed, was captured and condemned to prison on French New Caledonia. French soldiers found guilty of certain infractions were reassigned to the infamous Bataillons d'Afrique, stationed in north Africa under harsh conditions.

Resistance and Collaboration

All sorts of peoples and states had to decide how to respond to growing European dynamism and pressure. The New Imperialism took place in the context of a world of empires and of competition between European states, the United States, Russia, China, Ethiopia, the Zulu, the Ottoman Turks, and others. The unsuccessful Indian Rebellion of 1857 was just the tip of the iceberg in terms of organized resistance to colonial rule. The revolutionary Phan Đình Phùng joined with the Can Vuong movement to lead anti-French campaigns in Vietnam. As noted, Samori Touré, a soldier-trader who sought to re-establish the Mande empire, resisted the French in west Africa, eluding them for years in the Guinea Highlands.

Some anticolonialist movements were well organized. The first Indian National Congress was held in 1885, the same year that the Berlin Conference concluded. Composed of generally Western-educated, well-off Indians, it did not call for an end to colonialism but for more rights and a greater role for them in governing India. That same decade saw a parallel development in Ireland, a British colony incorporated into "Great Britain and Ireland" in 1801. Irish nationalists pushed for Home Rule. The House of Commons introduced multiple pieces of legislation to grant Home Rule, but they were always stymied, in some cases by the House of Lords. There was a first Pan-African Congress in 1900.

Sometimes resistance was subtle, like work-site slowdowns or using European ignorance of native languages to call European colonials bad names. In Rudyard Kipling's novel *Kim*, the eponymous protagonist is of European descent but grows up in the streets of Lahore, passes as a native, and dislikes the British. One ignorant British drummer boy with whom Kim had to associate, "resented his silence and lack of interest by beating him, as was only natural ... He styled all natives 'niggers'; yet servants and sweepers called him abominable names to his face, and, misled by their deferential attitude, he never understood. This somewhat consoled Kim for the beatings."

Others took advantage of Europeans. Buganda's Mutesa I welcomed both Protestant and Catholic missionaries so that he could play them off each other. Tippu Tip, who helped Stanley cross the African continent, parlayed his dominance in eastern Congo into a governorship under Leopold II, and the Belgian king's colonial state only displaced him with great difficulty, using armed force in the 1890s. Menelik II used French money to finance a railway. Some went to work for European colonials. In Vietnam, Hoang Cao Khai accepted the position of viceroy in Tonkin and helped track down anti-French revolutionary Phan Đình Phùng. Bou El Mogdad Seck worked as a translator for the French in Senegal, facilitating Faidherbe's conquests there. Thus did indigenous collaboration sometimes facilitate European involvement.

Real Colonial Control?

The so-called "rise of the West" from the 1500s should not be understood as the absolute "decline of the rest." Non-European actors from the Qing in China to Buganda's Kabaka Mutesa to Ethiopia's emperors wielded great clout. But, by the late 1800s, Europe (and the United States) had leapfrogged other world areas technologically, developing "tools of empire" that made conquest feasible, which only accelerated during the Second Industrial Revolution, leading to more powerful steam engines and improved weaponry. Surveying and the gathering of geographical, topographical, and other scientific, as well as commercial, data were other tools of imperialism, which tipped the scale against native peoples, "whose control over their destinies could be eroded as surely by map coordinates and museum specimens as by steamships, bullets, and treaties of cession." Many advances, for instance in cartography and medicine, developed alongside colonial expansion. For all the attempts at resistance, Europe's superiority in weapons and technology prevailed, with few exceptions. As Hilaire Belloc's ditty put it, "Whatever happens, we have got/The Maxim gun, and they have not."

That said, European control was never complete, and we should never mistake rapid conquests for total control. There are innumerable maps depicting the dramatic expansion of European rule during the Scramble for Africa, oftentimes two maps comparing an extremely limited European presence in the 1870s and a map around 1900 or 1914 with all borders drawn across Africa, all colonies color coded according to the ruling European power (see Map 2.1). In reality, more often than not, real colonial control was more limited.

Consider France's protectorate in Tunisia, established by the 1881 Bardo Treaty with the Tunisian bey. Even if in practice Tunisia was very much subject to French wishes, the French still had to contend with the bey's government. Because the treaty guaranteed the extraterritorial sovereignty for citizens of European states – at the time there were some 11,000 Italians and 7,000 British citizens there – this meant that the French competed for authority with the bey, local Tunisians, and foreign powers. When the French declared their "co-sovereignty" with the bey after World War I to boost their power – going from just *protecting* his regime to being *sovereign* in Tunisia – this unwittingly boosted the bey's authority because France recognized it as equal to its own. In short, the French were never fully in control.

Another telling incident is that of the Stairs expedition in the CFS. To occupy his colony, Leopold II sent missions to stake out claims before the Germans, British, Portuguese, or French outmaneuvered him. In 1891 the chartered Compagnie du Katanga sent out two such expeditions, one under the command of Captain William Grant Stairs who, like many others working for the CFS, was not Belgian (he was British). Stairs targeted Msiri, head of the Garanganja kingdom, to make him recognize the authority of the CFS. In response to an earlier demand to place himself under Leopold II, Msiri had responded, "I am the master here, and as long as I'm alive, the Kingdom of Garanganja will have no other master but me." Msiri was uninterested in submitting to another central African empire; he wanted to rule his own.

When the Stairs group arrived at Msiri's headquarters in Bunkeya, Msiri initially welcomed it: since Stairs was British, Msiri thought he could use him as an ally against the Belgians. When Msiri found out that Stairs worked for the

The Civilizing Mission and the Race for Empire, 1879–1902

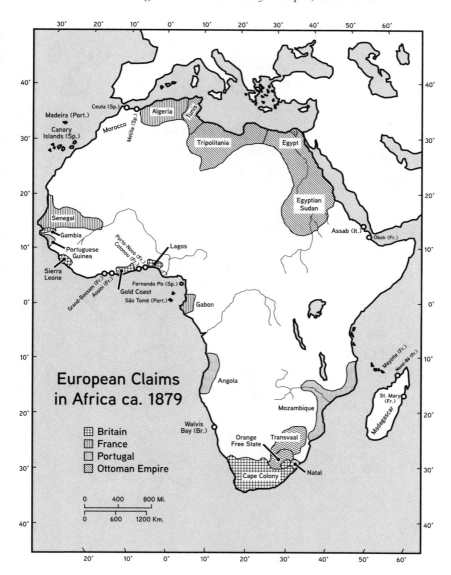

Map 2.1 European claims in Africa: ca. 1879 and 1914. *Source*: Maps drawn by Stanard Design Partners, Cincinnati, Ohio (USA).

The Civilizing Mission and the Race for Empire, 1879–1902

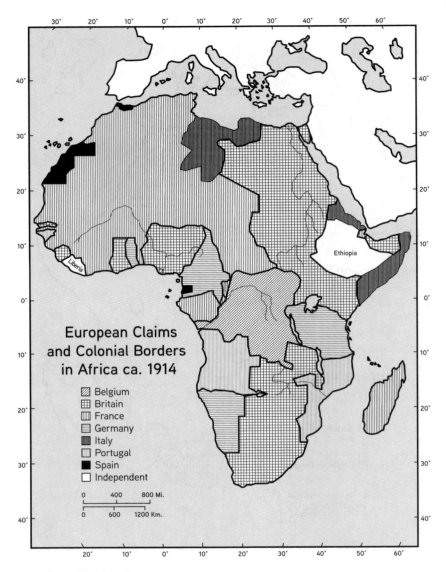

Map 2.1 (Continued)

Belgian king, he grew alarmed, and refused Stairs's pleas to hoist the CFS flag. After arguing the matter over for a series of days, Stairs finally just hoisted the flag, and Msiri and his men left Bunkeya for a nearby village to regroup.

Stairs dispatched one Captain Bodson and some dozen soldiers to retrieve Msiri, but he refused to return. Threats were exchanged. Bodson drew his revolver and shot Msiri three times, killing him. Bodson died at the hands of one of Msiri's bodyguards, by gunfire. With Msiri's death, the area did fall to the CFS – locals had grown tired of Msiri's exactions, especially his constant ivory raiding. The Bodson fiasco also reveals how Europeans were not the only ones vying for power in central Africa, and that they were relatively weak when confronted by organized polities. In this case, they had to stoop to assassination and trickery to get their way.

Expansion at Century's End

Between 1898 and 1902, a series of events capped this era of European empire building. Britain's decisive victory over the Mahdist state in 1898 reasserted Anglo-Egyptian control over the Upper Nile. The French finally captured Samori Touré, exiling him to Gabon. The United States, which had joined the race for empire, annexed Hawai'i and went to war with Spain. Americans had long criticized Spanish colonialism in Cuba. After losing its mainland American colonies in the early nineteenth century, Spain had made Cuba even more profitable, in particular sugar cultivation, of interest to United States importers and investors. Profits grew despite uprisings and prolonged anticolonial wars from the late 1860s to 1880. José Marti launched another war of independence in 1895, dying soon after it had begun, which led to growing criticism of Spain in the United States. In 1898 the USS *Maine*, sent to Cuba to protect Americans, exploded, which the United States used as a pretext to intervene. A brief war (April to August 1898) resulted in Spain's defeat and the US takeover of the Philippines, Cuba, and Puerto Rico. Thus in the Philippines, which had been under some form of Spanish influence or control from the sixteenth century, freedom from Spanish rule was followed by a new foreign regime. Rebellion ensued, followed by a savage US suppression that resulted in some 5,000 American and 200,000 Filipino dead.

North of the Philippines, China's Boxer Rebellion tried to expel foreign influence, and its outcome only exemplified Europe's and Japan's expansionism. Tired of foreign meddling, Boxer rebels in 1899 attacked Christians and foreigners. Part of the Qing imperial household supported the uprising, illustrating once again how China's leadership was caught between reformers and traditionalists. Kaiser Wilhelm II's July 1900 *Hunnenrede*, or "Hun speech," with which he saw off his China-bound troops, underscored European callousness:

> Should you encounter the enemy, he will be defeated! No quarter will be given! Prisoners will not be taken! Whoever falls into your hands is forfeited. Just as a thousand years ago the Huns under their King Attila made a name for themselves, one that even today makes them seem mighty in history and legend, may the name German be affirmed by you in such a way in China that no Chinese will ever again dare to look cross-eyed at a German.

In the end, US, German, French, Japanese, Italian, Indian, Austrian, and British troops crushed the uprising and extracted even more concessions from the Qing. French and British cooperation against rebels in southern China underlined the rapprochement between those two powers. A subsequent Anglo-Japanese treaty (1902), in which Britain – still possessor of the world's most powerful navy – recognized Japan as a leading Pacific power signaled the latter's continued rise.

The Boer War

The year 1902 also marked the conclusion of a war between Britain and the two Boer states of Transvaal and the Orange Free State. In short, the British had gone to war with the Boers over gold. The 1886 discovery of gold in Transvaal attracted thousands of foreigners, called *uitlanders*, who soon outnumbered Boers. Transvaal restricted *uitlander* rights in order to maintain Boer control. In 1895 the British South African L. S. Jameson and the South African prime minister Cecil Rhodes hatched a plan to raid Transvaal from Rhodesia to incite a rebellion among *uitlanders* and to overthrow the government. The *uitlanders* did not respond, the "Jameson Raid" failed, and its conspirators were rounded up and jailed. Rhodes resigned.

In 1899, again pressing the point about *uitlander* rights, the British pushed the Orange Free State and Transvaal into war. Both sides fought without arming Africans. Britain sent a massive force averaging some 250,000 men – its maximum strength hit 450,000 – compared to a *total* Boer population of some 200,000 and a fielded force of 45,000. Horatio Kitchener, the victor of Omdurman, commanded the British colonial troops, and Britain's press cheered as its forces routed the Boers in the field by mid-1900. Some 15,000 Boer "commandos" turned to guerilla warfare, and held out for two more years. Finally, Boer leaders signed the 1902 Peace of Vereeniging, ending both the war and Transvaal's and the Orange Free State's independence.

Despite victory, British public opinion was shocked. Kitchener had resorted to brutal measures, including a farm-burning campaign that destroyed more than 600 farms in the Orange Free State and made thousands homeless. Britain's War Office built camps to "concentrate" and control whites and blacks, which by the war's end held some 100,000 Boers and 110,000 Africans. Poor conditions and careless organization led to exposure and disease. More than 28,000 Boer civilians died in concentration camps, most of them women and children, "more than twice the number of men on both sides killed in the fighting of the war. The death rates were even higher in the African camps." Why, the British public asked, had the country sent so many men so far away to fight a savage war costing taxpayers £200 million? Many were surprised at the imperialistic jingoism that accompanied the war, as it had much of the overseas conquest of the late nineteenth century. The British saw themselves as sitting at the apex of human civilization and history, imbued with rationalism and faith in people's shared humanity. How could Europe have embarked on another round of violent conquest overseas?

Explaining Imperialism's Causes

Capitalism and empire

One person raising such questions was the Englishman J. A. Hobson, whose book *Imperialism: A Study* (1902) offered an economic explanation: imperialism was a symptom of structural imbalances inherent in industrial capitalism. Low wages paid to workers led to weak purchasing power, underconsumption, and limits on profitable domestic investment. Capital moved inexorably in the direction of more profitable investments in colonies. Related to this was a search for protected markets. Many European governments had adopted freer trade by the mid-1800s, but a depression beginning in 1873 led Austria (1874), Russia (1875), Italy (1887), and France (1892) to raise tariffs to protect domestic industries. By the early twentieth century, Germany had imposed a whopping 25 percent tax on industrial and agricultural imports. Countries thus sought colonies for markets. Hobson's solution was structural reform: higher worker wages to increase consumption. The Bolshevik leader Vladimir Lenin later elaborated on Hobson's theory in his work *Imperialism: The Highest Stage of Capitalism* (1916), agreeing that industrialists invested in colonies because capitalism had become "overripe" and because the masses were impoverished. But Lenin went further, developing a rigid interpretation focused more on the profits financiers made from colonial investments. Lenin believed that capitalism was incapable of reform and that imperialism was its last gasp before inevitable collapse.

It made sense to many that the drive for profit that flowed from industrialism gave rise to overseas expansion. As European wealth grew, investors sought new investment opportunities. Westward expansion in the pursuit of more land by European settlers in the United States and Australia found a counterpart in Russia's extension eastward. Many became convinced that colonies could be ideal zones for investment and control over exclusive markets and natural resources. Britain's war against the Boers seemed to confirm this. Raw materials, especially precious metals, were of longstanding interest to Europeans, and they gained value in an era of growing industrialism. There were gold rushes in California (1849), Australia (1851), and Transvaal (1886), and a rush after diamonds were discovered at Kimberley (1867).

But the more scholars delved into the details of the economics of empire, the more it seemed that Hobson and Lenin had based their argument on a coincidence of increased overseas investment during the New Imperialism. For imperialism to be "economic," economic interests with a stake in conquest – in trade, industry, or investment – had to be identifiable groups of capitalists who put colonial dependencies to their own use, or who formed an essential part of the economic interests to which home governments had to pay attention. Only then could one say that a government and its overseas possessions had become "tools of capitalism." These conditions did not exist until perhaps the last years of the nineteenth century, after most imperial expansion already had taken place.

Later study confirmed that it was not capital's inexorable search for profits that drove this new era of empire. Portuguese colonialism after 1850 was thwarted by investor resistance: "it was rare that any private investor would be willing to invest in any major project in Portuguese Africa." With exceptions, British colonies did not attract large amounts of British finance. An astounding proportion – 75 percent – of all British private and public capital was either invested within Britain or Ireland or in foreign countries, not the empire. Viewed globally, the British empire was not money making, and colonial investments were no more profitable than those made at home. By and large, individual colonies were not profitable. The trading company that pioneered German involvement in southwest Africa went bankrupt in the mid-1890s. The French state had to encourage investment in Indochina because it was so slow to happen on its own. When Henry Morton Stanley presented the findings of one of his central African voyages to the Manchester Chamber of Commerce, its members declined to take up his call to invest there.

Although colonial trade grew, it remained small, and its expansion did not track the massive enlargement of empire from 1879 to 1902. Britain's trade with its colonies at the empire's height was small, and colonial trade constituted only 9.5 percent of both French total exports and imports. Protectionism in Europe did not drive colonial expansion, nor did protected colonial markets benefit European industries, in the aggregate. Big tariffs in Germany and France *followed* much colonial expansion, for example France's 1892 Méline tariff or Germany's 25 percent tariff on industrial and agricultural goods. Moreover those two tariffs hardly slowed trade between Germany and France, which meant that exporters did not need the security of colonial outlets. And countries that never abandoned free trade – Belgium, Britain, the Netherlands – became colonial powers anyway.

To be sure, some companies and individuals made fortunes. Leopold II, who was one of Europe's richest men, first depleted his fortune in the Congo before making it back, and then some. Cecil Rhodes became fabulously wealthy from mining in southern Africa. More importantly, although colonies might not have been altogether profitable, the *idea* that money was to be made drove much conquest.

The Civilizing Mission and the Race for Empire, 1879–1902

A revival of missionary activity

If it was not capital's inexorable search for profits that drove imperialism, what was it? Kipling's poem and Berry's work in Georgia illustrate how a renewed missionizing movement and belief in the "civilizing mission" were factors. Although the French Revolution of 1789 had sapped the church's authority in Europe, it endured. Many women remained churchgoers, finding there a social outlet in an age when men went to cafes and pubs. Even nonbelieving men took pride in the moral character of their wives and daughters and valued the stability that the church provided. Later in the century many bourgeois turned, or returned, to the church, seeing it as a bulwark of social stability in a time of growing uncertainty. Catholic religious orders revived. In France the number of nuns grew from 37,000 in 1851 to 162,000 in 1901, an increase that vastly outstripped population growth. Visions of the Virgin Mary and popular religious pilgrimages to Santiago de Compostela, Lourdes, and elsewhere underscored rejuvenated faith.

Missionary activity revived from the 1830s, and Protestants and Catholics often competed overseas, although it was seldom imagined that the redemption of souls would one day involve the taking of political power. The Church Missionary Society founded Fourah Bay College in Freetown, Sierra Leone, in 1827, which trained missionaries. French Cardinal Lavigerie founded the Catholic Pères Blancs, or White Fathers, in Algiers in 1868. Relations between missionaries and governments grew stronger from mid-century on, even in the overtly secular French Third Republic (after 1871) where church–state conflict reached crisis proportions in 1906 when a new law forbade Catholic involvement in education; some clergy had to be dragged out of schools. Yet, in the colonies, clergy and colonial officials shared common ground, a marriage of convenience that lasted. Nationalism was key: "No less in the twentieth century than in the nineteenth, and irrespective of church or denomination, missionaries have shared the nationalist sentiments of their home communities." Many missionaries nonetheless saw themselves as part of an international endeavor, their partners being Protestant or Catholic peers from wherever. As we saw with the story of Martha Berry, the dedication to proselytizing so-called backward peoples was widespread, driving many to embark into the unknown to "save souls." Missionary orders were diverse and never constituted one movement, rather a variety of religious forms and evangelizing programs that differed from place to place. Not everywhere did proselytizing accelerate: in India, policy shifted to de-emphasize missionary activity.

Science, explorers, and geographical societies

This era must also be understood against the background of a growing European faith in science. This was the age of Auguste Comte's positivism, and of Charles Darwin's voyage on HMS *Beagle* and his *On the Origins of Species* (1859) and

The Descent of Man (1871). Science was king. In Africa, the "classic" period of exploration (1840s to 1870s) was an era of grand but dangerous adventure. Pioneers included the German Friedrich Hornemann, who traveled in northern Africa (1798–1801), and the Scot Mungo Park. Of the 45 Europeans who departed on an expedition with Park in January 1805, only 11 were alive by mid-August, the rest having died of fever or dysentery. Park himself drowned in west Africa that year. Another Scot, Alexander Gordon Laing, was probably the first European to see the famed Timbuktu. He died – likely decapitated – not long afterward in the Sahara, in 1826.

National geographic societies promoted explorers and exploration, such as those founded in Paris (1821) and Berlin (1828). Britain's Royal Geographical Society (founded in 1830) was explicitly linked to imperial expansion. Societies financed voyages, conferred medals, held receptions and banquets to honor returning explorers, published travel accounts, and offered prizes. France's Société de Géographie offered a 10,000 franc prize for the first non-Muslim to reach Timbuktu. The effort cost Laing his life, but the Frenchman René Caillié made it there in 1828 and returned to claim the prize. Geographers and scientists like Joseph Banks and Sir Roderick Murchison were "sub-imperialists," adept at exploiting the research opportunities that conquest created for them. "Mapping the world and subjecting it to scientific inventory were principal accomplishments of nineteenth-century European civilization." French geographical societies sponsored explorations in mainland southeast Asia, as well as voyages by Pierre Savorgnan de Brazza and others in equatorial Africa along the Ogowai and Congo rivers. National heroes spurred the appetite for geography.

Others like Richard Burton and John Hanning Speke joined the race to locate the Nile's origins, Speke discovering it in 1858. De Brazza had carried out major reconnoitering for the French government in central Africa, and was commissioned to begin another in 1879. De Brazza competed with Stanley, who traversed central Africa in 1874–1877. The German explorers Hermann Wissman and Carl Peters ventured to east and central Africa in the 1880s, as did numerous explorers from England, Scotland, France, Belgium, and elsewhere. As this cascade of names suggests, early voyages had turned into a flood by the 1870s and 1880s as Europeans sought to fill in the remaining "blank spots" on their world maps.

Discovery stoked imaginations. There was talk of tapping into millions of ready consumers in the Congo, or innumerable customers in China. For many Frenchmen, Algeria became a window onto Africa and the world, firing incredible dreams. Captain François Élie Roudaire conjured up the idea of creating an interior sea south of Algeria and Tunisia, briefly captivating the French public with a project that, naturally, remained unrealized. Others envisioned a trans-Saharan railway linking Senegal and Algeria, or a Cape-to-Cairo railway linking Britain's east African possessions from Egypt to South Africa.

The Civilizing Mission and the Race for Empire, 1879–1902

European explorers viewed the world with reference to that which they knew, and understood it within the framework of their education and previous experiences. Burton commented on village life in east Africa in his journal of 1858, when he and Speke were exploring around Lake Tanganyika: "The African is in these regions superior in comforts, better dressed, fed, and lodged, and less worked than the unhappy Ryot [peasant] of British India. His condition, where the slave trade is slack, may, indeed, be compared advantageously with that of the peasantry in some of the richest of European countries." Europeans were quick to disparage Africans as being lazy, unwilling to work, or incapable of decent agricultural production. They believed the soils of tropical Africa were productive, when in fact laterite soils are generally poor. The Frenchman Paul du Chaillu wrote:

> I am convinced that the people will never prosper till they turn their attention more to agricultural operations ... The men despise labour, and force their women and slaves to till the fields; and this tillage never assumes the important proportions it deserves, so that the supply of food is never abundant; the tribes, almost without exception, live from hand to mouth, and, with a fertile soil, are half the time in a state of semi-starvation.

One famous explorer was also a missionary, the Scotsman David Livingstone, who began his career in the 1840s with the London Missionary Society in southern Africa. From 1853 to 1856 Livingstone traveled northward to Victoria Falls, westward to Luanda in Angola, and eastward again to the mouth of the Zambezi. He went on other voyages in 1859–1864 and 1867–1873, seeking the Nile's source. His *Missionary Travels and Researches* and other works spurred interest in Victorian England in "opening" the continent to the "three Cs": Christianity, commerce, civilization. He was the first European to cross the African continent, and his discoveries included Victoria Falls (1855), and Lake Nyasa, Lake Tanganyika, and Lake Victoria (all 1858). It was Livingstone's last voyage that helped make another explorer famous, the Welsh American journalist Henry Morton Stanley. Livingstone's peregrinations beginning in 1867 lasted so long that rumors spread that he had perished. A newspaper sponsored Stanley on a trip to "find" Livingstone, which Stanley did in 1871 at Ujiji on Lake Tanganyika. Beginning in 1874, Stanley made his own crossing of the continent from east to west, taking 999 days and arriving nearly dead at Boma in 1877.

Geographical societies promoted exploration, and ethnographers' search for knowledge shaped the form of colonial administration that followed. "Blueprints for colonialism were prepared not so much in Europe's official foreign ministries as in the scholar's study, the traveler's diary, and the playwright's tale of Oceanic shipwreck and African adventure." Much activity focused on Africa, but there were counterparts elsewhere. Between 1828 and 1830, Briton Charles Sturt explored Australia, known to Europeans only from the late eighteenth century.

Later expeditions by the likes of Ludwig Leichhardt, Robert O'Hara Burke, and Ernest Giles scoped out the island continent. The British carried out extensive projects in India to survey the colony. The Frenchman Henri Mouhot's description of Angkor Wat in Cambodia stirred public interest. Ernest Doudart de Lagrée led an expedition to explore the Mekong River in 1866–1868, followed later by Francis Garnier along the Mekong, who was killed at Hanoi in 1873.

Such men – and they were all men – have long been perceived as lone explorers, sailing uncharted waters or blazing trails through the jungles of southeast Asia or the African bush. In their own travelogues, explorers portrayed themselves as sympathetic, brave, rational, and accomplished. Newspapers, novels, and later motion picture productions reinforced this image. Some became national heroes, had statues built to honor them, and became famous; for instance, Stanley was a revered figure in England during the Victorian era.

But explorers were hardly lone adventurers, and their dependence on locals illustrates exchanges between Europeans and non-Europeans and the power of the latter. In Africa, local outfitters were crucial to assembling caravans, which were often composed of dozens if not hundreds of porters, women, and children, spawning a veritable travel industry on both coasts, run mainly by Indian and Arab merchants. Local rulers had to grant permission to cross their territory. Explorers' voyages were often "parasitic" in the sense that they advanced the interests of local rulers who themselves competed for lands, for instance the emperor of Ethiopia. Stanley's east–west transcontinental voyage in 1874–1877 saw him arrive on the Atlantic coast nearly dead after 999 days. He had Tippu Tip to thank for providing him with essential assistance on the upper Congo, somewhere mid-voyage. Local guides led the way, and existing routes determined how – and how fast – explorers got to where they were going. This was also true in Australia, where the Aborigine Wylie helped the explorer Edward John Eyre survive his journeys of exploration. When Burton and Speke (1857–1859), Verney Lovett Cameron (1873–1875), and Stanley traveled inland from the east coast to Tabora and then on to Ujiji on Lake Tanganyika and beyond, they followed well-established routes developed by Arab-Swahili traders who had flourished during the rule of Seyyid Said. Few Europeans knew the local languages so they almost always depended on Africans as guides and translators. Polyglots like Burton, who is said to have spoken some 25 languages, were rare.

While some adventurers developed a deep respect for non-European cultures, others did not. Many criticized Asian societies for having retrogressed, or Africans for being backward savages or lazy drunkards. Descriptions of drinking or smoking hemp during meetings or negotiations with African leaders insinuated that Europeans exercised self-restraint and kept a clear state of mind and in control. Some explorers did mention partaking of drink or smoking hashish, and it seems unlikely that others spent hours in meetings with Africans whom they claimed were smoking or drinking palm wine or *pombe* (millet beer) without imbibing themselves.

The Civilizing Mission and the Race for Empire, 1879–1902

Explorers sometimes decried their porters' laziness or savagery, or how they tended to abscond. Yet, reading against the grain of their accounts shows that it was often the Africans who were in control, not the other way around. The Belgian Jérôme Becker traveled three times to central Africa in service of Leopold II's CFS during the 1880s. While suffering a bout of fever during one trip, he fell back to the rear of the caravan. Exhausted, he collapsed against a tree. At that moment he saw a lioness and her cubs nearby. As he reached for his gun, his porters restrained him, fearing that he might miss and provoke the lioness to attack. Instead, the Africans resorted to a customary tactic: making noises and gesticulating wildly to make the lioness go away. It worked. The African porters, not the explorer's heroics, saved the day.

Medicine and empire

The tools that Europeans had to treat tropical and other illnesses were limited, suggesting that medical know-how played a limited role in driving the New Imperialism. Sickness plagued Europeans moving through tropical areas, which meant that they were often out of their minds not just because of drinking and smoking. Many still believed in the miasma theory that blamed disease on bad airs from swampy areas; thus the term "malaria," from the Italian *mala aria*, "bad air." Ronald Ross did not make the connection between mosquitoes and malaria until 1897–1898. Europeans generally had little idea how to treat, let alone cure, tropical diseases. Some contemporary handbooks suggested that tight-fitting clothing might help, others loose-fitting clothing. The Swede C. B. Wadström designed "air-conditioned" homes for tropical areas, whose air circulation would carry off bad "vapors." Some explorers swore by abstinence from alcohol as a prophylactic, others the opposite. Others drank large quantities of alcohol regardless. Long before Kipling wrote of the "white man's burden," people spoke of the "white man's grave" in tropical Africa. Much of Africa and south Asia remained out of the reach of Europeans not only because of the power and resistance of indigenous societies, but also because of disease.

Self-medication for malaria, dysentery, yellow fever, and other afflictions could be worse than the illness it was intended to treat, and could profoundly alter the mind. The three or four most mentioned substances used to treat tropical sicknesses were arsenic, quinine, and opium, the latter usually as laudanum, a tincture of opium often used to treat dysentery or diarrhea. Arsenic is poisonous, and high doses of quinine cause side effects like ringing in the ears. Opium directly affects the nervous system. When Jérôme Becker took over one of the CFS's earliest posts, at Tabora in east Africa, the supplies left there by the doctor who preceded him included not only quinine and different emetics (to induce vomiting) but also poisonous agents like lead sulfate (which is toxic, corrosive, and a cumulative poison); tannin; cantharidin (which causes blistering but which can be used as a counterirritant or an aphrodisiac); citric acid; Epsom salts (used as a laxative or topically to relieve pain); aloe; benzene (a flammable solvent); rhubarb; and kermesite (an expectorant). Becker's travelogue description of his abstemiousness belies the fact he was heavily drugged: "Apart from quinine, Warburg elixir, iodine (for external use!), laudanum, common purgatives, zinc sulfate, sel de Saturne, ammonia, silver nitrate, and some caustic substances whose effects everyone knows, I touched nothing at all!"

Explorers' limited medical knowledge illustrates how colonialism was anything but a simple story of the export of European knowledge to uncivilized peoples in backward places. In Europe itself, the nineteenth century was an era of terrible preventable diseases like rickets, and of epidemics, for example of cholera. Most fatalities during the Crimean War (1854–1856), as during the American Civil War, were caused by disease. When cholera came to Italy from Indochina via France in 1884, it radiated across the country, killing more than 7,000 people in Naples alone. When a renewed outbreak occurred in 1910–1911, tens of thousands died. During the Boer War, 72 percent of all British fatalities resulted from fecal–oral diseases such as typhoid, diarrhea, and dysentery.

Colonial encounters shaped European medical knowledge, and advances against disease often followed from experience overseas. The use of quinine against malaria was initially isolated, with some experiments being carried out by the 1820s. The British armed forces used it prophylactically as early as the mid-nineteenth century. Gin and tonic, a quintessential British drink, resulted from the practice of mixing gin and sugar with quinine to make a highball drink to mask quinine's bitterness. The French conclusion that quinine prevented malaria resulted in part from trial and error during conquests in west Africa. One scholar has estimated that from the 1890s down to World War I, the French made greater strides against infectious disease in French Algeria than in France, as did the British in India than in Europe.

That said, most progress against disease came not from new medicines but from development of the most basic knowledge. "The triumph of nineteenth century medicine was prevention, not cure; and the key was the provision of clean water. A better water supply had been the most important single cause of the great mortality improvements over the midcentury." Typical European death rates in the tropics for soldiers dropped 90 percent from the early nineteenth century to 1914, meaning that by the end of the nineteenth century Europeans were freer to move in the tropics than ever before.

Scientific racism and social Darwinism

Scientific thinking manifested itself in a changed racism, which was another factor underpinning overseas expansion. Many have long thought of racial thinking and racism as "American" problems because of the legacies of slavery, whereas racism in Europe was thought to be a deviation from Enlightenment ideals. In truth, racial thinking was no aberration but an integral facet of modern European history. To understand race in the era of the New Imperialism is to grasp a fundamental aspect of modern European history.

The eighteenth-century Enlightenment led to a focus on science and the natural order of the world, and Enlightenment *philosophes* built upon thinkers of the scientific revolution like Isaac Newton by applying rational, scientific thinking to the study of humankind. The idea became widespread that humankind was not preordained by any religious or supernatural determinants; rather, education made us what we are. This was John Locke's *tabula rasa*, the idea that the human mind was a blank slate at birth. Such thought was put into practice in early nineteenth-century French policy in its small overseas possessions. Whatever the form of government in France – republic, empire, monarchy – the country pursued a policy of assimilation in the colonies. In 1833 Paris extended to free persons in the colonies all civil and political rights enjoyed by French citizens. The Second Republic (1848–1851) manumitted all slaves and made the colonies part of France. Napoleon III reversed this somewhat after seizing power and declaring a Second Empire in 1852, but assimilation continued. The 1870 Crémieux Decree naturalized all Jews in France's largest overseas territory, Algeria. French assimilation policy, halting as it was, revealed a basic assumption that all humankind was in some fundamental way equal.

Beliefs about race changed as science grew in importance. The Enlightenment heritage of dividing the world into comprehensible categories contributed to the view that the world's peoples were divided into races. Entire new fields of scientific study like anthropology, phrenology, and physiognomy legitimized divisions based on physical characteristics and external appearance. Some today inaccurately call this "pseudo-science" – at the time, it *was* science. While Enlightenment thinkers and those who followed them claimed to embrace only rational, science-based approaches, they never shed their inherited aesthetic beliefs that held up the Greeks and the Romans as the ideal; this meant that scientific methods and conclusions were often detached from empirical evidence. Growing contacts with Africans and Asians seemed to confirm that the world was divided into a hierarchy of races, and that Europeans were superior.

Racialist thinking was European-wide. There is a tendency to project Nazi antisemitism into the past and to see European racism as peculiar to Germany or as especially directed toward Jews. In fact, scholars from across the Continent and Britain classified peoples according to their "race," including Europeans, and fundamental contributions were made by the Frenchmen the Comte Arthur de Gobineau and Georges Vacher de Lapouge and the Britons Francis Galton and Robert Knox, among others.

Scientific racism manifested itself in social Darwinism, the eugenics movement, and the pursuit of "racial purity." Charles Darwin described the evolution of organisms in *On the Origins of Species*, extending this to humans in *The Descent of Man*. The philosopher Herbert Spencer applied Darwin's biological theory to human society, popularizing the idea that societies or races were governed by a law of the "survival of the fittest," an expression coined by Spencer. It was thought that some societies, races, and nations would survive while others would decline, even disappear; thus one needed to pursue racial "strength" or "purity." This could be seen in the United States where 50,000–100,000 people were sterilized between 1900 and 1950 to stop "undesirables" from reproducing. The success of Europe's rapid conquests in the late nineteenth century only seemed to confirm Spencer's views and the idea of white supremacy.

Public attractions underscored a hierarchical view of races. Albert Geoffroy Saint-Hilaire set up a zoo in Paris in the 1860s with "exotic" guides from far-flung places. After noting that many visitors were more interested in their guides than the animals, he put people behind the fences. Such "human zoos" were widespread. Organizers of the 1904 St. Louis World's Fair exhibited several Africans, one of whom, Ota Benga, ended up in the monkey house at New York's Bronx Zoo. The German Carl Hagenbeck made a living touring so-called exotic animals and peoples across Germany in *Völkerschauen*, or "people shows." Advertising exaggerated the Asian or African features of these people and relied on racist tropes to drum up business, reinforcing European ideas about their superiority and their right to rule.

Population pressures and emigration

Demographic pressures triggered a search for outlets for excess population. Earlier European expansion, from the fifteenth century, had not included mass migration. When the British temporarily took over the Dutch East Indies during the Napoleonic Wars, for example, there were only several hundred Europeans or people of European descent in Batavia, a city and area that had been the center of Dutch trading activity in northern Sumatra for hundreds of years. As late as 1855, Batavia had a civilian population of merely 4,145, including "mestizos and other coloureds," whites born in the Indies (Creoles), and 840 people born in Europe. By contrast, the second half of the nineteenth century was a period of massive European emigration as population growth and land hunger drove people elsewhere. Especially in an age of growing nationalism, many disliked seeing their fellow citizens leave, especially if other nations benefited as a result. Italy produced millions of expatriates, leading many to complain that the country was educating and rearing emigrants during their nonproductive years – as children – only to lose them during their productive years, exacting a steep economic price and benefiting rival nations.

Demographic pressures help explain the New Imperialism, but only in part. Many countries needed no outlets for "excess" population. In the last decades of the century in Germany, domestic demand for labor soared and emigration dropped. France's empire expanded more than any other between 1880 and World War I, yet from 1861 to 1910 only 0.2 persons per thousand emigrated from France. France had a presence in Senegal dating back many decades, but as late as 1921 Dakar, the capital of Afrique Occidentale Française (AOF; French West Africa), counted only 1,661 Europeans out of a population of 34,101. The 1931 census of Italy's African colonies showed a mere 4,188 Italians in Eritrea and only 1,631 Italians in Somaliland. By comparison, roughly two million Italians left for the United States alone between 1901 and 1910.

Existing colonies, renewed expansion

Existing colonial holdings and the diplomacy related to them constitute another factor hastening expansionism. EIC activity in India, Boers in southern Africa, and settlers in Algeria provoked resistance along the colonial "turbulent frontier." When officials took steps to secure those frontiers by attacking real or perceived threats at or beyond them, they extended those frontiers. This expansion produced yet more resistance, leading to a cycle of conflict and conquest. In Indochina, where the French had taken southerly Cochinchina by 1859, French forces pushed northward and inland, justifying this as means to secure Cochinchina's frontiers. As Mughal power weakened in the nineteenth century, the EIC raised military forces to put down local disturbances, and political annexation followed. As land-hungry Boers extended their holdings eastward and northward from the Cape Colony, they provoked peoples like the Xhosa, leading to borderland clashes, further expansion, and renewed resistance. Local officials often did not consult home governments before taking action. The man on the spot sometimes made decisions leading to expansion despite official policy.

Nationalism and social imperialism

National pride manifested itself in overseas conquests, which many believed reflected the nation's strength. Many in newly united Italy and Germany viewed British power with envy, and wanted colonies – their own "place in the sun" – to show they, too, had achieved great power status. France's defeat in the Franco-Prussian War made it imperative to possess colonies, to show that it remained a great power. Even if numerous acquisitions overseas did not really make up for the loss of the provinces of Alsace and Lorraine – as the nationalist Paul Déroulède put it, "I had two daughters, and you offer me twenty domestic servants" – the search for prestige was an impetus nonetheless. Competition heightened at the *fin de siècle*, leading to conquest not for the sake of colonial rule but to forestall potential gains by rivals.

Resolving tensions within the nation-state was a priority for many. The French abbé Raboisson, a devout Catholic, thought empire would diffuse "the soul and the religion of France" across the world while resolving tensions among social classes at home. Newly united Germany was rent by regional, class, economic, and religious divisions. It industrialized at breakneck speed, yet its government remained dominated by the landed aristocracy. By 1870 Germany was the Continent's dominant military power, and needed no strategic world outposts because it had no empire. But "social imperialism" worked through the creation of a "magic triangle": the state would acquire overseas colonies to secure markets and raw materials; this would ensure steady, continuous economic growth at home, appeasing workers, which would, in turn, sustain the country's social hierarchy and political status quo. Surely this is what finally helped persuade Chancellor Bismarck of colonialism's potential usefulness. As the economist Joseph Schumpeter argued, imperialism was an atavism. To stay at the top of the social and political structure, the aristocracy, which had been in decline since the late eighteenth century, could prove its relevance and power by directing expansion overseas.

Colonial interest groups

There was some mass support for empire, as evidenced by interest groups that goaded governments into action. In Britain, the Primrose League (founded 1883), Imperial Federation League, British Empire League, Imperial South Africa Association, and the women's Victoria League (1901) were prominent. In France, a loose coalition known as the *parti colonial* grouped politicians and pro-empire activists and overlapped with organizations like the Union Coloniale Française (founded 1893), the Comité de l'Afrique Française (1890), the Comité de Madagascar, the Comité de l'Asie Française, and the Comité du Maroc. The Sociedade de Geografia de Lisboa (1875), Gesellschaft für Deutsche Kolonisation (1884), and Istituto Coloniale Italiano (1906) (among others) promoted colonialism in Portugal, Germany, and Italy, respectively. Generally these groups were small and included specialists or others predisposed to support colonialism but, because they were politically connected and focused, their influence was disproportionate.

Individuals also lobbied for imperial expansion, like the French politician Jules Ferry, the journalist Paul Leroy-Beaulieu, the academic Gabriel Charmes, and the history professor Paul Gaffarel. Their counterparts included Carl Peters in Germany and Lord Cromer, Cecil Rhodes, John Buchan, and Winston Churchill in Britain. Skeptics of empire included Roger Casement, Edmund Dene Morel,

J. A. Hobson, and many socialists and communists, but they were "outsiders" to the halls of power in these years. And virtually no Europeans opposed imperialism *tout court*. Skeptics usually advocated reform, not the end of empire.

A "new" wave of imperialism?

By 1900 European states and the United States ruled over 500 million people, about half the world's non-European population. This radical development intrigued contemporaries, many of whom believed that they were witness to a distinct stage of history. Many at the time, and since, called this the New Imperialism to distinguish it from the "old" empire building of the sixteenth to eighteenth centuries.

But was this late nineteenth-century wave of overseas conquest really so new? The nineteenth century world was in many ways a "British world," and Britain enjoyed colonial possessions, economic might, and naval supremacy. A British "imperialism of free trade" continually expanded by incorporating areas of the globe into a growing trade network. Britain and the United States exercised informal empire in Latin America, the latter seen in the Monroe Doctrine, military interventions, and the Mexican–American War. Even if there were setbacks, most notably the 1857 Sepoy Uprising, Britain's empire continued to expand, for example in South Africa, especially following the discovery of diamonds at Kimberley.

Some scholars have extended this line of reasoning to argue that France remained an imperial power throughout the century through informal empire. Historians traditionally saw the French Revolution as a decisive break with the old regime and overseas colonialism, "empire" becoming in the early nineteenth century synonymous with Napoleon's rule. Historians of France have tended to focus more on the nation-state, industrialization, social class formation, and France's dramatic nineteenth-century revolutions rather than on developments overseas. But France, too, maintained a large "informal" empire, which took the form mainly of overseas investments. "Egypt, for example, could be viewed as a cultural and economic French colony for much of the nineteenth century." The country's formal overseas possessions were small, but trade with them soared in the early nineteenth century. France lost Saint-Domingue (Haiti) but by 1826 its remaining sugar-producing islands – Martinique, Guadeloupe, and Bourbon (Réunion) – collectively produced the same volume of sugar for export as Saint-Domingue had before it was lost. The conquest of Algeria, which began in 1830, offered France "a substitute for the riches of Saint-Domingue rather than a new colonial departure." Key figures in Algeria had gained experience in the earlier overseas empire, for instance the colony's first governor, General Bertrand Clauzel, who had served in Saint-Domingue and under Napoleon. Napoleon III's projection of French influence and Catholicism during the Second Empire (1852–1870) included growing involvement in Indochina and Senegal, support for the abortive Mexican empire under Maximilian I (r. 1864–1867), and negotiating with the Ottomans to put Roman Catholic authorities in charge of granting access to Christian holy sites in Palestine, then under Ottoman control.

Still, there are powerful reasons for regarding the empire building of the last two decades of the nineteenth century as a distinct era. First, there was the astonishing speed and extent of European conquests. As noted, in the 25 years or so after 1880, Europeans came to exercise control over 500 million people, or about half of the world's non-European population. Second, there was Europe's dynamism and expansionism, which manifested themselves in a massive outflow of people. Between 1870 and 1914, 55 million Europeans moved overseas, mainly to Australia, the United States, Canada, and Argentina. Third, there was the role of industry and new technologies. Finally, there was the novel influence of mass politics as well as the compelling force of nationalism. Nationalistic publics, encouraged by press accounts of daring exploits in exotic locales across the globe, pressured governments to rally the nation around the flag by means of conquests overseas.

Conclusion

The New Imperialism had no one single cause. Capital, industry, and advanced technologies were tools of conquest; nationalism propelled state rivalries; and racism and the so-called civilizing mission confirmed Europeans in the righteousness of their rule. But the degree to which population pressures, geographical societies, missionaries, or interest groups were factors depended on where you looked, and when.

Whatever the causes, by the first years of the twentieth century, western European states and the United States had staked out massive claims across the globe and held special privileges or concessions in the Ottoman and Qing empires. Recently agreed colonial frontiers crisscrossed south Asia, Africa, and the Middle East, borders that resulted more from foreign (European) actions and negotiations, even chance, than they did from local interests, languages, religious identities, or ethnicities. British rule in India was more direct than ever. In 1901 Edward VII became Britain's new king and India's new emperor. This was shown off in Delhi at an elaborate imperial durbar organized by the viceroy, Lord Curzon, a durbar being a traditional public reception held by an Indian prince, a practice appropriated by the British. British rule extended to Australia, New Zealand, Canada; islands, concessions, and exclaves across the globe; Burma and Malaya; and African territories stretching almost from the Cape to Cairo, and in the Gambia, Sierra Leone, Gold Coast, and Nigeria. The French had a presence in Algeria and Tunisia and were assembling three huge colonial federations in Africa: AOF, Afrique Équatoriale Française (AEF; French Equatorial Africa), and Madagascar. The French also ruled smaller islands around the globe, exclaves in

India, as well as French Indochina and French Guiana in South America. Leopold II claimed the CFS, and the Netherlands exercised more control in the Dutch East Indies than it had for centuries, in addition to ruling islands in the Caribbean and Dutch Guiana (Suriname). The United States claimed Alaska, Hawai'i, and the Philippines. Germany had a far-flung colonial empire stretching from Africa to Qingdao to Oceania. Italy had eked out territories along the Red Sea and on the Horn of Africa, and the Portuguese controlled exclaves in India and east Asia, including Macau, and claimed Portuguese Guinea, Angola, and Mozambique in Africa. These mostly new colonial regimes forced Africans, Asians, and others to choose between resistance, adaptation, or cooperation, at least for the time being.

Citations

Page	Source
36–7	"Your map of Africa..." Quoted in Eugen Wolf, *Vom Fürsten Bismarck und seinem Haus: Tagebuchblätter* [From Prince Bismarck and His House: Diaries], 2nd ed. (Berlin: Egon Fleischel, 1904), 16 (my translation).
38	"Where is the Gold Stool?..." Hodgson's address to Ashanti chiefs, January 1900, quoted at http://www.bbc.co.uk/worldservice/africa/features/storyofafrica/4chapter6.shtml, accessed September 11, 2017.
38	"The white man..." Kwadwo Afodo, quoted in Thomas J. Lewin, *Asante Before the British: The Prempean Years, 1875–1900* (Lawrence: Regents Press of Kansas, 1978), 220.
39–40	"I have occasionally seen..." and "became mere slaves..." Edgar Canisius, "A Campaign amongst Cannibals," in Captain Guy Burrows, *The Curse of Central Africa* (London: R. A. Everett & Co, 1903), 75, 75–76.
42	"We have to beat them..." Quoted in Daniel Vangroenweghe, "The 'Leopold II' Concession System Exported to French Congo with as example the Mpoko Company," *Revue Belge d'Histoire Contemporaine* 36, nos. 3–4 (2006), 323–372 (quotation at n. 18 on p. 335).
43	"resented his silence..." Rudyard Kipling, *Kim* (1901) (London: Puffin, 2011), 156.
44	"whose control over their destinies..." Robert A. Stafford, "Scientific Exploration and Empire," in *The Oxford History of the British Empire*, vol. 3: *The Nineteenth Century*, edited by Andrew Porter, 302.
44	"I am the master here..." Quoted in Alex. Delcommune, *Vingt années de vie africaine: récits de voyages, d'aventures et d'exploration au Congo Belge, 1874–1893* [Twenty Years of African Life: Stories of Voyages, of Adventures, and of Exploration in the Belgian Congo, 1874–1893], vol. 2 (Brussels: Vve Ferdinand Larcier, 1922), 274.
47	"Should you encounter the enemy..." Wilhelm II, "Hun Speech" (July 27, 1900), German History in Documents and Images. At http://germanhistorydocs.ghi-dc.org/sub_document.cfm?document_id=755, accessed September 21, 2017.

48	"more than twice the number of men..." Paula M. Krebs, "'The Last of the Gentlemen's Wars': Women in the Boer War Concentration Camp Controversy," *History Workshop Journal* 33 (1992), 41.
50	"it was rare..." Valentim Alexandre, "The Portuguese Empire, 1825–90: Ideology and Economics," in *From Slave Trade to Empire: Europe and the Colonisation of Black Africa 1780s–1880s*, edited by Olivier Pétré-Grenouilleau (London: Routledge, 2004), 144.
51	"No less in the twentieth century..." Andrew Porter, "Church History, History of Christianity, Religious History: Some Reflections on British Missionary Enterprise since the Late Eighteenth Century," *Church History* 71, no. 3 (2002), 567.
52	"Mapping the world..." Stafford, "Scientific Exploration and Empire," 318.
53	"The African is..." Richard Burton, "The Lake Regions of Central Equatorial Africa," *Journal of the Royal Geographical Society* 29 (1859), 362.
53	"I am convinced..." Paul B. Du Chaillu, *Explorations and Adventures in Equatorial Africa; with accounts of the manners and customs of the people, and of the chace of the gorilla, crocodile, leopard, elephant, hippopotamus, and other animals* (London: John Murray, 1861), 16.
53	"Blueprints for colonialism..." George Steinmetz, *The Devil's Handwriting: Precoloniality and the German Colonial State in Qingdao, Samoa, and Southwest Africa* (Chicago: University of Chicago Press, 2007), 25.
54	"parasitic." Dane Kennedy, "Imperial Parasitism: British Explorers and African Empires," in *Echoes of Empire: Memory, Identity and Colonial Legacies*, edited by Kalypso Nicolaïdis, Berny Sèbe, and Gabrielle Maas (London: I. B. Tauris, 2015), 19–34.
56	"Apart from quinine..." Quoted in Johannes Fabian, *Out of Our Minds: Reason and Madness in the Exploration of Central Africa* (Berkeley: University of California Press, 2000), 65.
56	"The triumph of..." Philip D. Curtin, *Death by Migration: Europe's Encounter with the Tropical World in the Nineteenth Century* (Cambridge: Cambridge University Press, 1989), 111.
58	"mestizos and other coloureds." Ulbe Bosma and Remco Raben, *Being "Dutch" in the Indies: A History of Creolisation and Empire, 1500–1920*, translated by Wendie Shaffer (Athens: Ohio University Press, 2008), 228–229.
60	"the soul and the religion of France." M. Raboisson, *Etude sur les colonies et la colonisation au regard de la France* [A Study of the Colonies and Colonization with regard to France] (Paris: Challamel ainé, 1877), 30 (my translation).
61	"Egypt, for example..." and "a substitute for the riches..." David Todd, "A French Imperial Meridian, 1814–1870," *Past & Present* 210 (2011), 160, 169–170.

Bibliography

Bosma, Ulbe, and Remco Raben. *Being "Dutch" in the Indies: A History of Creolisation and Empire, 1500–1920*. Translated by Wendie Shaffer. Athens: Ohio University Press, 2008.

The Civilizing Mission and the Race for Empire, 1879–1902

Brunschwig, Henri. *French Colonialism 1871–1914: Myths and Realities.* Translated by William Glanville Brown. London: Pall Mall Press, 1966.

Cohen, William B. *The French Encounter with Africans: White Response to Blacks, 1530–1880.* Bloomington: Indiana University Press, 1980.

Cohn, Bernard S. *Colonialism and Its Forms of Knowledge: The British in India.* Princeton: Princeton University Press, 1996.

Curtin, Philip D. *Death by Migration: Europe's Encounter with the Tropical World in the Nineteenth Century.* Cambridge: Cambridge University Press, 1989.

Davis, Lance E., and Robert A. Huttenback. *Mammon and the Pursuit of Empire: The Political Economy of British Imperialism, 1860–1912.* Cambridge: Cambridge University Press, 1986.

Fabian, Johannes. *Out of Our Minds: Reason and Madness in the Exploration of Central Africa.* Berkeley: University of California Press, 2000.

Headrick, Daniel R. *Tools of Empire: Technology and European Imperialism in the Nineteenth Century.* Oxford: Oxford University Press, 1981.

Lewis, Mary Dewhurst. *Divided Rule: Sovereignty and Empire in French Tunisia, 1881–1938.* Berkeley: University of California Press, 2013.

Robinson, Ronald, and John Gallagher, with Alice Denny. *Africa and the Victorians: The Climax of Imperialism* (1961). Garden City, NY: Anchor, 1968.

3
Resistance and Consolidation, 1902–1912

Black shapes crouched, lay, sat between the trees, leaning against the trunks, clinging to the earth, half coming out, half effaced within the dim light, in all the attitudes of pain, abandonment, and despair. Another mine on the cliff went off, followed by a slight shudder of the soil under my feet. The work was going on. The work! And this was the place where some of the helpers had withdrawn to die.

Joseph Conrad, *Heart of Darkness* (1902)

In the spring of 1902, Hanoi, the capital of French Indochina, had a problem: rats. The city's new sewers were such an ideal breeding ground that "the rodent community quickly grew to unimaginable proportions and began to spill out of its subterranean haven in search of food." Worst of all, rats began to make their way into homes in the European part of town, through pipes and toilets. Authorities recruited Vietnamese workers to catch them, and the number of rats trapped climbed from 7,985 in the first week to a record 20,114 on June 12. Yet the problem continued unabated.

Rat catchers having failed, the authorities shifted gears, announcing a one-cent bounty for each rat tail turned in, since the disposal of mass numbers of corpses would be too difficult. People turned in tens of thousands of tails:

> While many desk-bound administrators delighted in the numbers of apparently eliminated rats, more alert officials in the field began to notice a disturbing development. There were frequent sightings of rats without tails going about their business in the city streets … the authorities realized that less-than-honest but quite resourceful characters were catching rats, but merely cutting off the tails and letting the still-living pests go free … more enterprising but equally deceptive individuals were actually raising rats to collect the bounty.

European Overseas Empire, 1879–1999: A Short History, First Edition. Matthew G. Stanard.
© 2018 John Wiley & Sons, Inc. Published 2018 by John Wiley & Sons, Inc.

The problem was particularly vexing to authorities because it followed on major urban renovations. Paul Doumer, governor-general of French Indochina as of 1897, wanted to make Hanoi a showpiece of French colonialism and rational planning. Yet it was the city's new sewer system that helped provoke the plague of rats.

The great rat massacre reveals how racism and the management of difference were central to empire. The "white" part of the city, segregated from indigenous quarters, was the area that received the greatest attention in the remaking of Hanoi. Running water and indoor toilets in the city's white areas signaled superiority and power in the most intimate spaces of people's living quarters. Europeans believed that the indigenous quarters of Hanoi were the source of rats and the plague that came with them – how ironic that it was the new sewer system that offered rats such favorable conditions in which to procreate. To catch rats, authorities did not recruit European but Vietnamese workers, believing that such work was beneath them. The massacre also shows the limits of French power. This cautionary tale about incentives and unintended consequences reveals how, despite their faith in the civilizing mission, colonial planning, and infrastructure investments, the French were unable to control many things. Anxieties about colonial power – or the lack thereof – often manifested themselves in heightened concern for and regulation of gender and sexual and race relations.

Hanoi's urban renovations also indicate a turn-of-the-century shift. By that point the French presence in Indochina dated back decades. Doumer relocated the capital from Saigon in the south because many viewed that city as old and having grown through accretions, "disorderly, venal, and ungovernable." Hanoi was a fresh start, a site for new investment, rational urban design, and long-term planning. Although more conquest had yet to take place and areas that were formally claimed by Europeans remained beyond their control – as in the case of Hanoi's sewers – the years after the century's turn were a period of consolidation, planning, reform, and building. Imperialism reached a new zenith.

The Apex of Imperialism

By 1910 more individuals claimed the title of "emperor" or some variant thereof than at any other time in history: the Meiji emperor (Japan), the Xuantong emperor (China), Sultan Mehmed V (Ottoman empire), Emperor Franz Josef (Austro-Hungarian empire), King-Emperor George V (United Kingdom, India), Sultan Abdelhafid (Morocco), Ahmad Shah ("king of kings") Qājār (Iran), Emperor Menelik II (Ethiopia), and Sunjong (Korea) until Japan forced him to abdicate that year. Kaiser Wilhelm II of Germany and Tsar Nicholas II of Russia both had titles that meant "caesar." Although this list had shrunk by the 1920s because of the disappearance of specific empires – Korea (1910), China (1912), Russia (1917), Germany (1918), Austria–Hungary (1918), and Ottoman Turkey (1923) – imperialism was not on the decline because other empires expanded – and considerably so.

By 1914 foreign powers claimed virtually all of Africa, a land mass more than three times the size of the continental United States. The only exceptions were Ethiopia and Liberia, the latter essentially a colony of US rubber firm Firestone. British power reached new heights in India. In Indochina France invested in Hanoi alongside other efforts to extend its dominion. Dutch colonial forces neared victory in a decades-long struggle against the Sultanate of Aceh in the western Indonesian archipelago, General J. B. van Heutsz and his lieutenant, Hendrikus Colijn, having brought virtually all of Aceh under their control by 1904. That year Van Heutsz was appointed Dutch East Indies governor-general. (He later became Dutch prime minister.) Notwithstanding nineteenth-century losses in the Americas, Europeans remained important powers there: Britain in Canada, the Falkland Islands, British Honduras, British Guiana, the Bahamas, Trinidad and Tobago, and numerous other islands; the Dutch in Dutch Guiana and islands like Curaçao and Sint Maarten (shared with the French); France in its half of Saint Martin, French Guiana, Guadeloupe, Martinique, other possessions in the Caribbean, and Saint Pierre and Miquelon to the north.

In addition, there was the growing power of two agrarian giants, Russia and the United States, both sprawling land-based empires. The Romanov empire had expanded to its greatest extent, underscored by the completion of the Trans-Siberian Railway in 1904, three times the length of the first US transcontinental railway, connected in 1869. By 1900 the United States comprised 45 states reaching from the Atlantic to the Pacific. The year 1902 marked the end of both the Boer War and an anticolonial Filipino uprising, the suppression of which made the United States master in the Philippines. The 1905 Platt Amendment made Cuba for all intents and purposes a US colony, and US corporate and direct influence was so great over Central American states that the term "banana republic" came into use to refer to semi-autonomous American states. More than the Romanovs, US leaders, like their western European counterparts, pleaded altruism, believing that the United States was in the influence business for the good of others.

Ottoman, Qing, and Japanese Empires

One question, the so-called Eastern Question, remained (as it had for some time) at the forefront of European diplomacy: what was to become of the sick man of Europe, the Ottoman empire? In an age of growing nationalism, multinational entities like the Ottoman and Austro-Hungarian empires were inherently threatened. The Ottomans already had suffered major losses as a result of nationalism, for example when Greece won its independence by 1830. Sultan Abdul Hamid II continued to rule the Turkish empire as he had since 1878, without a constitution, and his failure to stem the tide of decline finally sparked a rebellion by younger, reform-minded Turks in 1908. This "Young Turk" revolt not only generated pressure for a new constitution but was motivated by a form of Ottoman Turkish nationalism, which further threatened the sultan's authority and the empire's very existence. The question of which European power would benefit most from the Ottomans' inevitable collapse burned in the minds of statesmen and military planners, fueling dreams and inducing anxiety.

China had become a victim of imperialism by the early 1900s, unable to determine its own fate and suffering defeat and humiliation during the Boxer Rebellion. There were parallels between the centralized Ottoman and Chinese empires and their inability to compete in the unsparing international state system at the turn of the century. Elites in both were divided between reformism and traditionalism. Chinese conservatives remained wedded to longstanding Confucian values and faith in a powerful state bureaucracy. Ottoman traditionalists continued to embrace a multinational empire dominated by Muslim Turks. When the Ottomans had sent learning missions to western Europe, their return brought not only technical knowledge but also ideas for reforming Ottoman government, challenging the sultan's authority. Likewise, in China students returning from abroad, for example Sun Yat-sen, brought back novel ideas. Ottoman "capitulations" gave Europeans special treatment, and "concessions" like those to Germany for the Berlin–Baghdad Railway had parallels in China's surrender of territory to Britain (Hong Kong), Japan (Taiwan), Belgium (a railway concession in Tianjin), Germany (Qingdao), and concession zones in cities like Shanghai. European states accepted the US-backed "open door policy," and there was no attempt to partition China. No such consensus existed regarding Ottoman territories.

Japan had reversed roles with China, transforming itself from a peripheral land to an imperial power in its own right. Japan's smaller size and ethnic homogeneity were advantages, and a strong sense of nationalism developed. The elite clique backing the Meiji emperor transformed state-led industrialization into military power. Building on its 1894–1895 victory over China, Japan joined in the race for empire. Japan was victorious in the Russo-Japanese War (1904–1905), extended its sphere of influence, and seized Korea, long a vassal state of China. Russia's defeat sent shock waves around the world: a non-European country had bested one Europe's largest military powers. Defeat sparked a revolution in Russia in 1905, which Nicholas II's government put down with difficulty. As news of Japan's victory spread, others questioned the supposed racial superiority of whites and wondered about their own potential to challenge Western power.

Resistance and Consolidation, 1902–1912

Atrocities, Resistance, and Accommodation

Japan's 1905 takeover of Korea opened a decades-long, oppressive colonization of the Korean peninsula that paralleled abusive regimes in European colonies. Further European conquests and violence belied rhetoric about the "civilizing mission." Atrocities occurred in the CFS under Belgium's Leopold II, where already by the 1890s, elephant hunting, rubber collecting, forced labor, and warfare had caused deep disruption. There was also the building of a railway from Matadi to Stanley Pool in the interior in 1890–1898. Without a railroad to bypass the waterfalls that blocked river traffic from the interior to the coast, "the Congo is not worth a penny," as Henry Morton Stanley remarked. This infrastructure project came at great cost: construction of the 241-mile-long railway killed 132 whites and 1,800 to 5,000 Africans and others. This chapter's epigraph from Joseph Conrad's *Heart of Darkness* expressed some of Conrad's horror at what he saw along the railway construction zone.

Heart of Darkness tells of the narrator Marlow's search for the enigmatic Kurtz, a successful ivory trader who has gone "up river" in the Congo and lost his grip on reality, creating a fiefdom of power and madness among the natives. By the time Conrad's novel appeared in 1902, it was more the forced collection of rubber than of ivory that underpinned Leopold's regime of atrocities as first a bicycle craze, and then automobiles, increased global rubber demand. The Congolese reported needing to go ever further into the forests to meet rubber quotas; wild animal attacks; and death by exposure or at the hands of colonial soldiers: "The white men sometimes at the post did not know of the bad things the soldiers did to us, but it was the white men who sent the soldiers to punish us for not bringing in enough rubber." African soldiers often enforced rubber collection, but it was for a system designed and directed by Europeans.

Indeed, authorities in the Congo – as elsewhere in the colonial world – recruited locals to do their dirty work, a dynamic captured in Édouard Manduau's painting *La civilisation au Congo* (1884) (Figure 3.1). Manduau was a European working in the Congo, and the painting depicts the meting out of a vicious penalty. An anonymous African man kneels, his face turned away. Two African men have immobilized him against a post, while another in a cap and a coat with red chevrons holds a whip at the ready. Others observe impassively nearby; a white man supervises, scribbling in a notebook. The prisoner's bloodied back, the official making Africans mete out the punishment, Manduau's sardonic title – all drive home to the viewer the darkness at the heart of European rule. African cultural production, including similar paintings like Tshibumba Kanda-Matulu's *Colonie belge 1859–1959* (ca. 1974–1976), also capture this ambivalent view of whites as dominant, yet always hiding behind – and dependent upon – a dark-complected person to do their dirty work.

Resistance and Consolidation, 1902–1912

Figure 3.1 Édouard Manduau, *La Civilisation au Congo* (1884). *Source*: Royal Museum for Central Africa.

"Red rubber" abuses gained notoriety thanks to reports from missionaries like the American George Washington Williams and the Englishwoman Alice Seeley Harris. In 1902 the Anglo-Frenchman E. D. Morel quit his job to take up full-time campaigning against Leopold II's regime. The British government commissioned the Irishman Roger Casement to investigate abuses in the Congo, which he described in the Casement Report, released in 1904. In 1906 Morel published *Red Rubber*, a scathing indictment. Stories and photographs circulated of mutilations, including severed hands. White officers of the colony's armed forces, the Force Publique, required soldiers to account for all bullets, to ensure that they did not stockpile ammunition for use in a rebellion. Any missing bullet required evidence that deadly force had been used: a hand or an ear cut off a corpse. Out on extended patrol, soldiers sometimes collected strings of dozens of hands; some smoked them over fires to stave off rot. Worse, because patrols sometimes lasted weeks at a time and food ran short, soldiers resorted to hunting. To account for missing bullets, soldiers caught living people and cut off their hands. Reports of abuses circulated, critics grew in number, and international pressure forced Leopold II to surrender the Congo to Belgium, creating the Belgian Congo in 1908.

Native peoples resisted such foreign impositions across the colonial world, for instance in German South West Africa. Although the European settler presence there was small, it placed great demands on land resources because the Germans viewed cattle ranching and mining as crucial to the colonial economy. The local Herero, San, and Nama peoples fared badly as settlers seized more and more land. Then an 1897 rinderpest epidemic decimated local cattle stocks. In 1904 Samuel Maharero, a paramount chief of the Hereros, led an attack against settlers, joined at first by some San and later by some Nama. Berlin decided that German authority could brook no threat and transferred power to Lieutenant General Lothar von Trotha who issued a Vernichtungsbefehl – a "destruction" or "extermination" order – against the Herero. German soldiers attacked, driving men, women, and children into the Omaheke desert. By the rebellion's end in 1907, the Herero population had dropped from 80,000 to 15,000 and the Nama from 20,000 to 10,000. The Dutch suppressed rebellions in these years, too, as did the Portuguese, putting down the Bailundo Revolt against Portuguese claims in Angola by 1904. In German East Africa, Africans countered colonial rule with both nonviolent and violent resistance, including the 1905–1907 Maji Maji revolt over forced labor and German misappropriation of natural resources.

Resistance sometimes took nonviolent forms, for example fleeing across colonial borders to avoid paying taxes. The Indian National Congress continued to make its case peacefully. It is unsurprising that strong nationalist movements emerged first in India since it had been a site of European imperialism for much longer than Africa or mainland southeast Asia. The All-India Muslim League joined anticolonial activism from 1906. Initially, Congress did not push for independence, but rather for greater autonomy. Indeed, Asian, African, Caribbean, and Indian reactions to a growing European presence were not uniformly hostile. Some gained from foreign interventions, institutions, and culture, such as some converts to Christianity. Rarely, elite members of the colonial world participated in government in Europe itself. By the late 1890s there were two Indian members of parliament in Britain, and by 1914 the first African had joined the French National Assembly.

Consolidation and Reform

The 1902–1912 period witnessed significant colonial reforms and consolidation. Scandals and brutalities provoked changes, and not for the first time. Multatuli (Eduard Douwes Dekkert) had published the book *Max Havelaar* to draw attention to abuses in the Dutch East Indies as early as the 1860s, for example. When Europeans rained down abuses on colonial subjects, individuals like Dekkert, Manduau, and Casement sometimes emerged to condemn them. Leopold II said that he was promoting the civilizing mission in central Africa, but it was missionaries who pointed out atrocities there, undermining his rule. Put simply,

Western attitudes toward colonialism varied, and Europeans and Americans were not one undifferentiated bloc of "colonizers."

Reforms included the extension of on-the-ground authority. Portugal had long claimed massive territories in Angola and Mozambique, but had only achieved any kind of real control in the years after 1900, embarking on reforms in Mozambique as of 1907. That same year Germany introduced major changes after the arrival of a new minister of colonies, Bernhard Dernburg, in response to the vicious assault on the Herero and the San and the criticism that followed. Although the "new" colonial administration in the Belgian Congo after 1908 was in large part inherited from the CFS, the new minister of colonies initiated a series of reforms to rectify abuses and distance the new regime from its predecessor.

Administration in the two largest empires in Africa – those of France and Britain – differed. The French adopted so-called "direct rule" across AOF, AEF, and Madagascar. They organized a centralized chain of command (on paper, at least) running from lower-level, local *commandants* to district commissioners to colonial governors, the latter reporting to the federation governor-general. The only role for Africans was as local *chefs*, appointed and removed by *commandants*. The British eschewed centralization, opting instead to follow British West Africa official Frederick Lugard's precepts of "indirect rule." Lugard was governor of Northern Nigeria from 1900 to 1906 and again after 1912, and of a unified Northern and Southern Nigeria from 1914, where he remained until after World War I. Indirect rule capitalized on existing power structures and elites to run empire at a low cost and with, in theory, minimal disruption. The British adopted some form of indirect rule in Nigeria and its other colonies in black Africa: the Gambia, Sierra Leone, Gold Coast, Kenya, Uganda, Nyasaland, and the Rhodesias. In either case, direct or indirect rule, district commissioners and colonial governors depended heavily on the cooperation of local elites to get anything done, but at the same time they also retained extensive powers on the ground, as they were largely unmoored from metropolitan control.

In South Africa, the 1902 Peace of Vereeniging concluded the Boer War and created the Union of South Africa, which consolidated white domination and excluded Africans from political power. Although Britain won the war, elections in 1910 brought Boers to power at the head of South Africa's responsible government. What followed was a most egregious case of land expropriation, the 1913 Land Act, which reserved only 7.3 percent of all land to native Africans, who composed some 80 percent of the population.

In south Asia, US rule extended in the Philippines, as did Dutch control in the East Indies and the British in India. The British rewarded loyal Indian princes and others with boons to cultivate acceptance of their dominion. The Raj witnessed consolidation including reforms in 1909 that changed the way provincial legislatures were formed and that furthered the role of elections in

Indian governance, even if the British retained executive power. In 1905 Viceroy Lord Curzon implemented a controversial and unpopular partition of Bengal; it was revoked in 1911. That same year, the viceroy organized an imperial durbar, co-opting a customary public reception for princes and other indigenous traditions in order to cement his authority. King-Emperor George V and Queen Consort Mary traveled to India for the event, the first and only time a ruling British monarch visited the colony.

Colonial dominion depended on cultural control as much as on military force, administration, or control over economic production. French began to supplant Chinese as the language of government in Vietnam, and *quốc ngữ*, an alphabet and writing system established by Catholic missionaries in the seventeenth century, became the mandatory written script for Vietnamese. Europeans centered education in sub-Saharan Africa around European languages and culture. The Dutch believed that a real education for anyone aspiring to a significant career in administration in the Dutch East Indies entailed a voyage to Europe and a stay in the Netherlands, and the same obtained for British India; Kipling, for example, was sent back to Britain for his education when he was five, and he did not return to India until he was 16 years old. By contrast, few Indians could go to Europe for higher education, and even fewer natives from the Dutch East Indies, French Vietnam, or sub-Saharan Africa – an unequal exchange that was indicative of who held power. The odd European might depart to the colonies for an "education," for instance poet Paul Verlaine or artist Paul Gauguin, but none for higher education.

Consolidation also revealed itself in the guise of regulated hunting and nascent conservation efforts. Innumerable images in magazines and books of hunters posing over lifeless elephants, hippopotamuses, and other large game conveyed the idea that Europeans were virile and in control. In truth, such hunters depended on native trackers and hunters, and on porters to carry their equipment. Richard Lynch Garner, who hunted extensively in Gabon in the early 1900s, relied on the chief hunter of the local Fang people, Donga Njango. For Europeans to dominate hunting, firearm controls were necessary, and colonial governments restricted firearm ownership to Europeans. In Gabon, one needed a government permit for any modern rifle. Unrestricted hunting slowly gave way to conservation efforts, including transcolonial cooperation and the creation of large reserves in some places.

The extension of European power manifested itself in the medicalization of colonialism. Europeans assumed a scientific and medical superiority that justified medical interventions, even radical ones. After all, such actions protected their charges, who in turn underpinned colonial profitability by providing labor, paying taxes, and buying manufactured goods. The Germans, French, and Belgians launched campaigns against sleeping sickness, which ravaged regions of central Africa. Belgian CFS agents had launched a major sleeping sickness campaign in 1903 involving lazarettos for infected individuals and *cordons sanitaires* around affected areas, including one of approximately 300,000 square kilometers in the Uele District in northern Congo. Many Africans considered the lazarettos to be death traps. The one drug that was partially effective against sleeping sickness, atoxyl, an arsenic compound, cured few and blinded many from the Belgian Congo to French Cameroon. Of course, when Africans avoided such European medical attention, the Europeans thought they were being irrational.

The Belgian takeover of the Congo in 1908 coincided with reforms to the sleeping sickness campaign. Lazarettos became more relaxed, taking the form of "villages." But the campaign continued to constitute a major form of control over Congolese populations. Belgians had already required travel documents for any Congolese moving beyond a defined home region. New medical passports superseded these beginning in 1910, a sign of what would become a hallmark of Belgian and some other colonialisms: an attempt to tightly control the movements of native peoples. The 1910 regulation also revealed the *limits* of colonial control because there simply were not enough Belgian personnel on the ground to fully implement it, and because many – subjects and administrators alike – chose to ignore it.

Colonial infrastructure projects also represented the consolidation of European mastery. Neo-Gothic churches and missionary stations that sometimes resembled medieval abbeys not only reminded settlers of home but established their authority and transformed the landscape. New urban areas represented in concrete form the power and permanence of colonial rule and the Europeans' supposed rationality in contrast to indigenous cultures. When Edwin Luytens designed India's new capital at New Delhi, and when Italy rebuilt Tripoli in Libya, European racial ideas found expression in colonial cityscapes. Architects and planners built segregated "white" areas for Europeans and "native" areas for Asians or Africans in the "colonial city," whether in Morocco, British India, or Hanoi (as in the case of the 1902 great rat massacre).

As European colonials built cities, they constructed their own idea of themselves. French urban design and architecture reinforced an ideology that held Europe to be modern, dynamic, and superior and the colonized to be backward, static, and inferior. Urban planners in Morocco hemmed in the parts of cities in which Moroccans lived, for example in Casablanca and Rabat, not accounting for population growth and fixing the colonized in time. Architecture and city planning pigeonholed local cultures by considering them unchangeable and simultaneously worthy of preservation – like relics – in the face of modernity's onslaught. In Madagascar, French urban planners and builders co-opted traditional forms of building and design, and through this incorporation of the native downplayed resistance to French rule and lessened the more "disruptive aspects of modernization."

Figure 3.2 Hanoi's Pont Doumer, around 1912. *Source*: Wikimedia Commons, https://commons.wikimedia.org/wiki/File:ASIE_-_VIET_NAM_-_TONKIN_-_HANOI_-_Le_Pont_Doumer.jpg.

As urban development in Hanoi mainly serviced "white" needs, so did infrastructure projects serve European interests, including ports, roads, hospitals, factories, agricultural stations, irrigation systems, plantations, dams, mines, processing centers, and bridges such as Hanoi's Pont Doumer, built in 1898–1902 (Figure 3.2). Railways "penetrated" or "opened up" colonial territories for global commerce and the development of legitimate (nonslave) trade. Infrastructure facilitated raw materials exports to the metropole for processing or re-export, and thus for sale and profit-making. By 1914, India boasted the largest rail network in the colonial world, some 40,000 miles, nearly twice as many as in Britain itself. Indian taxpayers financed it all. Almost all British initiative and investment was directed toward equipping India with basic facilities rather than with manufacturing capabilities, which meant that India depended on Britain for all its major materials for rail construction and operation, from locomotives to rolling stock to signaling equipment. The same applied to projects in quasi-colonial situations, such as in China, where Europeans had from the late 1800s negotiated significant railway concessions, both for investment opportunities and to access markets.

Colonial administrators often depended on missionaries for their work because the cost of administration was so high. It says much that France's Third Republic (1870–1940), although intensely anticlerical, supported Catholic missions in the French empire, and that missionaries and officials of the secular Third Republic on the ground in the colonies agreed as often as they disagreed.

Peoples the world over used Christianity to serve their own purposes. At the same time missionaries and the religion they brought with them were disruptive and divisive. Both Chinua Achebe's novel *Things Fall Apart* (1958) and Ngũgĩ wa Thiong'o's *The River Between* (1965) depict how conversion tore families and communities apart. Many missionaries considered those who did not embrace Christianity as uncivilized – as "beyond" civilization – while in Africa locals who did convert were viewed as outsiders by their native communities. Yet converts could never become assimilated to European culture because of European racism, which meant that they often found themselves in limbo, caught between colonizer and colonized. For some, however, Christianity did offer a way forward and a new identity.

Elsewhere Europe's religions had less of an impact, such as in Vietnam. There, although a sizable Catholic minority developed, it remained dwarfed by the country's Buddhist population. In India, the British vacillated between permitting and disallowing proselytism, and ultimately Christianity failed to gain many converts. In Muslim regions, for example Algeria or Northern Nigeria, Europeans did not push missionary activity as much as they did in other areas of Africa or in south Asia.

Overseas empire insinuated itself into European diplomacy. The near miss at Fashoda led France and Britain to sign an *entente cordiale* to regulate colonial affairs in 1904. Two other rivals at risk of going to war were Britain and Russia because of competition for empire in central Asia, as captured in the spying and intrigue at the heart of Kipling's novel *Kim* (1901). Russia and Britain reached their own colonial agreement in 1907, the former not only wishing to stop worrying about Britain in Asia but also suffering insecurity following defeat in the Russo-Japanese War. Concern about Germany motivated Britain: Japan's 1905 victory over Russia essentially sank the latter's fleet, and suddenly Germany's navy loomed large. Wilhelm II wanted Germany to have its "place in the sun" and assume its rightful place among the great powers, and he believed that a large navy was one way to achieve this. As an island nation dependent on seaborne trade, Britain had a longstanding "two-power" policy whereby its navy had to be at least as large as the next two largest combined. German leaders thought that a bigger German navy might make Britain more averse to conflict and possibly even draw it closer to Germany to form an alliance. But German overtures amounted to nothing. The British had already signed an agreement with Japan in 1902, ceding to Japan greater power in the Pacific, and subsequent agreements with France and Russia tied Britain more closely to them and to Continental affairs. British hostility toward German ambitions hinged on a defense of the existing state of affairs, seemingly unconscious that no status quo in international relations derives from nature; it has to be made, remade, or shored up through deliberate action. Britain's refusal to adapt to pressures on the status quo in the form of a larger German navy contributed to great power tensions. That said, Germany's build-up was indeed aggressive: the country was a dominant land power, had no need for a large navy, possessed huge domestic resources, traded mostly with Continental neighbors, and had few overseas colonies.

European and Non-European Migrations

Emigration to and migration between colonies accelerated. Some 52 million Europeans emigrated between 1860 and 1914: more Germans, Scandinavians, British, and Irish during the mid- to late nineteenth century, and more Spaniards, Italians, Russians, Poles, and other Slavic peoples in the decades before World War I. Fewer left Austria–Hungary, Belgium, France, the Netherlands, or Portugal. Most departed for the United States; others went to Argentina, Uruguay, Canada, Australia, New Zealand, Cuba, or Brazil; and many fewer moved to Africa or Asia. This emigration was massive compared to that of the earlier era of empire building in the Americas. By 1650 there were fewer than one million people of European descent in the Americas, including those born locally. In the first decade of the twentieth century alone, half a million Spaniards emigrated to the New World, that is *after* Spain's loss of colonies in 1898.

Although Europeans were better able to survive in the tropics than they had been in the nineteenth century, few men and even fewer women emigrated there. Disease remained an issue, as did isolation. Soldiers in remote French New Caledonia suffered high suicide rates: between 1903 and 1906 there were 2.88 suicides per thousand, and between 1909 and 1913 there were 1.41 per thousand, making suicide the leading cause of death. In one of Joseph Conrad's lesser-known works, "An Outpost of Progress," two men sent to a distant trading outpost in the Congo, isolated for months, get into a fight over a trivial matter; one shoots the other, killing him, and then hangs himself. Thus did tropical colonies remain sparsely populated by Europeans. In 1886, the year after Leopold II declared the CFS, there were only 254 whites there. Three decades later, during World War I, there were still only some 5,500 Europeans in the Congo, a country that is today the world's eleventh largest by area. In neighboring French Congo, a tiny pre-1900 European presence grew only slowly after the turn of the century. By 1912 there were only some 18,000 Germans in all German overseas colonies combined. A 1931 census of Italian north and east Africa showed 4,188 Italians in Eritrea and only 1,631 Italians in Somaliland. Despite centuries of British involvement in India, in 1900 the colonial service there consisted of 4,000 British civilians, 69,000 British army personnel, 250,000 Indian civil servants, and 130,000 Indian soldiers. While Britons held all the top posts in both army and government, it was Indians who made the Raj work.

Europeans were not the only ones moving overseas. A small but growing number of Africans and Asians migrated temporarily or permanently to Europe, reshaping Europe and then their own cultures upon their return. Indians also moved in large numbers, voluntarily or otherwise, within Britain's empire and to and from other colonies. For example, Mohandas Gandhi studied law in London in the late 1880s and started practicing in the Cape Colony in the 1890s. For all intents and purposes, indentured labor replaced slave labor in many colonies. Britain had abolished slavery in 1833, but the first ships loaded with indentured laborers from India, the *Hesperus* and the *Whitby*, set sail for the Caribbean in 1837, inaugurating a system of indentured labor that was not ended by Britain until 1919. France had abolished slavery in 1848; its first ships of indentured servants arrived at Indian Ocean islands like Réunion soon thereafter. These laborers fulfilled the needs of labor-intensive regimes, for example on Indian Ocean or Caribbean sugar cane plantations. The pejorative term "coolie" obscured them as individuals, each with a life story. For instance, Sujaria from Bhurahupur signed up as an indentured servant and left India in 1903, giving birth to her son Lal Bahadur on the ship *Clyde* on the way from India to British Guiana – these were just two of innumerable lives caught up in the system. Although it is considered brutal today, indenture was not necessarily a bad thing for all individuals. Major D. G. Pitcher, the British officer tasked with examining recruitment of indentured laborers in India in the 1880s, strove to correct abuses in the system. George Grierson, a civil servant, noted that for many Indian women emigration was an opportunity to escape patriarchy, an observation that was confirmed when Indian men tried to prevent women from accepting indenture contracts.

Gender, Sex, Race, and Anxieties

Few women left Europe for the colonies until well into the twentieth century. Individuals like Karen Blixen, whose life story was portrayed in the film *Out of Africa* (1985), or the author and sometime British colonial official Elspeth Huxley, stood out not only because for their intelligence and personality, but because they were among the few women in a male-dominated world, namely British Kenya. In India in the nineteenth century, European men outnumbered women three to one. In the Belgian Congo, there were almost no white women until after World War I. Just because men predominated in colonial situations, this does not mean colonies were exclusively male spaces – far from it. Of course, women constituted fully half the population of the colonized world.

Even though discovery, exploration, and conquest are intrinsically gender-neutral activities, they were cast as "manly." Young men pursued them to prove their virility and manliness. Explorers wrote about "penetrating" the "virgin lands" of the African continent, which many artists depicted as a young woman. Novels like H. Rider Haggard's *King Solomon's Mines* (1885) sexualized exotic lands. Haggard's story recounts Allan Quatermain's African adventures, a voyage leading to the mines of the book's title. The story is set up with the possession of an old map whose image takes the shape of an inverted female body, spread-eagle, with only those parts indicated that are suggestive of female sexuality, such as the hills called "Sheba's breasts." The book's great success enabled Haggard to retire to a country house to write full time. That Europeans considered exploration and conquest as "male" activities is unsurprising insofar as women had largely been excluded from the public sphere in Europe by the late 1800s: a man's place was in the public sphere, a woman's in the domestic arena. Still, it followed from such characterizations of conquest and exploration that those who had not explored or who had been conquered were unmanly, or had been emasculated. Many of the British disparaged Indian men as effeminate, thus rendering them less threatening, less likely to rebel, in colonial minds.

Colonial soldiers used sexual violence as a weapon. Roger Casement's report of atrocities in the Congo detailed sexual attacks against women. The historian Nancy Rose Hunt retells the story of Boali, whose deposition was collected as part of Leopold II's 1905–1906 commission of inquiry into Congo abuses, which followed Casement's report. Living in the concession of the Anglo-Belgian India Rubber Company, Boali's husband went out to gather rubber one day and was assaulted by a sentry. When she rejected him he shot and wounded her. She reported that he thought she was dead, and "to get hold of the brass bracelet that I wore at the base of my right leg, he cut off my right foot." So great was her fear of being raped that Boali pretended to be dead despite excruciating pain.

Gender differences, concepts of race, and power became prominent, intertwined aspects of conquest and colonial rule. People drew on sexual identity or sexual difference to mark off racial or ethnic differences, and vice versa, and by doing so implicated gender in presuppositions of racial or ethnic difference. White men from Europe oftentimes talked about women in the same ways as they talked about non-Europeans: in terms of male domination over the subordinate, of men being superior to women. Difference was essential: it was biological, natural. Difference justified the authority of white, European males over non-Europeans and women. Drawing on ideas of ethnic difference to define distinctions between genders meant delineating both. Europeans were anxious about white women in the colonies, fearing that native men might have sexual relations with them; this occasionally resulted in hysterical "race" scares.

Sexual transgressions were significant because they could upend what was believed – by most whites – to be the proper dynamic between gender, sex, race, and political power. The taking of local mistresses by European men provoked nervousness because control over sex was crucial in an age of eugenics: "racial purity" was essential, and white prestige was essential to upholding colonial authority. This was a recent development. In the Dutch East Indies, for instance, "whites" were not a single tight social class, despite depictions in textbooks and newspapers of unity. Religion had been a marker of distinction in the East Indies in the early years of Dutch involvement, but the nineteenth-century rise of scientific racism and increased presence of the Dutch in south Asia led race to supplant religion as the differentiator of people and communities.

Race and gender intersected with notions of social class distinctions, which connected to insecurity about bourgeois or middle-class notions of what the bourgeoisie itself was. Bourgeois culture and identity at home in Europe were not stable and self-evident, and colonies did not represent islands of people upholding bourgeois culture in a sea of non-European culture. In the Dutch East Indies, the moral authority of bourgeois values was played out because of the possible ways middle-class values could be altered or dropped. A line had to be drawn between Javanese and Europeans, and crossing that line – literally embodied in Indo-Europeans, those descended from a Dutch parent and an Indonesian parent – threatened European, middle-class supremacy. A Javanese person could not become European but a white person could become Javanese, which was to be avoided since poor or mixed-race Europeans detracted from white prestige. Discourse within and about the Indies then informed concepts of race, gender, and social class in the Netherlands: "The making of racial discourse ... [was] formative in the making of a middle-class identity rather than as a late nineteenth-century addition to it."

Although people saw conquest as a manly thing and colonies as places of male domination, women gained in importance as colonialism endured. Europeans in south Asia or in sub-Saharan Africa were more often than not young men far from home and isolated. Many sought local mistresses or concubines, a role taken by women under compulsion or negotiation, or voluntarily. As noted, this elicited fears of racial mixing and of its negative effects on men. Thus did many come to see it as imperative for women to go to the colonies to domesticate their men. Because of the dearth of white women in the colonies, those who did go had a great deal of power. Unwed English women who went to India for marriage (or who were taken there), for example, faced a "seller's market."

Colonial societies sometimes witnessed the upending of traditional gender roles. Forced labor requirements, for instance, often fell on men, which compelled women to do additional work, such as in Leopold II's Congo, where collecting rubber removed men from regular activities for days at a time. Change was not always negative. European colonial regimes did not enter into idyllic precolonial societies of gender equality or harmony. As noted, women in India sometimes answered the call of indentured labor recruiters because of the possibilities offered by a new life or because of the terrible conditions under which they lived. Indian women facing recruiters had more power than their male counterparts because the British required that a certain percentage of coolies be women: if recruiters did not meet the quota, the boat would not sail from India. It is true that Indian women on colonial plantations sometimes suffered terribly at the hands of men, including jealous husbands, and that they endured rape or disfigurement, or were even killed. But, because there were more Indian men, women had power, even if it was relative; depending on the individual circumstances, they could be seen as victims or as "concubines with leverage."

Empire and Globalization

"Opening up" supposedly backward regions, valorizing "untapped" resources, and spreading international commerce and development were stated justifications for imperialism. International trade increased dramatically in the last decades of the nineteenth century in this second era of globalization – the first dating back to Columbus's voyages and the inauguration of interactions between the Americas and the "Old World" of Eurasia and Africa. Did the New Imperialism accelerate or impede globalization? Or were imperialism and globalization two sides of one phenomenon?

From the mid-nineteenth century, European states embraced more free trade, and many lowered their tariffs. Although some states introduced significant tariffs in the last two decades of the century, others remained "free trade," namely the Netherlands, Britain, and Belgium (the latter two being the globe's most industrial economies), and international trade increased dramatically. Although China and Japan's isolationism had never completely closed those two countries to foreign trade, their "opening up" around mid-century facilitated international commerce. Britain's "free trade" imperialism from the end of the Napoleonic Wars in 1815 linked formal and informal colonial territories within an expanding "British world." A massive outflow of European emigrants made the world more "connected," and even more so did major communications and travel advances: railroads, telegraphs, telephones, steamships, and the Suez Canal. A sign of greater connectedness was that Europe's last famines occurred in the 1840s. Thereafter, better communications and transportation meant that famine disappeared from the Continent (with the exception of Russia). In many ways there was a melding of cultures across the globe, for instance sartorially (well-off men from Japan to Paris now wore suits) and linguistically (as English, French, and German were spoken more widely than ever).

Although this second era of globalization coincided with the rapid European expansion of the late nineteenth century, European trade with overseas colonies remained small. Britain, the largest imperial power, relied on its colonies for only a third of exports and a quarter of imports. Colonial trade usually focused on only one or two overseas possessions. French commerce benefited little from the empire because foreign trade constituted a small part of France's total trade, and of that colonial commerce constituted only 9.5 percent of all exports and imports. Trade within European empires was small, concentrated in a few colonial possessions, and did not increase in proportion to the growth in overseas control toward the century's end.

Numerous colonial ventures failed, although fortunes were made in the colonial world. Europeans dreamed of tapping into unimaginably large markets in China, or the Congo. The discovery of gold and diamonds in South Africa stoked visions of underground riches and another El Dorado, that myth of a city of gold in the Americas dating back to the sixteenth century. In reality, many colonial enterprises were flops. In 1889, faced with high costs and the potential for further revolts, the German government took over the possessions of the German East Africa Company, officially establishing German East Africa. A similar situation obtained in German South West Africa. The royal chartered Imperial British East Africa Company, which had moved into east Africa both in pursuit of profit and to stabilize the situation in Buganda, failed. In 1895–1896 the British government took over in both east Africa and Uganda. Some companies made huge profits, and individuals like Cecil Rhodes became immensely rich from diamonds. As noted, Leopold II exhausted his fortune setting up the CFS and waging war against rivals like Tippu Tip, but made it back in the end-of-the-century rubber and ivory boom. For better and worse, such exploitation involved Africa – and Europe – in expanding networks of global trade.

That said, the overt negative nationalism that grew in strength in Europe toward the century's end led many states to enact measures to impede international commerce. States instituted import taxes, such as France's Méline tariff. The more rail lines that were built, the more it became clear that they were *national* rail networks. France's rail network resembled a spider's web, centered on Paris. The Transcontinental Railroad in the United States (completed in 1869) tied the nation together from east to west, as did Russia's Trans-Siberian Railway (completed in 1904). Such networks encouraged trade *within* more than *between* nations. European states sought colonies to carve out exclusive access to key raw materials, to secure markets for national exports, and to exclude competitors. Steps were taken to erect imperial trading "blocs" to support the metropole. By the early twentieth century, politicians like Britain's Joseph Chamberlain were openly calling for the creation of exclusive imperial trading blocs.

Despite such impediments, globalization continued and even accelerated. The country of greatest immigration, the United States, took in more than eight million foreigners between 1871 and 1890 and nearly 12.5 million between 1891 and 1910. Millions of Italian, east European, and other long-term migrants were joined by innumerable Indians, Chinese, and others, many of whom were availing themselves of opportunities offered within imperial formations, such as indentured laborers from India who went to South Africa, British Guiana, or Mauritius. In 1900 the percentage of long-term international migrants reached 3 percent of the world's total population. (As late as 2005, in a supposedly "globalized" world, the number was only 2.9 percent.) In the years leading up to World War I, trade grew to unprecedented levels. Refrigerated train cars and ships lowered the price of foodstuffs, for example meat and grain imports to

Europe from Australia, South America, or Russia. Rubber booms in central Africa, South America, and then southeast Asia were directly connected to the bicycle and then the automobile in Europe and the United States, many miles distant. International trade grew so much in the antebellum era that it would not be until at least after World War II, probably not truly until after 1989 that the percentage of trade across the world that was international or "global" would regain levels reached in the years before 1914.

But would this globalization have continued without European imperialism? After all, freer and greater volumes of trade developed earlier in the century with the end of the Atlantic slave trade, the development of the "legitimate trade" in sub-Saharan Africa, and the rise of informal British hegemony – that is, without formal empire. Even if many colonial subjects went on the move, most European emigrants ended up in noncolonial territories, in particular the United States. Despite a drive to carve out exclusive access and trading rights, international trade and exchanges thrived. What is clear in any case is that the post-World War I years marked a caesura in globalization as international cooperation plummeted along with prices, production, wages, and employment rates. Nations erected massive trade barriers, for example the US Smoot–Hawley Tariff (1930), and international trade dropped precipitously.

Conclusion

Although European overseas colonial regimes committed many atrocities and faced resistance, in many ways the first decade of the twentieth century was one of consolidation and reform. Colonies came under greater European influence, for example through building projects that transformed cityscapes or infrastructure projects to facilitate European profit-making, or continued large-scale emigration. Nevertheless, the more Europe's colonial empires developed, the greater the growth of anxieties centering on gender, sex, and race. Despite such fears and fissures, the first years of the twentieth century represented a new apex of empire. Thus, it comes as no surprise that overseas colonies played a significant part in the outbreak of war in 1914, and that they played a big role once the war had begun, helping to transform it into a global conflagration.

Citations

Page *Source*
67–8 "The great rat massacre" is drawn from Michael G. Vann, "Of Rats, Rice, and Race: The Great Hanoi Rat Massacre, an Episode in French Colonial History," *French Colonial History* 4 (2003), 191–204.

71   "The white men sometimes..." Quoted in Arthur Conan Doyle, *The Crime of the Congo* (New York: Doubleday, 1909), 65.

76   "disruptive aspects of modernization." Gwendolyn Wright, "Tradition in the Service of Modernity: Architecture and Urbanism in French Colonial Policy, 1900–1930," *Journal of Modern History* 59, no. 2 (1987), 291–316 (quotation at 315).

79   "half a million Spaniards." Antony Beevor, *The Battle for Spain: The Spanish Civil War, 1936–1939* (New York: Penguin, 2006), 9.

79   "high suicide rates." Philip D. Curtin, *Death by Migration: Europe's Encounter with the Tropical World in the Nineteenth Century* (Cambridge: Cambridge University Press, 1989), 16.

81   "to get hold of the brass bracelet..." Quoted in Nancy Rose Hunt, "An Acoustic Register: Rape and Repetition in the Congo," in *Imperial Debris: On Ruins and Ruination*, edited by Ann Laura Stoler (Durham, NC: Duke University Press, 2013), 43.

82   "The making of racial discourse..." Ann Laura Stoler, "Cultivating Bourgeois Bodies and Racial Selves," in *Cultures of Empire: A Reader*, edited by Catherine Hall (New York: Routledge, 2000), 104.

83   "concubines with leverage." Gaiutra Bahadur, *Coolie Woman: The Odyssey of Indenture* (Chicago: University of Chicago Press, 2014), 150.

Bibliography

Bahadur, Gaiutra. *Coolie Woman: The Odyssey of Indenture*. Chicago: University of Chicago Press, 2014.

Betts, Raymond F. *Assimilation and Association in French Colonial Theory, 1890–1914* (1960). Lincoln: University of Nebraska Press, 2005.

Brocheux, Pierre. *Indochina: An Ambiguous Colonization, 1858–1954*. Berkeley: University of California Press, 2009.

Conrad, Sebastian. *German Colonialism: A Short History*. Translated by Sorcha O'Hagan. Cambridge: Cambridge University Press, 2012.

Darwin, John. *Unfinished Empire: The Global Expansion of Britain*. New York: Bloomsbury Press, 2012.

Daughton, J. P. *An Empire Divided: Religion, Republicanism, and the Making of French Colonialism, 1880–1914*. New York: Oxford University Press, 2006.

Hochschild, Adam. *King Leopold's Ghost: A Story of Greed, Terror, and Heroism in Colonial Africa*. Boston: Houghton Mifflin, 1998.

McClintock, Anne. *Imperial Leather: Race, Gender and Sexuality in the Colonial Contest*. New York: Routledge, 1995.

Pakenham, Thomas. *The Scramble for Africa*. New York: Random House, 1991.

Vanthemsche, Guy. *Belgium and the Congo, 1885–1980*. Translated by Alice Cameron and Stephen Windross. Revised by Kate Connelly. Cambridge: Cambridge University Press, 2012.

4

Empires at War, 1912–1922

We don't want to fight
But, by Jingo, if we do,
We won't go to the front ourselves,
  We'll send the mild Hindoo.

English ditty (before 1914)

An enduring memoir of World War I is Ernst Jünger's *Storm of Steel*, first published in 1920. A German officer who was awarded Germany's highest honor for valor on the Western Front, Jünger exulted in the rush of battle. His memoir describes countless skirmishes, battles, and bombardments; he was wounded numerous times and always returned to the front as soon as he could.

In May 1917, while Jünger was stationed in north-central France, a melee broke out between his men and soldiers whom they thought, logically enough, to be British or French. The battle over, Jünger and his men spread out over the battlefield to survey the damage. "From the meadow arose exotic calls and cries for help," he recalled. He stumbled across wounded soldiers, neither French nor British, but Indian, one calling himself a "poor Rajput": "So these were Indians we had confronted, who had travelled thousands of miles across the sea, only to give themselves a bloody nose on this god-forsaken piece of earth against the Hanoverian Rifles."

Jünger fought on the Western Front, where fighting had commenced in August 1914, the month traditionally viewed as the opening of the war. But, well before then, conflict was underway elsewhere. Why fighting broke out in the first place is a question that has fascinated historians for more than a century.

European Overseas Empire, 1879–1999: A Short History, First Edition. Matthew G. Stanard.
© 2018 John Wiley & Sons, Inc. Published 2018 by John Wiley & Sons, Inc.

As this chapter shows, the dynamics of overseas imperialism was one of the war's fundamental causes. That Jünger skirmished with colonial troops on the Western Front is unsurprising considering that Europe's colonial powers mobilized hundreds of thousands of men from overseas to fight. Many more from colonial territories and beyond worked behind the front lines. Even if World War I was in essence a war of nationalism, the fact that fighting took place across continents and at sea made this global conflict a struggle not only between nations but also between empires. Moreover, the mobilization of colonial subjects and the drawing up of specific wartime colonial agreements had major ramifications for the postwar situation.

The Outbreak of Conflict

The assassination of Archduke Franz Ferdinand on June 28, 1914, is widely regarded as the spark that started World War I, ending a long period of peace in Europe. A Bosnian Serb nationalist murdered the archduke, who was heir to the Austro-Hungarian throne, during an official visit to Sarajevo, Bosnia–Herzegovina's main city. Austria–Hungary had administered the Ottoman Balkan provinces of Bosnia and Herzegovina since 1878 and annexed them outright in 1908. The archduke's visit aimed to tie these newly acquired areas more closely to the Habsburg crown, but the date of the visit was poorly chosen: it was Serbia's national day. Many Serbs envisioned a "Greater Serbia" embracing all Serbs, including Bosnian Serbs living under Habsburg rule. To them Austria–Hungary's land grab meant that Bosnia's Serbs had merely exchanged one foreign ruler for another. An attack on the heir to the throne would strike a blow at foreign rule, perhaps even destabilize the Habsburg crown. The reasoning was similar to that of anarchists hoping to bring down governments through terrorist attacks or political murders, for example the 1901 assassination of the US president William McKinley.

The archduke's death unleashed a chain of events that led to global war. Because the impending collapse of the Ottoman "sick man of Europe" threatened to reveal another long sufferer, Austria–Hungary, Vienna decided to use the assassination as a pretext to humiliate Serbia and to crush Serbian nationalism, nationalism being the greatest threat to the multinational Habsburg empire. Austria received assurances of support from Berlin, its main ally in the Triple Alliance (the other being Italy), and presented the Serbs with an ultimatum so punitive that it knew the Serbs would not comply. When Serbia did not completely meet the terms of the ultimatum, Vienna had its pretext for war.

As Austrian pressure on Serbia mounted, Russia warned Vienna and Berlin to back down. Russia, smarting from defeat in the Russo-Japanese War, felt the need to appear strong. Believing the Balkans to be within its sphere of influence, and opposed to the Catholic Habsburgs bullying its Orthodox Serb allies, Russia threatened war. When Austria–Hungary attacked, Nicholas II ordered Russia's army to mobilize, which Germany – sharing a long border with Russia – viewed as a direct threat. Germany declared war on Russia and launched its Schlieffen Plan, which had been many years in gestation, invading Belgium and France to knock them out before then concentrating on Russia. Although it was not obligated by the Triple Entente alliance to go to war with Russia and France, Britain was a guarantor of Belgian neutrality and was wary of German ambitions. After debate, Britain declared war against Germany on August 4. Japan, Britain's ally since 1902, did the same within a couple weeks. The Ottoman empire, not only pursuing lost territories but fighting for its survival, joined in by the year's end.

Nationalist feelings rallied populations to the flag and sustained the conflict for years, making World War I a war driven by nationalism. Because the main belligerents brought their colonies into the war with them, it also became a clash of empires. Once begun, the war immediately spread beyond Europe.

Conflict before 1914

In truth, fighting had already begun. In Ireland, which had long been a British colony, the prewar years witnessed the so-called Home Rule Crisis. After the 1912 Third Home Rule Bill, pro-British "Ulster unionists" in northern Ireland started arming themselves to prevent Ireland from breaking free, and Irish nationalists began arming themselves to achieve independence.

There were also three wars between 1911 and 1913 over the "Eastern Question," at least in part. The first of these was between Italy and the Ottoman empire. In 1908 Austria–Hungary had annexed Bosnia–Herzegovina outright, taking advantage of upheaval during the Young Turk revolt. Abdul Hamid II's powerlessness to stop the Austrians only exacerbated the crisis surrounding his regime. Italy capitalized on Turkey's weakness by declaring war to seize Ottoman north African territories. The ensuing Italo-Turkish War (1911–1912) was one of colonial expansion and the first to see the use of aircraft – Italy used airplanes for reconnaissance and to drop bombs – and another Ottoman defeat. Italy took the Dodecanese islands and Cyrenaica, Tripolitania, and Fezzan in north Africa, the latter three becoming the colony of Libya. Still, Italy remained unable to control its Libyan provinces for years because of local resistance and the exigencies of war in Europe beginning in 1914.

After Austria–Hungary's 1908 land grab and Turkey's 1911–1912 defeat, nationalists in southeastern Europe began circling the failing Ottoman empire. Just as many Serbs dreamed of a "Greater Serbia," so did Bulgarians long for a "Greater Bulgaria" and Greek nationalists a "Greater Greece" or Megale Idea. There were many ethnic Greeks living in the Ottoman empire, primarily in Istanbul or the Anatolian peninsula, some populations having lived there for so long that they spoke only Turkish. The Megale Idea envisioned reclaiming lands of the erstwhile Greek-speaking Eastern Roman (or Byzantine) empire, with its capital at Constantinople – Istanbul, the Ottoman capital. The result was two "Balkan" wars over Ottoman territories in southeastern Europe. In 1912 Bulgaria, Serbia, Greece, and Montenegro banded together to attack, and by 1913 they had taken almost all the remaining territories held by the Ottomans in Europe, part of the area becoming independent Albania. Dissatisfied with the division of the spoils, Bulgaria provoked another war in 1913. This time Serbs, Greeks, and Romanians sided with Turkish forces to defeat Bulgaria within weeks.

Although it is accurate to say that Archduke Ferdinand's assassination ended a long period of general peace in Europe, this was more true from the vantage point of Lisbon, London, and Berlin, but less so from that of Istanbul, Rome, Sofia, or Athens. While there had been no European-wide war since 1815 and no major interstate war since the 1870–1871 Franco-Prussian War, the Italo-Turkish and Balkan wars resulted in hundreds of thousands of casualties and involved seven countries altogether. Still, Ferdinand's assassination was a watershed. Within weeks of his murder, France and its colonies, Belgium, Germany, Russia, Austria–Hungary, Serbia, Japan, and Britain and its empire (including India, Australia, New Zealand, Canada, and its African and Asian colonies) were at war in a conflict that ended up involving even more countries and consuming some 17 million lives.

Imperialism and the war

Ever since the fateful days of July 1914, historians have debated the war's causes, why it became global, and why it continued for so long. From the outset, all the belligerents produced histories that impugned their enemies. In 1919 the Versailles Treaty imposed on Germany by the Allies included Article 231, the so-called war guilt clause, which pinned the blame on Germany. In subsequent years, scholars apportioned blame more equally before the pendulum swung back with Fritz Fischer's *Germany's Aims in the First World War* (1961), which again found Germany to be at fault. Since then, the pendulum has veered back, and today most historians agree that the blame for the war is widely shared, even if Germany bears disproportionate responsibility.

Assigning blame to a country is one thing, but examining all causes is another. Numerous factors drove Europeans to first gamble on war, and then to keep fighting: nationalism, the international alliance system, militarism, war planning, an arms race, and a mood conducive to conflict that included embracing irrationalism and turning away from rational, scientific thinking. Another explanatory factor was overseas imperialism. Before 1914 many feared that tensions overseas might spill over into a war within Europe, as seen in the negotiations, conferences, and agreements that were aimed at easing colonial frictions, including the 1884–1885 Berlin Conference, the 1890 Anglo-German Treaty, and the 1904 Anglo-French *entente cordiale*. Unsurprisingly, many pinpointed imperialism as one of World War I's root causes.

Although the conflict was global, and while developments of the half century before 1914 had made Europe's state system the center of global imperial networks, it was in fact European events, not colonial clashes, that sparked the war. Remember that many Italians had viewed France's protectorate in Tunisia as an affront, and that the French in turn had perceived Britain's unilateral takeover of Egypt in 1882 as an aggression, believing Egypt to be within France's orbit of influence. Britain and Russia had played the dangerous "Great Game" as their zones of influence abutted each other in central Asia, and the Fashoda Crisis brought France and Britain to the brink of war. The Boer War stoked tensions between Britain and Germany, and two Moroccan crises risked war, the second of which was followed by actual fighting between Italy and Turkey. Yet none of these or other such near encounters led to a European-wide war.

But overseas imperialism did contribute to the start of World War I in three fundamental ways. First, the dynamic of overseas imperialism forged and solidified the European alliance system that helped cause the outbreak and spread of the war. The near miss of the Fashoda Crisis induced France and Britain to sign an *entente cordiale* to avoid colonial conflicts; it led to the coordination of military affairs, including a division of naval responsibilities as France took a larger role in the Mediterranean, and Britain beyond. Britain and Russia's 1907 agreement was also designed to avoid colonial clashes – in central Asia. Because France and Russia had signed a secret alliance in 1894, by 1907 a Triple Entente existed, which aligned Britain, France, and Russia. Designed to regulate colonial issues, these agreements involved Britain more intimately in Continental affairs and cemented relations between the three countries.

Second, two crises over Morocco in 1905 and 1911 deepened divisions between the Triple Entente and the Triple Alliance. (The latter originated with an 1879 defensive alliance between Austria–Hungary and Germany, which Italy joined in 1882.) Morocco's fate was an open question in the twentieth century's first decade. It had never formed part of the Ottoman empire, and enjoyed political independence under sultans Abdelaziz (r. 1894–1908) and Abdelhafid (r. 1909–1912). The British, French, Spanish, and Germans jockeyed for influence there, setting up language schools, promoting emigration across the Mediterranean, and sending doctors to establish their presence. Competition emerged into the open in 1905 when Wilhelm II, on a Mediterranean cruise, landed at the Moroccan port of Tangier to assert German claims. By making a show of force, Germany hoped to persuade the British that backing the French in a conflict was not worth it, which would break the Franco-British *entente cordiale*. The crisis and the Algeciras Conference that resolved it had the opposite effect: France and Britain drew closer together in the face of a volatile rival.

A second "Moroccan" crisis occurred in 1911, this time after Germany sent the SMS *Panther* to the Moroccan port of Agadir, supposedly to protect German citizens there, but in reality as a diplomatic gamble to disrupt the growing Franco-British comity. The true situation became clear when it turned out that the Germans who were supposedly in need of protection were in fact absent; they had yet to arrive when the *Panther* showed up. Diplomacy also resolved this second crisis as Germany recognized a Franco-Spanish protectorate over Morocco and received territories from France around German Cameroon as compensation. Wilhelm II had provoked these crises to drive a wedge between France and Britain, but he failed to do so, his reckless behavior bringing Britain and France even closer together. As the Triple Entente coalesced, so did the defensive alliance between Italy, Austria–Hungary, and Germany, who now felt surrounded.

Competition for empire overseas also reinforced an impulse toward war by nurturing negative nationalism and a mindset wherein conflict was seen not merely as sometimes unavoidable but as a good thing. Nationalism promoted the idea that Europeans were superior, but always in competition with other races or nations. Many came to believe Herbert Spencer's idea that existence was a life-and-death struggle, something that was confirmed only as they themselves outcompeted other "races" across the globe. Inherent in the social Darwinist impulse behind overseas expansion was an anxiety that furthered a propensity to make war. J. A. Hobson expressed this when pondering about a potential partition of China: if that happened, Europeans would become rentiers, masters of tributary empires, drawing incomes from abroad while manufacturing, agriculture, and production were shifted overseas. The more successful Europeans were, the more wealth and services and other resources would flow to them, producing indolence and, ultimately, decline. Only those on the colonial frontier, who were tested constantly, would remain hardy, and truly "white." As one student of the British empire puts it, settlers on the frontier were "quite different from the stunted, undernourished Tommies who were emerging from a dark and decaying urban England." To take it to its logical conclusion, with natives killed off or subjugated, the colonialist would become as soft and complacent as his or her metropolitan counterparts. Then what? The only way to forestall this dreary eventuality was to remain in fighting shape, and this could be achieved only through war.

Global War of Empire

Africa south of the Sahara

It was unclear what would happen in Asia and Africa in the case of a European war, Europe's colonies generally being subject to neutrality clauses in various agreements. In August 1914 the British and French swept aside neutrality provisions in west Africa, and it took their troops just days to overrun German Togoland. French, British, and Belgian colonial soldiers also attacked German Cameroon, which held out until 1916. When South Africa mobilized to invade German South West Africa, some Boers resisted out of sympathy with Germany and because the British were calling on them to defend the British empire little more than a decade after being defeated by the British in the Boer War. South Africa's government suppressed such resistance, and by July 1915 German South West Africa had surrendered unconditionally.

In east Africa, the German East African governor Heinrich Schnee and the governor of British Kenya decided not to fight, the latter declaring his colony uninvolved and out of Europe's war. German Colonel Paul von Lettow-Vorbeck preempted Schnee by assembling black African troops, called *askaris*, to do battle, attacking entente colonial troops on Lake Tanganyika. Lettow-Vorbeck embarked on a campaign that extended through much of east Africa and lasted beyond the end of hostilities in Europe. British colonials, Belgian Force Publique soldiers, Portuguese Mozambican troops, and later South African soldiers were all unable to engage Lettow-Vorbeck's forces directly. He and his *askaris* ranged widely, conducting raids into British Uganda and Kenya. More often than not, Portuguese, Belgian, and British forces did not even know where Lettow-Vorbeck and his troops were.

After failing to keep the Congo neutral, Belgium engaged its colonial army, the Force Publique, in Cameroon, southern Africa, and east Africa. The Force Publique was not really a military force but rather a police force, and was surprisingly small, considering the vastness of Belgium's colony: in total it was barely the size of one 15,000-strong German division. In April 1916 Force Publique officers offered Governor Schnee an armistice demanding compensation, territory, and an admission that Germany was responsible for starting the war. Schnee declined, and Belgian colonial troops led by Charles Tombeur attacked, taking the territories of Ruanda–Urundi within weeks. British colonial troops also engaged, and by September the Belgians had captured the capital of German East Africa, Tabora, sealing Belgium's greatest field victory of the entire war. All told, the war in Africa mobilized many thousands of people including soldiers and porters, the latter often accompanied by their wives and children.

South and east Asia

Japan viewed the outbreak of war in 1914 from a great distance, "like a fire on the far bank of the river." Loosely allied with Britain since their 1902 agreement, Japan joined the entente and declared war on Germany on August 23. Like Italy's decision in the spring of 1915 to abandon its erstwhile Triple Alliance allies and join the entente powers, Japan's entry into the fray was a move calculated to maximize potential benefits, specifically geographical expansion. In coordination with Britain, Japan attacked German possessions, taking Qingdao by the end of 1914. Japan also seized some of Germany's Pacific islands which, cut off and half a world away from Germany, were unable to resist.

The Netherlands remained neutral during World War I, and the Dutch East Indies remained outside the conflict. Britain brought its empire into the war, which meant that India joined it on the entente side, where it made a huge contribution. Although white settlers in Australia and New Zealand had achieved internal autonomy by 1914, which meant that their governments answered to their own parliaments, Britain brought both into the war without consultation. Both had expressed support for Britain during the 1914 July crisis that saw Europe stumble toward war, and they rallied to the cause. In its first action of the war New Zealand's forces attacked and took over German Samoa, and Australians overwhelmed German New Guinea. Most Kiwis and Australians fought further afield, mobilized first to Egypt and then to fight the Ottomans.

Holy War and the Near East

By joining the war in November 1915, the Ottomans brought the Near East into the conflict. Germany had cultivated a relationship with the Turks, and the Ottoman empire plumped for the Central Powers (Germany and Austria–Hungary, joined later by Bulgaria), even when this allied it with its perennial rival, Austria–Hungary, which it had confronted for centuries along a shared border. The Ottoman empire lasted the duration of the conflict, which was surprising considering the repeated losses and outright military defeats it had suffered over the preceding century. With the Ottomans' entry into the war, the British decided to expand the theater of the conflict, attacking in 1915 at Gallipoli along the Dardanelles Straits connecting the Mediterranean and Aegean seas to the Sea of Marmara and, beyond that, to Istanbul on the Bosphorus. A victory for the Ottomans, Gallipoli was a disaster for the British, although it was the soldiers of the Australia and New Zealand Auxiliary Corps (ANZAC) who bore the brunt of the defeat. Ottoman military reformers had done well, with assistance from German military officers.

When the Ottoman sultan and Muslim caliph Mehmed V brought his empire into the war, Muslim clerics issued a fatwa, or Islamic legal decree, whereby all Muslims, wherever they found themselves, must fight jihad (holy war) on behalf of the caliphate, and thus for the Ottomans. Mehmed wanted to win over the hearts and minds of Muslims everywhere, especially those in British India, French Algeria, and other colonies of his enemies. This call for jihad was odd considering that the Ottomans themselves were aligned with the Christian powers of Germany and Austria–Hungary, and both entente and Central powers courted Muslim favor. Germany, for instance, propagandized among captured Muslim French colonial prisoners of war, even building a mosque for them at one camp.

Ultimately, the appeal for jihad fell flat. Muslim troops from west Africa or Algeria, for example, generally remained loyal to France. Like everyone else, Muslims wanted to be on the winning side, and many calculated that this meant staying loyal to local authorities, whether or not they were Christian. Some Muslims viewed the call from Istanbul as an appeal from a Turkish leader at war with other nations rather than as a command from a religious man fighting for Islam. In fact the Arab sharif of Mecca and other Muslim Arabs worked *against* the sultan, taking advantage of the war to revolt against Ottoman overlordship. Thus the Ottoman position remained precarious, with the need to defend long frontiers and to face internal rebellion from Arabs who chafed against Turkish rule from Istanbul.

Wartime Colonial Agreements

In an effort to win the war at any cost, the British and French made contradictory promises that came back to haunt them at the war's end. One set of promises was made by the British to Arab leaders. After its defeat at Gallipoli, Britain sought to bolster its war efforts in the Near East by fomenting rebellion among the Ottomans' Arab subjects. Its relative success with Arab nationalists, compared to the weak response to the sultan's call for jihad, revealed the war to be more about nationalism than anything else. The British High Commissioner to Egypt, Henry MacMahon, sent a letter to Hussein, the sharif of Mecca, in October 1915 promising that Britain would "recognize and support the independence of the Arabs." In return, Hussein was expected to assemble forces to assist the British effort. When Britain expanded the war theater by attacking Mesopotamia and Palestine, it did better than at Gallipoli. The sizable armies assembled by the British needed assistance against formidable Ottoman forces, and one British officer in particular – T. E. Lawrence ("Lawrence of Arabia") – worked with Hussein to raise an Arab army to attack the Ottoman flanks. By March 1917 the British had captured the Ottoman administrative center in Mesopotamia, Baghdad, by late 1917 Jerusalem, and by late 1918 Mosul.

In May 1916 the British signed another agreement to bolster their war efforts, this time with the French. According to the secret Sykes–Picot Agreement, Britain and France would divide most non-Turkish Ottoman territories in the Middle East between themselves after the war, France gaining Syria and Lebanon, and Britain Palestine and Mesopotamia (present-day Iraq and Kuwait). The British and French made clear to allied states, specifically Greece and Italy, that they would overlook attempts to take advantage of Ottoman defeat by making land grabs in the Turkish heartland. The "Eastern Question" was, in the eyes of the British and French, largely settled.

At the same time, the British promised Zionist leaders support for the establishment of a Jewish state in the Near East. Modern Zionism had emerged in the late nineteenth century, led by Theodor Herzl, an Austro-Hungarian journalist whose witnessing of rabid antisemitism in France during the bitter Dreyfus affair helped persuade him of the need for a Jewish national state. The Dreyfus affair, which centered on the unjust conviction and imprisonment of Captain Alfred Dreyfus, a Jew, revealed French antisemitism. Herzl reasoned that if Jews could not assimilate and get by in the secular French Third Republic – the land of *liberté, égalité, fraternité* – it was impossible for them to do so in any foreign state. The solution was a Jewish homeland. In Palestine, a small Jewish population living amongst the much larger Arab population had begun to grow as a result of immigration. The British foreign secretary, Arthur Balfour, cautiously announced in the Balfour Declaration of November 1917 that Britain "looked with favour" on the prospect of a "Jewish home" in Palestine. Thus in the heat of battle did exigencies of the moment drive the British and the French to make promises and agreements that were not entirely compatible with one other.

People on the Move

Nothing better illustrates how imperialism moved people around than World War I (Map 4.1). Colonial resources, soldiers, and workers played a key role in the European theater, and the export of the conflict to Europe's colonies put people on the move. Not all colonial powers mobilized their colonial subjects as soldiers or workers for the European theater. Portugal, which sought to remain neutral, did not. Italy halted its brief experiment of putting Libyan troops into action after it resulted in thousands of deaths. The British navy blockaded Germany throughout the war, so that German officials could not bring in colonial troops, even if they had wanted to do so. The Belgian authorities refused to mobilize the Congolese for action in Europe out of fear that exposure to European ideas and peoples would undermine colonial control. The Congolese who did fight in Europe were among the few residing there in August 1914. All told, some two dozen fought in Belgium, many if not all of whom had been captured by September 1914 and who spent the remainder of the conflict in a prisoner-of-war camp in Germany.

France embraced the use of colonial troops and workers (Figure 4.1). Lower French birth rates in the nineteenth century led to fears of demographic decline, especially as other countries' populations steamed ahead – after Germany unified, France faced a much larger country to its east. Many believed that overseas empire could compensate. France was a country of only some 40

Empires at War, 1912–1922

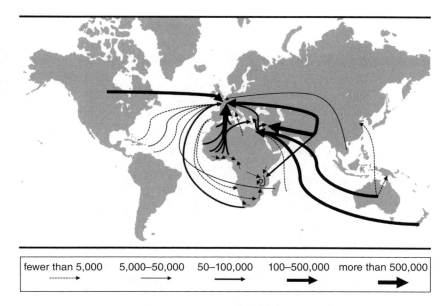

Map 4.1 Colonial troop movements during World War I.

Figure 4.1 *Spahis* from Morocco in Ribecourt, France, around 1915–1920. *Source*: Library of Congress, http://www.loc.gov/pictures/resource/ggbain.22168.

Empires at War, 1912–1922

Figure 4.2 Grave of Nedjimi Bouzid Ben Tayeb in Saint-Charles de Potyze Military Cemetery, Ieper (Ypres), Belgium, 2013. Born in 1884 in Boghari, French Algeria, he "Died for France on November 4, 1914." *Source*: Photograph by the author.

million people in 1914, but a land "of 100 million Frenchmen" if colonial subjects were included. Some were wary of arming colonial subjects, but the army officer Charles Mangin argued in *La force noire* (The Black Force, 1910) that the country should tap into colonial human resources for national defense. Mangin had fought in colonial wars, including under the command of Marchand at Fashoda, and his argument won the day. France eventually mobilized more than 500,000 Vietnamese, Algerians, west Africans, Malagasy, Tunisians, and others, the most famous of whom were the *tirailleurs sénégalais*, soldiers recruited not only in Senegal but across AOF. These men did some of the toughest fighting, for instance at Verdun, and also worked behind the lines. Some 87,000 men from the empire died, including colonial subjects and colonials of French descent (Figure 4.2).

As this chapter's epigraph suggests, the British also relied on colonial troops, including Indian soldiers for frontline fighting in the first years of the conflict, as

Ernst Jünger discovered in northern France. All told, Indians made a huge contribution: authorities increased taxes in India to help pay for the war, and the Indian Army provided 1,440,000 volunteers. The British dominions also contributed, in both European and non-European theaters. Although New Zealand contributed comparatively few men in absolute numbers, its support as a percentage of its total population was tremendous. As noted earlier, ANZAC soldiers were central to the efforts at Gallipoli, and combat in the Middle East involved Australian, Kiwi, and Indian soldiers. Some 6,700,000 men from Britain itself fought in World War I, of whom some 715,000–760,000 died, and more than 2,618,000 from the colonies and dominions fought, of whom more than 202,000 perished. What is more, all of the troops from the colonies were overwhelmingly financed by their country of origin.

The French, British, and – after it joined the war in April 1917 – the United States also recruited Asians for work behind the front, especially the French from among the Vietnamese. Entente forces brought some 140,000 Chinese workers to carry out manual work on the Western Front. They arrived in the spring of 1917, and tens of thousands were still living and working in Europe in 1919–1920, well after the conflict was over. This was a significant change. "Both the earlier Ming and Qing governments had strongly discouraged Chinese from going abroad, and even persecuted those who had." China's new republican government allowed it, hoping to shed its second-tier status by participating in the war alongside the Allies.

Colonial subjects were not sitting around in 1914 waiting to be recruited as laborers or soldiers, or as porters to lug supplies. French recruitment in west Africa put great pressure, including coercion, on local elites, and the first African elected to France's National Assembly, Blaise Diagne, went to west Africa to press people into service. One Nwose, from British-ruled eastern Nigeria, described how he "volunteered" for military service.

> We came back one night from our yam farm, the chief called us and handed us over to government messenger. I did not know where we were going to, but the chief and the messenger said that the white man had sent for us and so we must go. After three days we reached the white man's compound. Plenty of others had arrived from other villages far away. The white man wrote our names in a book, tied a brass number ticket round our neck and gave each man a blanket and food. Then he told us that we were going to the great war … We left and marched far into the bush. The government police led the way, and allowed no man to stay behind.

Many challenged the colonial authorities, who reciprocated with violence. In 1912, the very year in which Italy claimed Libya from the Ottomans, Omar Mukhtar led a rebellion to overthrow colonial rule, which continued during World War I. The Portuguese did not mobilize Africans to fight in Europe but they did for the war in Africa, especially in Mozambique. In 1917 forced labor and other impositions provoked the Barue rebellion along the Zambezi River, an area over which the Portuguese had only recently asserted any kind of real control. The French authorities violently suppressed a Kanak rebellion in New Caledonia in the same year.

War Continues in Europe

The fighting that made World War I a conflict of unprecedented attrition and industrialized killing took place on the Western Front. There, two battles in 1916 epitomized the war: Verdun and the Somme. Colonial troops fought at both, helping to determine the course of a war that affected relations between Europe and the world profoundly.

In 1916 German leaders launched a battle against the French stronghold of Verdun in northeastern France to "bleed" the French army white. General Erich Falkenhayn reasoned that France would throw everything it had at Verdun to keep it, causing "the forces of France [to] bleed to death." Once France was defeated, the British would be forced to yield. To achieve this result, Falkenhayn had 1,220 pieces of artillery moved to the short stretch of front at Verdun, including massive Big Bertha guns, each of which needed nine tractors to move and whose shells each weighed a ton. Over the course of the months-long battle German artillery fired some 22 million rounds and the French artillery 15 million. At the end, there were around 400,000–500,000 wounded and a total of 250,000 dead or missing on both sides, many *tirailleurs sénégalais* among them. The Battle of the Somme was a British offensive that took the pressure off Verdun, which led to a comparable loss of life. On July 1, 1916, the very first day of the battle, the British suffered 60,000 casualties, among them some 20,000 dead. Commanders halted the offensive only in November 1916, when there were some 600,000 German, 195,000 French, and 420,000 British dead and wounded, including British colonial troops from the Caribbean.

While the European war fronts remained in stalemate, Japanese and Australian forces made advances in the Pacific. Germany and Austria–Hungary, blockaded and hemmed in, began to suffer severe food shortages which led to the "Turnip Winter" of 1916, when it seemed that everything in Germany was made of turnips, the only foodstuff available in abundance. Germany gambled on restarting unrestricted submarine warfare, provoking the US entry into the war in 1917. The same year Russia, unable to successfully pursue a war of attrition in an industrial age, dropped out of the conflict, essentially defeated by Germany. A German gamble in the spring of 1918 to push across the Western Front and take Paris failed, and German troops were retreating by late spring. By October 1918, Germany, Austria–Hungary, and the Ottoman empire had been defeated, and Germany signed an armistice with the entente powers that ended fighting on November 11, 1918.

Attempts at Peace

The war's victors gathered in Paris in 1919 to craft a durable peace. The negotiations were contentious, lasted months, and involved innumerable sessions and backroom meetings. It was mainly discussions between the "Big Four" – the British prime minister David Lloyd George, the US president Woodrow Wilson, the French prime minister Georges Clemenceau, and the Italian prime minister Vittorio Orlando – that determined the contours of the final peace treaties. Other victors like Japan, China, Belgium, Romania, and Portugal played smaller roles. Russia, which experienced two revolutions in 1917 and had withdrawn from the war, was not invited, nor were the war's losers, namely Germany, Austria, Hungary, the Ottoman empire, and Bulgaria.

But the fighting was not yet over because the armistice of November 11, 1918, halted combat mainly in western Europe. Elsewhere conflict continued, again proving that this was a global and not merely a European war. The war in east Africa did not end until Lettow-Vorbeck and his *askaris* surrendered in late November. Russia's revolution of November 1917 led to a civil war that lasted until 1922, which pitted the Bolshevik Red Army against the anticommunist Whites. Russia and Poland were at war into 1921, which ultimately determined their shared border. When the Big Four examined maps of eastern Europe in Paris in 1919, they might as well have been looking at maps of the dark side of the moon, so far removed were they from the reality on the ground in the east.

For Britain, conflict continued closer to home, following the Irish Easter Rising of 1916. At the time of the rising, the same Roger Casement who had reported on abuses in Leopold II's Congo was trying to import German arms into Ireland in a bid to expel the British. Casement was caught, tried for treason, and hanged in London on August 3, 1916. The continued crackdown on Irish nationalism led many of the Irish to turn away from Home Rule and to take more extreme positions. The troubles continued and Irish nationalists declared a republic. The war of Irish independence did not conclude until 1921, and was followed by civil war within Ireland from 1922 to 1923.

Warfare also continued beyond the 1918 armistice in the former Ottoman lands in what turned into a postwar "scramble for empire," and, as in eastern Europe, it was local developments rather than any Paris agreements that shaped the peace. Victorious against the Turks, the entente powers occupied much of the Ottoman empire and compelled the sultan's government to sign the Treaty of Sèvres in August 1920. In accordance with the Sykes–Picot Agreement, Britain and France took possession of the Ottoman territories of Syria, Lebanon, Palestine, and Mesopotamia, even though this contravened their wartime assurances to Arab and Jewish nationalists. Italy and Greece expected to make gains in Turkey itself, Greek leaders hoping to finally realize the Megale Idea of a greater Greece. This led to an Italian invasion and a Greco-Turkish War (1919–1922), during the first part of which Greek forces advanced rapidly, occupying much of western Anatolia. Under the leadership of the World War I commander Mustafa Kemal, known as Atatürk, Turkish forces fought back, and by 1923 had defeated and expelled all foreign forces and established Turkish sovereignty. (Because Greek revolutionaries had secured Greece's independence by defeating the Ottomans by the 1830s, Turkey's victory in the Greco-Turkish War created a unique coincidence in world history whereby two countries fought each other to achieve their national independence.) Following victory, Atatürk abolished the caliphate, moved the capital from Istanbul to Ankara, and began secularizing what had been a Muslim state. There also followed massive exchanges of populations: Greece expelled its Turks, and Turkey forced Greeks out; some 900,000 "Greeks" (Ottoman Christians) and 400,000 Greek Muslims were resettled. The Turkish republic signed a new peace with the Western powers, the Treaty of Lausanne, in July 1923.

Just as the attack on the former Ottoman lands represented a kind of scramble for empire, so too did many of the 1919 negotiations in Paris as the victors tried to seize not only pieces of the defunct Ottoman empire but also former colonies of Germany, which had been stripped from the latter by the Treaty of Versailles. This flew in the face of Woodrow Wilson's Fourteen Points, one of which was the right to self-determination. France, Britain, Belgium, and Portugal grabbed pieces of the former German empire in Africa, including Togoland, Cameroon, and German East Africa. Japan took over Kiautschou and some of Germany's Pacific islands. Some British dominions became mandate powers, in effect colonizing states: South Africa became the mandatory power over South West Africa, Australia over former German New Guinea and Nauru, and New Zealand over former German Samoa. As noted, the British and French occupied large parts of the former Ottoman empire. Italy cemented its hold on the Dodecanese islands, seized in the 1911–1912 Italo-Turkish War. The Big Four sidelined delegates to Paris from colonized lands, including members of Egypt's Wafd Party, Arab leaders, and Ho Chi Minh from Vietnam (see Chapter 5).

Japan's gains at Paris, including its takeover of Kiautschou, led to protests in China. When the victors announced the terms of the Peace of Paris, including Japan's occupation of Germany's erstwhile possessions in the Shandong peninsula, the Chinese were outraged. This was a highly sensitive topic considering the degree to which Chinese had been subject to manipulation at the hands of outsiders. Moreover, China had been allied with the entente and had provided thousands of workers for the war effort, and Wilson's call for self-determination should have placed all of China under Chinese rule. The result was the May Fourth Movement, a massive outpouring of protest beginning on May 4, 1919, which catalyzed Chinese nationalism.

Such land grabs by the Western powers and Japan appear unseemly today. In contrast to the Bolshevik leader Vladimir Lenin's anticolonialism, President Wilson's calls for self-determination, the postwar granting of US and British women the right to vote, and so forth, the imperial, authoritarian impulses of European statesmen appear backward and short-sighted. But to impose our contemporary judgments on past actors does a disservice to them and distorts our understanding of how change took place at the time. Today people regularly criticize imperialism, neocolonialism, and related hegemonic impositions on supposed victims. From such a viewpoint, the empires of the 1920s and 1930s were violent, unfair, and working against the course of history, or History, as some would have it, where the past is the prologue toward an inevitable present of greater liberty and enlightenment. But, if we were to place ourselves in the times, the situation appears more ambivalent. Even following the disappearance of the Ottoman, Romanov, Habsburg, and German empires, the world remained a world of imperial formations. Indeed, the Paris peace negotiations and post-1918 land grabs reveal the scale of European postwar ambitions and an enduring commitment to an imperial future. Europe's overseas empires after 1919 were larger than at any other time previously and, following Turkey's 1922 victory over Greece, the abolition the caliphate and Turkey's emergence under Atatürk's leadership as a secular, Western-oriented republic, Europe had recreated the Mare Nostrum of the Roman empire.

The League of Nations

The League of Nations, with its "mandates" system, was a new, early form of international supervision of the colonial situation. With backing from President Wilson, the League of Nations came into existence in the spring of 1919 (even though the US Senate never ratified the Treaty of Versailles), establishing three classes of mandates: Class A mandates were former Ottoman territories, considered nearly ready for self-rule but needing a period of stewardship; Class B mandates were former German protectorates in Africa; and Class C mandates included former German South West Africa and German territories in Oceania.

Mandates represented an unprecedented attempt to control and regulate colonial practices. Before the war some had talked about international governance but they were seen as dreamers. There had been international involvement in colonial situations, for instance E. D. Morel's humanitarian campaign against atrocities in Leopold II's Congo. Morel justified intervention by arguing that the Congo was international in nature because its establishment had depended on its recognition by foreign powers, obtained around the time of the 1884–1885 Berlin Conference. Britain and other colonial powers were wary of such reasoning because it paved the way for scrutiny of their own colonial authority. The very placement of former Ottoman lands and German colonies under League of Nations supervision, whatever the class of mandate, represented a significant shift because powers had to report on their mandates. This was a real attempt to inaugurate a new kind of colonialism, even if in many cases mandatory powers in practice ruled these newly acquired territories as colonies. A good example is the Belgians, who took over Ruanda–Urundi from Germany as a Class B mandate but in 1925 unified Ruanda–Urundi with the Belgian Congo administratively.

The mandates system survived, even if neither the League of Nations nor the Treaty of Versailles did. The Paris peace treaties were on shaky ground from the start. Despite years of fighting together as allies, the Big Four were divided. The lack of wartime coordination is reflected in how it was not until 1918 that the entente placed their Western Front armies under joint command, under the French field marshal Ferdinand Foch. The Big Four entered the peace negotiations divided, and signed the final treaties at odds with each other. Although the league eventually failed, it set a precedent, and when the United Nations emerged after World War II, mandates were converted into United Nations trust territories.

The Results of War

By the time Lettow-Vorbeck and his soldiers surrendered in east Africa, nearly 10 million men had been killed in the war, some 20 million more wounded, and 7 million to 10 million civilians left dead. The Spanish influenza pandemic that followed killed tens of millions. All told, colonial powers may have mobilized more than four million men from beyond Europe for the war, either to fight or to work. Despite the many casualties among them, whether of African porters who perished or ANZAC troops who fell at Gallipoli, there are good reasons why historians focused on the war's European theaters for so long. France alone lost one and a quarter million souls, more than 4 percent of its population. The Ottoman empire and Russia each lost some three million men. Serbia suffered worse, losing as much as a fifth of its prewar population.

The war highlighted imperialism's complexities, and how empire was anything but a story with two sides, one European and one beyond Europe. There were significant numbers of Boers who opposed the British during the war, which meant that whites of European (largely Dutch) descent faced off against other whites in southern Africa. *Askaris* who dutifully fought for Lettow-Vorbeck in east Africa shared a devotion to their German officer that trumped other loyalties. Many veteran *tirailleurs sénégalais* returned to Africa more skeptical of whites' claims to superiority after their experiences in or behind the trenches on the Western Front, and yet many of those same veterans became some of the most loyal French subjects, proud to have gone to Europe, worn a uniform, and fought for France. Many donned their uniforms proudly for postwar commemorations of victory and remembrance.

As we have seen, although the years 1914–1918 normally bookend World War I, conflict started in 1911 and continued through 1922. The last Chinese workers were not repatriated from the Western Front until 1920. Peace treaties were signed beginning in 1919, but the Russo-Polish War and Ireland's war against

Britain continued into 1921 and Russia's Civil War to October 1922, the same month that an armistice was signed ending the Greco-Turkish War. The Irish Civil War continued into 1923, the same year the Turkish Republic signed a new peace treaty with the victors of World War I.

The conflict and the peace that followed had several concrete results, many of which affected the peoples and cultures that fell within the orbit of Europe's overseas empires. The war led to devastation in Europe, from northern France to the Balkans to eastern Europe. Psychologically, the conflict ended a long period of "progress" and optimism in Europe. Its massive costs precipitated a shift as the United States switched from being a net debtor to a net creditor, while Britain, the prewar flywheel of the gold standard system and global finance, shifted from being a net creditor to a net debtor. Economic problems developed, in particular a breakdown of cooperation between European nations, and the imposition of peace treaties by the victors on the losers as they redrew much of the map of Europe.

Beyond Europe and the United States, Africans and Asians were exposed to European culture in new ways. Many of the hundreds of thousands who had been brought to Europe to work or fight in support of the entente war effort died, but even more survived and returned home. (A vanishingly small number remained in Europe.) As noted, many became more loyal as a result, such as many *tirailleurs sénégalais*, who were proud veterans. Nonetheless, they had seen much on their voyages to and from Europe and during the war, and they recounted this to people back home, including stories of fighting alongside British or French soldiers in the trenches. Many soldiers and workers, stationed there for months or even years, interacted with civilian populations, either behind the lines or while on leave. Back home they spoke of the boredom and excitement, of death and destruction, and of how Europeans were just as easily terrified during attacks as they were and, when shot or hit with shrapnel, Europeans died just as they did. This undermined the idea of European supremacy.

Four long, inward-looking years of total war and investment in destructive rather than constructive capacity undermined the connections between the colonial world and Europe. Fewer Europeans traveled overseas and Europe exported less, leaving colonies more to their own devices. Funds that might have been invested in development, trade, or communications linking Europe with its colonies went into the war effort. Colonial economies developed import substitutes to make up for the lack of goods from the metropole. In some cases, the United States and Japan moved in to take advantage of the situation, seizing a larger market share for their exports – for instance, textiles woven in Japan – and developing stronger commercial ties.

Despite millions of civilian and military war dead, and millions more in the Spanish influenza epidemic, European states kept control over massive overseas empires into the postwar era, further evidence of the great power they wielded. One reason this situation continued, however, is not because of European strength but because other powers retreated or declined after World War I, not least President Wilson suffering a stroke in September 1919 and the US Senate failing to ratify the Treaty of Versailles, which ushered in an era of isolationism. Although the Treaty of Brest-Litovsk took Russia out of World War I by early 1918, Russia remained mired in conflict for years, both against Poland and in a civil war between its White and Red armies. Implementing a socialist state absorbed huge energies. Then Stalin's rise to power plunged the Soviet Union into inward-looking industrialization, revolution, and totalitarian terror, beginning in 1928. A stock market crash the following year pushed the United States further into isolationism. Another former (and future) giant, China, was wracked first by civil disorder, then civil war, and then foreign invasion at the hands of the Japanese beginning in 1931. All this left the global scene mainly to Europe's colonial powers.

Conclusion

A broader view of World War I reveals that warfare was already underway, even in Europe itself, before Franz Ferdinand's assassination in 1914. Overseas imperialism played an important if not obvious role in causing the war, and the conflict was one not only of national but also of imperial competition. There was great destruction in Europe but also tremendous loss of life elsewhere – battles raged in Africa, east Asia, and beyond – and Europeans mobilized colonial subjects to fight and work, putting millions of people on the move. Imperial entwinements increased in complexity as wartime colonial agreements complicated a postwar context in which Europe's imperial ambitions grew, leading to another scramble for overseas territories and a new height of empire.

Citations

Page *Source*
87   "From the meadow arose exotic calls..." Ernst Jünger, *Storm of Steel*, translated by Michael Hofmann (Penguin, 1961), 149.
92   "potential partition of China." J. A. Hobson, *Imperialism: A Study* (London: James Nisbet, 1902).
92   "quite different from the stunted..." Bill Schwarz, *Memories of Empire: The White Man's World* (Oxford: Oxford University Press, 2011), 145.
93   "like a fire on the far bank of the river." Aritomo Yamagata, quoted in Margaret MacMillan, *Paris 1919: Six Months that Changed the World* (New York: Random House, 2003), 312.
95   "recognize and support..." Letter from Sir Henry McMahon to Sharif Hussein, October 24, 1915, at http://www.balfourproject.org/translation-of-a-letter-from-mcmahon-to-husayn-october-24-1915, accessed September 24, 2017.

99 "Both the earlier Ming..." Xu Guoqi, *Strangers on the Western Front: Chinese Workers in the Great War* (Cambridge, MA: Harvard University Press, 2011), 32.

99 "We came back one night..." Quoted in Saheed Aderinto, "Isaac Fadoyebo at the Battle of Nyron: African Voices of the First and Second World Wars, ca. 1914–1945," in Trevor R. Getz, ed., *African Voices of the Global Past: 1500 to the Present* (Boulder, CO: Westview Press, 2014), 110–111.

100 "the forces of France..." Quoted in Alistair Horne, *The Price of Glory: Verdun, 1916* (New York: Harper & Row, 1967), 36.

Bibliography

Brown, Judith M., and Wm. Roger Louis, eds. *The Oxford History of the British Empire*. Vol. 4: *The Twentieth Century*. Oxford: Oxford University Press, 1999.

Cleveland, William L. *A History of the Modern Middle East*. 3rd ed. Boulder, CO: Westview Press, 2004.

Fogarty, Richard S. *Race and War in France: Colonial Subjects in the French Army, 1914–1918*. Baltimore: Johns Hopkins University Press, 2008.

Gerwarth, Robert, and Erez Manela, eds. *Empires at War, 1911–1923*. Oxford: Oxford University Press, 2014.

Guoqi, Xu. *Strangers on the Western Front: Chinese Workers in the Great War*. Cambridge, MA: Harvard University Press, 2011.

Jarboe, Andrew Tait, and Richard S. Fogarty, eds. *Empires in World War I: Shifting Frontiers and Imperial Dynamics in a Global Conflict*. London: I. B. Tauris, 2014.

Joll, James, and Gordon Martel. *The Origins of the First World War*. 3rd ed. Abingdon, UK: Routledge, 2007.

Moyd, Michelle R. *Violent Intermediaries: African Soldiers, Conquest, and Everyday Colonialism in German East Africa*. Athens: Ohio University Press, 2014.

Pedersen, Susan. *The Guardians: The League of Nations and the Crisis of Empire*. Oxford: Oxford University Press, 2015.

Strachan, Hew. *The First World War in Africa*. Oxford: Oxford University Press, 2004.

5

The Colonial Era, 1922–1931

> *It is alarming and also nauseating to see Mr. Gandhi, a seditious Middle Temple lawyer, now posing as a fakir of a type well-known in the East, striding half-naked up the steps of the Vice-regal palace ... to parley on equal terms with the representative of the King-Emperor.*
> Winston Churchill on Gandhi's meeting with the viceroy of India (1931)

A story tells of two Indian chess players in Lucknow in the 1850s, at the time the EIC was advancing across northern India. The two well-to-do men indulged their passion for chess by playing together regularly. Likewise did the people of Lucknow entertain themselves with music, gambling, and other distractions. Meanwhile, the company racked up success after success and, even as it closed in on Lucknow's nawab, or local governor, the players continued with their games, oblivious to what was happening around them. "The political condition of the country was growing from bad to worse. The company's forces were advancing toward Lucknow. The whole city was in a panic. The inhabitants rushed to the villages. But the two chess-players were absolutely unconcerned."

Although it was set in the mid-nineteenth century, Munshi Premchand's "Shatranj ke Khiladi" (The Chess Players) was published in 1924, and was more a commentary on the India of the postwar years. The Indians' lack of resistance, Premchand was saying, meant that the British were able to take and rule India without a fight. "Not a single drop of blood was spilled. Never in history had an independent kingdom been conquered so swiftly and without a blow struck in defense. It was, on the contrary, cowardice at which even the most cowardly would weep." While it was also a denunciation of British colonialism, "The

European Overseas Empire, 1879–1999: A Short History, First Edition. Matthew G. Stanard.
© 2018 John Wiley & Sons, Inc. Published 2018 by John Wiley & Sons, Inc.

Chess Players" was more a critique of Indians in the face of foreign rule, and a wake-up call. Premchand wanted his fellow Indians to leave their games of chess, or whatever their diversions, and awaken to their situation.

Although weakened by four years of war, Europe's colonial powers in the 1920s ruled empires larger than ever, and there were few signs that this would ever change. Europeans sustained their overseas ambitions despite their sometimes faltering self-confidence and serious economic problems. Knowing what we know today about events in the decades that followed, we must resist the tendency to read into the interwar years the eventual success of independence movements. At the time, large-scale successful nationalist or anticolonialist actions like Gandhi's Salt March in 1930 were exceptions that proved the rule, namely that imperialism endured. That said, the violence with which Europeans countered colonial resistance signaled both fundamental weaknesses and that the question of who wielded power was never settled. Reforms and changes during the interwar years further reveal that Europe's overseas empires were never finalized; rather they were always "unfinished empires," to borrow historian John Darwin's phrase.

The Massacre at Jallianwala Bagh

Having been brought into World War I by Britain without consultation and having sacrificed much as a result, India was rewarded with a massacre. Sunday, April 13, 1919, was Vaisakhi, a festival day in Punjab, a day of thanksgiving for Sikhs. Fearing insurrectionary activity, Colonel Reginald Dyer had banned all public meetings. When peaceful protesters assembled at the public garden called Jallianwala Bagh in the city of Amritsar, Dyer decided to make an example of them. He ordered his Gurkha soldiers to open fire on the unarmed protesters, at times commanding them to aim at the thickest parts of the crowd. They killed hundreds of men, women, and children and wounded hundreds more.

At the time some considered the Jallianwala Bagh or Amritsar massacre as representing British strength and resolve. Kipling praised Dyer as "the man who saved India." Although he was reprimanded, Dyer returned to Britain a hero. But why would a longstanding colonial authority resort to force under such circumstances? Because, by 1919, opposition to the British Raj had called its legitimacy into question. Dyer and others *knew* that they lacked legitimacy, hence the recourse to violence, rather than negotiation, discussion, or other peaceful means. Rather than showing power, the massacre revealed a fear of losing control.

Indeed, anti-imperialist sentiment took increasingly organized and strident forms in India. Having worked within the system for years, Indian National Congress leaders realized that their efforts to speak to British reason were leading nowhere, and they faced continued high-handedness from authorities, as suggested in this chapter's epigraph, a contemptuous statement about Gandhi made in 1931 by the future British prime minister Winston Churchill. Some Indians began to call for independence. Indian nationalism also revealed the interconnectedness of the colonial world and the exchanges within it because Congress also fought against indentured labor in places like Guiana or Natal in South Africa. Gandhi, a London-trained lawyer, got his political start fighting for Indian rights in South Africa, developing his ideas and tactics there before taking them back to India.

Gandhi's response to the Amritsar massacre was the non-cooperation movement of 1920–1922 which included a boycott of British goods. Although a success, it ended with his arrest and the suppression of the movement, followed by growing divisions among nationalists, which sapped their ability to take concerted action. As India inched toward greater self-rule, more and more Muslims – about a fifth of the country's population – came to fear that they might trade a British Raj for a Hindu one, which induced them to move away from Congress and into the ranks of the Muslim League, founded in 1906. Muhammad Ali Jinnah, who despite declining health headed the league throughout the interwar years, preached the need for a separate state.

Congress persisted in its demands for greater self-governance. After his release from jail, Gandhi continued his noncompliance. The Raj had long monopolized and taxed the sale of salt in India, the revenue from which had helped to finance India's administration. Thus this monopoly and tax on a natural product became symbolic of India's oppression. In early 1930 Gandhi undertook an act of civil disobedience by marching to the sea at Dandi to make salt, thereby contravening the state's monopoly and tax. Hundreds of supporters accompanied him, and there were nonviolent marches on salt works elsewhere and stepped-up boycotts of British goods. Images from the Salt March were broadcast across the world. Although Gandhi is usually remembered as a humble man clad in simple, homespun cloth, he was an expert at mobilizing the masses using modern media and means, in particular photography, newspapers, and railways.

Gandhi's looming presence in history and popular memory gives the impression that opposition to the Raj was united and peaceful, but this was not the case. Indian nationalists were diverse, constituting a movement without any predestined path from colonial oppression to independence. Gandhi's views not only were unique, but often ran counter to those of other Indians. He shared the notion of Premchand's "The Chess Players" that Indians needed to awaken and throw off their self-imposed subservience. But, whereas many wanted to expel Europeans from India, in *Hind Swaraj* (Indian Home Rule, 1909), a political tract spelling out many of his ideas, Gandhi welcomed them to remain. His ally and fellow nationalist leader Jawaharlal Nehru was drawn to socialism, which often put him at odds with Gandhi, although Nehru generally deferred to him

The Colonial Era, 1922–1931

Figure 5.1 Gandhi with Jawaharlal Nehru during a meeting of the All India Congress, July 1946. *Source*: Getty Images, http://www.gettyimages.ie/detail/news-photo/indian-statesmen-mahatma-gandhi-and-jawaharlal-nehru-known-news-photo/2667560#indian-statesmen-mahatma-gandhi-and-jawaharlal-nehru-known-as-pandit-picture-id2667560.

(Figure 5.1). Gandhi envisioned a united India, whereas Jinnah used religion to mobilize for a separate state. Some Indians advocated direct action, even violence, and others launched terrorist attacks. Surya Sen led an assault on a British armory at Chittagong in Bengal in 1930, after which he was forced into hiding. The British authorities arrested and hanged him in 1934. Gandhi responded with the concept of *satyagraha*, or passive resistance and truth and firmness. Many of Gandhi's public fasts protested violence – whether by the British, Hindus, Muslims, or others; this meant that his approach was only one manifestation of anticolonialism, albeit a major one.

The Horrors of Settler Colonialism

Whatever the burdens of colonial rule in south Asia, India never became a site of large-scale British settlement. European migration abroad or to colonies slowed after World War I, particularly in the 1930s. Demographic losses stemming from World War I compounded economic upheaval, a breakdown in international cooperation and trade, and restrictions on immigration in the

United States and elsewhere. In the British case, despite the 1922 Empire Settlement Act (renewed in 1937), "during the worst years of the Depression migrants entering Britain outnumbered those leaving it." But the decline was more apparent than real. There were fewer emigrants *compared to* the massive numbers who left year after year from the nineteenth century down to 1914. Still, there were colonies where the white population declined after World War I, for instance British Nyasaland, or the Belgian Congo, where between 1930 and 1936 the white population dropped from 25,679 to 18,683. It is important to note that, despite such declines, there was a reorientation of emigration. In the British case, for example, out-migration, although down overall, became increasingly *colonial* as more Britons opted to emigrate to the empire and fewer to the United States or other foreign countries. This suggests "the maintenance, even intensification, of Imperial connections."

Foreign rule was almost always most destructive and disruptive in those areas that became settler colonies. There were parallels with eighteenth- and nineteenth-century colonization in North America: again and again settlers of European descent relegated natives to marginal lands while they took the best farming and grazing grounds for themselves. Consider British Kenya, where the authorities encouraged veterans to settle after World War I. The absolute numbers of whites remained small: by 1921, there were 9,651 settlers compared to two million Africans. As the English colonial medical officer Norman Leys put it, "The whole European colony … is no more than equal to the population of a large street in a European city." But, because settlers gobbled up vast tracts of land, the effects were significant. By 1931 Kenya's European population hit 15,290 – a 58 percent increase – setting the stage for a tripling of the white population after 1945.

Colonization was dramatic in Algeria, where a European population of 715,000 on the eve of World War I grew to 1,200,000 by mid-century. French Algeria was a race-based settler colony whose economy and society served Europeans, and which denied natives the same rights as Europeans, for instance through a legal *code de l'indigénat* which included infractions and penalties that applied only to Algerians. After 1884 a small number of Algerians who met certain requirements could vote in city council elections, for example those holding a doctorate, but only slightly more than 1 percent of the indigenous population satisfied them. In addition, Algerians bore a double tax burden because the colonial government retained traditional taxes and imposed new (French) ones. Yet it was European settlers (*colons*) who decided on spending, which overwhelmingly benefited their community. There remained a major gap between *colons* and native Algerians. They shared neighborhoods, but lived next to, not with, each other as ethnicity prevailed over differences of wealth, status, and power. There was little intermarriage or children of mixed parentage because people mixed only as economic relations necessitated.

The Colonial Era, 1922–1931

This is not to say that Algerians and settlers were two monolithic blocs. Algerians were divided by ethnicity and language between Arabs and Berbers (Kabyles). They were also divided by gender, profession, where they lived (urban or rural), and over time by the degree to which they assimilated to French culture; all remained overwhelmingly Muslim, however. French men and women also differed among themselves. Some settlers were large landowners, while others held small parcels of land. Settlers and the government in Paris clashed on many issues, such as Paris's 1870 Crémieux Decree, which naturalized all Algerian Jews and was resented by many *colons*. What guaranteed solidarity among the French was that they were far outnumbered by the native population, meaning that at times of crisis, either real or perceived, divisions between Europeans melted away. After the controversial Crémieux Decree, for example, settlers united to put down the uprising led the following year by El-Mokrani (see Chapter 1).

Another settler colony was South Africa, where whites of European descent dominated after World War I. The 1910 Act of Union had made South Africa a dominion, which meant that it was to a large degree "self-governing" within the British empire – except that the majority of the population, who were non-whites, had severely limited political rights. Because the union resulted from Britain's victory in the Boer War, it was ironic that two Boers (in more recent times called Afrikaners) won the union's first elections in 1910: Louis Botha and Jan Smuts were both moderates of the South African Party, which soon added the smaller pro-British Unionist Party to its ranks. The Afrikaner J. B. M. Hertzog formed the Nationalist Party in 1914 to push for greater Afrikaner rights and more distance from the British. The Nationalist Party's backbone in its early years was the Broederbond, a secret organization formed in 1918 that connected elites and coordinated a strategy for greater Afrikaner rights and power. When whites spoke of South Africa's "race problem," they were referring not to European–African divisions but to tensions between Afrikaners and the British. Tensions had come to the forefront during World War I as many Afrikaners felt sympathy toward Germany, and some had hoped to use the opportunity to distance South Africa from Britain. These were dashed when the Botha–Smuts government suppressed any opposition.

Whoever was in power, whether pro-Afrikaner or pro-British, discrimination against Africans and other nonwhites was a given. The 1913 Native Land Act restricted black Africans to a mere 7.3 percent of South Africa's land, even though they represented the vast majority of the population. The 1936 Native Land Act "rectified" this egregious land grab but only increased the lands that Africans could legally own and work to a mere 13 percent of South Africa's territory. This brutal expropriation took the best land, thereby impoverishing black South Africans, who had to negotiate a steady deterioration of their living conditions, the exhaustion of arable land in the few areas where they could own land, and a depletion of resources.

The Botha–Smuts government suffered at the polls for fighting Germany during World War I and crushing domestic opposition. After the war, the Nationalist Party joined with the South African Labour Party to win elections, and proceeded to establish laws in favor of whites and Afrikaners. They were spurred on by the Rand Rebellion, a 1922 upheaval where whites protested against the use of black labor in mines on the Rand during the postwar economic downturn. The 1923 Native Urban Areas Act designated many urban areas "white," allowing blacks only temporary entry, for example to work as domestics. The 1924 Industrial Conciliatory Act set up negotiation mechanisms for white laborers only, which meant that black workers remained without recourse in work disputes. The following year saw the government pass the Wages Act which set white wages higher than black wages. The 1926 Mines and Works Amendment Act set a color bar in employment that favored white workers. White mine workers were very soon earning on average 11 times what black mine workers did.

Resistance grew against political, economic, legal, and social discrimination. In 1912 the South African Native National Congress (SANNC) was formed, which later became the African National Congress (ANC). Like Congress in India, the SANNC at first appealed to authorities on the basis of reason, working within the system to demand political rights, more land, an end to job discrimination, and other common-sense reforms. As the 1920s became the 1930s, it became increasingly clear that the (now renamed) ANC was getting nowhere as the government only passed more restrictive and more discriminatory legislation. Working within the system was like politely knocking on a door for years and getting no answer.

True Control on the Ground?

After the war, from India to Algeria to South Africa, Europeans ruled larger parts of the world than ever before, and seemingly more intensely. But, considering the numerous rebellions and the anticolonial agitation they faced, how much did Europeans really control the areas they claimed? Quick resorts to violence suggest a tenuous hold despite the confidence apparent during the 1919 Paris peace negotiations. The Jallianwala Bagh massacre was but the tip of the iceberg. Italy managed to re-establish control in Libya only haltingly after 1919, and at a terrible cost in human lives. Britain struggled against growing nationalism in Egypt during and after the war, where the Wafd Party pressurized the authorities (Wafd meant "delegation" because the Egyptians sent a delegation to represent their interests at Paris, not dissimilar to the presence of Ho Chi Minh in Paris that summer or of representatives of other would-be Arab states). Britain declared Egypt independent in 1922, under King Fuad and Prime Minister Sa'd Zaghloul, but retained such important powers that Egypt continued, for all intents and purposes, as a kind of British protectorate. As noted, the British Raj faced non-cooperation in many forms. In Syria, a revolt against French control lasted from 1925 to 1930. The Dutch faced rebellion in Java and Sumatra in 1926. The Nuer in Sudan resisted British rule, which led to a British campaign in the 1920s that resulted in the 1929 killing of Guek Ngundeng, prophet of the Lou Nuer, after which the rebellion ceased. In 1930–1931 a mutiny at Yen Bay in Vietnam threatened French control there, and was met with violent suppression.

Another revolt took place in Morocco. Spain's Moroccan protectorate, established in 1912, signaled a minor renaissance of its empire, this time closer to home. Much has been made of the nineteenth-century decline of Spain's empire, ending with ignominious defeat at the hands of the upstart power of the United States, a defeat so traumatic that it provoked the Generacíon del '98 movement, a soul-searching movement in literature and the arts. After World War I, Spanish colonialists turned to the Maghreb, one military publication waxing lyrical as to how Morocco was "a fatal attraction, an irresistible urge, a mysterious calling, whose voice of enchantment is heard, from time to time, leading us fatally and irremediably, shackling our will, forcing us sometimes against our own desires, toward the fields of Africa." In Africa, Spain also controlled Equatorial Guinea, Western Sahara, the Canary Islands, Ceuta, and Melilla, and its Moroccan protectorate showed that the imperialistic spirit was alive and well even among the lesser of the European powers. Now, after the war, a rebellion led by Abd el-Krim against the Spanish and French developed into the so-called Rif War. Because the revolt dated back to the prewar years, this meant that, all told, the Spanish were at war in Morocco from 1909 to 1927, and only finally prevailed with French assistance.

In Morocco and elsewhere, Europeans used surplus military equipment to suppress anticolonial rebellions. Italy first used airplanes over north Africa in its war against the Turks in 1911–1912, and continued to use armed force to reassert its control after World War I. The British used airplanes and chemical weapons to quell an uprising in Iraq against the terms of the Versailles peace settlement. Martin Thomas has characterized French postwar reassertion of authority in many areas of its empire as a "new phase of French imperial expansion" that "was no less brutal than the earlier era of colonial conquest." Even if rebellions proved that European authority was not so sure-footed, again and again Europeans' technological superiority allowed them to prevail, for the moment.

The degree to which empire continued to put non-Europeans on the move also suggests the durability of European power and influence overseas. Inter- and intra-colonial migration – voluntary, induced, or compulsory – continued at high levels. As we have seen, many of the thousands of Chinese workers who went to work on the Western Front remained in France into 1919 or even 1920, after which they returned home. Dutch authorities arranged for tens of thousands of Chinese, Indians, and Javanese to be sent to labor-intensive plantations in Java or in Dutch Guiana. Indians likely made up the largest contingent of those moved around by colonialism as labor recruitment relocated untold numbers across the globe. Consider just one corner of the British empire: "From August 1925 the British India Steam Navigation Company was contracted by the British government to ferry up to 2,100 southern Indian labourers *per fortnight* from Avadi and Negapatam in the southern state of Tamil Nadu to the Malayan ports of Penang and Port Swettenham." To grasp the scale of Indian out-migration, compare the number of Europeans in Kenya by 1931 mentioned earlier (15,290) with the number of Indians there the same year: 39,644. In British Tanganyika in 1931, there were only 4,651 residents of British origin compared to 23,422 Indians. Such numbers indicate the degree to which Britain was dependent on colonial subjects to run its empire, and how Indians took advantage of the situation. These figures also suggest the ease with which the British were able to move vast populations around, not only within but even beyond the British empire – for example to Dutch possessions – revealing the power of postwar colonial states.

Confidence in the Civilizing Mission

In many ways, Europeans emerged less confident from World War I. Four years of conflict and millions dead brought the long, optimistic, and prosperous nineteenth century to a crashing end. Representative of this was the Dada movement, born in Zurich in 1916, which was not only anti-art but also anti-war, antibourgeois, and antisociety. The German writer Kurt Tucholsky's *White Spots* (1919) expressed profound disappointment with society for not standing up against war. Robert Graves conveyed intense disillusionment with English society in his war memoir *Good-bye to All That* (1929), and he meant what he wrote: he left England and settled in Majorca, Spain. Erich Maria Remarque's antiwar *All Quiet on the Western Front* (1929), based on his trench experiences, railed against the generation that had plunged Europe into the abyss of war.

After the conflict, some sought an escape from an immoral, decaying Europe in the colonies, just as the French artist Paul Gauguin had departed for the tropics in the late nineteenth century to escape European civilization and its discontents. After World War I many began to lament the effects of imposing European norms on the colonial world, reflecting a profound ambivalence about the so-called civilizing mission. Some suffered an underlying *malaise du colonisateur*, a feeling that Europeans were doing something wrong, as reflected in colonialism's negative effects. In *Les paysans noirs* (Black Peasants, 1931), the colonial administrator Robert Delavignette, later head of France's École Coloniale, expressed his respect for local cultures and ambivalence about French action in AOF. The university-educated Frenchman Georges Trial, who was first a mechanic in the merchant marine and then a professional hunter and guide in 1920s Gabon (AEF) wrote: "After a long stay among [Africans], I am not at all persuaded that we have worked very effectively to make Africans any happier in bringing to them our civilization." He envisioned a dreadful future, an Africa "crisscrossed with railroads, planted with metallic poles bearing high-tension electronic wires, empty of its big game, widow of its razed forest, as banal, and as desperately sad and ugly, as Europe itself."

All this said, the impression that Europe was sapped of confidence results in part from scholars' longstanding focus on British and French experiences with the war. The Belgians, who were victims of wartime suffering at German hands, emerged from the war in many ways more confident, as signaled by the number of Belgian missionaries leaving for the Congo, which increased dramatically after 1919. Because the Treaty of Versailles stripped Germany of its colonies, many Germans became more strident rather than hesitant colonialists, and many organized to reclaim the country's lost territories. Italy's fascist government, in power as of 1922, used overseas imperialism to bolster its legitimacy. Portugal's authoritarian Estado Novo regime, led by António Salazar as of 1926, made empire a cornerstone of Portuguese identity, reconceiving the country as a multicontinental lusophone entity.

The civilizing mission remained a laudable one for many. E. M. Forster's *A Passage to India* (1924) reveals both the sense of duty felt by many of the English as well as the benefits that colonial officials enjoyed, namely power and prestige. In one of the novel's scenes, Mrs. Moore, recently arrived in India from England, has a heated discussion with her son Ronny Heaslop, who works in the Indian Civil Service. In reaction to his mother's liberal attitudes, Heaslop blows up:

> "We're not out here for the purpose of behaving pleasantly!"
> "What do you mean?"
> "What I say. We're out here to do justice and keep the peace. Them's my sentiments. India isn't a drawing-room."
> "Your sentiments are those of a god," she said quietly, but it was his manner rather than his sentiments that annoyed her.
> Trying to recover his temper, he said, "India likes gods."
> "And Englishmen like posing as gods."

Whereas some had questioned colonial rule before 1914, after the war debate about colonialism dried up, and empire's enthusiasts could confidently hurl invective at nonwhites, as seen in this chapter's epigraph. Although figures like Winston Churchill loomed large in their inveterate support of colonial rule, some of Britain's leading intellectuals whose thinking and writing provided the underpinning for empire during the interwar era were women, including

The Colonial Era, 1922–1931

Elspeth Huxley, Margery Perham, and Rita Hinden. Huxley's engrossing *Red Strangers* (1939) immersed the reader in the world of the Kikuyu in Kenya. Some of the French had been dubious about late nineteenth-century expansionism because it distracted people from pressing priorities, including Germany's seizure of Alsace and Lorraine in 1871. With the recuperation of Alsace–Lorraine in 1919, this motivation evaporated. Even ostensibly anti-imperialist socialists fell into line. The Belgian socialist Jules Mathieu said in 1920: "Twelve years ago our party still fought over the appropriateness of a Belgian colonial policy. But I think that all now consider the Belgian colonial endeavor as a done deal and that we ought not have any other concern other than to get through it with honor." In sum, there was broad consensus.

Development, economics, and empire

European confidence manifested itself in colonial investment. World War I had proven the value of colonies as sources of manpower and of raw materials. Perhaps years of pro-empire propaganda had also started to take effect, as the empire became increasingly "present" in Europe in the form of products like sugar and tea, or at the cinema, in novels, and in colonial monuments. The war's victors sought to further develop their overseas territories to boost their value and profits. Albert Sarraut, the former governor-general of Indochina and twice minister of colonies, argued in *La mise en valeur des colonies françaises* (The Development of the French Colonies, 1923) that the era of conquest and exploitation was past and it was now a time for development. Even if French plans and corresponding initiatives like the British Colonial Development Act of 1929 did not materialize at anything like the level called for by Sarraut and like-minded officials, "development" became a byword for empire in the interwar years.

Despite talk about colonial investment, however, Europeans always wanted empire on the cheap. Colonies had to be self-financing. The Dutch East Indies was typical: "colonial development was financed by taxes and tributes extracted from the local population." Projects were designed to exploit raw materials and indigenous labor for the metropole's benefit. Take the Congo–Océan Railway connecting Brazzaville to Pointe-Noire on the Atlantic, a kind of parallel to the Matadi–Léopoldville line built in Leopold II's Congo in the 1890s. Construction of the 510-kilometer (317-mile) Congo–Océan line – longer than the distance from Boston to Philadelphia – lasted from 1921 to 1934. With limited heavy machinery and transportation, human labor was essential, and the French brought in workers from Chad and Cameroon, some 17,000 of whom lost their lives. The Congo–Océan line was not designed to meet demand from African passengers or merchants; rather it was a French-conceived link connecting AEF's capital, Brazzaville, to the coast. Similar examples abound, including the

Tokar–Trinkitat Light Railway in Sudan, built in 1921–1922 for transporting cotton from the interior to Port Sudan on the Red Sea for export.

Colonial budgets depended on export taxes, or taxes on workers and their households, or both. Just as infrastructure projects emphasized exports, so were colonial economies oriented to benefit European capital and the governing regime. Several colonies became heavily dependent on one or two exports: rubber in Vietnam, copper in the Belgian Congo, diamonds in Sierra Leone, gold in South Africa, rubber and tin in Malaya, agricultural products in Algeria, cocoa in the Gold Coast, oil in Trinidad and Tobago, and peanuts in Senegal. Emphasis on particular sectors reshaped regional economies.

Although Europeans continued to invest most money at home, colonies did become a significant target for private investment. Events in Russia contributed to this. Before 1914, Russia was a major destination for British, Belgian, and especially French investments. Following the Bolshevik Revolution, much of Russia's economy became closed off to foreigners, and European powers diverted investments to their colonial territories. The Chinese Revolution of 1911–1912, the May Fourth Movement of 1919, and postwar claims by Chinese nationalists on concessions and railways discouraged foreign investment there. "Of the total capital invested in the [Belgian Congo] between 1887 and 1959, one-third was subscribed between 1921 and 1931." By 1908 France's empire was second only to Britain's in size, and by 1924 it had become France's number one trading partner, a position it would not relinquish until the end of the colonial period. For some industries the colonies offered key raw materials or important outlets.

Europe's Colonial Administrations

There were important postwar administrative developments. In Britain's empire, the 1926 Balfour Declaration conferred "dominion" status on several so-called white overseas colonies, granting them formal autonomy in domestic affairs. The 1931 Statute of Westminster confirmed sovereignty, adult suffrage, and responsible government in the dominions while maintaining their allegiance to the British crown. Some places gained nominal independence, for example Egypt (1922) and Iraq (1932), yet, because of the nature of signed agreements, the British maintained de facto control in many ways; in practice it mean that such areas were not truly independent. The 1935 Government of India Act was an attempt to forestall further disobedience and anticolonial revolts, but in practice it did little to change the nature of power under the British Raj.

Colonial rule intensified, including medical initiatives like the campaign against sleeping sickness in the Belgian Congo. A first campaign launched in 1903 was brought to a halt by World War I. After the war, the Belgians panicked about a demographic crisis in the Congo, and launched special sleeping sickness missions in the 1920s that reached out to Africans in new ways. For many, this was their very first contact with the colonial state.

The French and Belgians implemented more direct colonial rule, the British adopted "indirect" rule where possible; in both cases, some level of cooperation and buy-in from locals was crucial. Consider the case of Nigeria. Its economy was agricultural, and the British promoted export crops like palm oil, cotton, and cocoa (which only intensified later during World War II). So few Europeans went there that by the 1920s there was only one Briton per 100,000 Africans. The colonial authorities worked through local leaders, making their role crucial. British administrators discussed new taxes as early as 1927–1928 and were to implement them in 1928–1929. Yet many in Nigeria, including many women, objected, leading to the so-called Women's War or Aba Women's Riots of 1929 in eastern Nigeria, in which rural women of several ethnicities protested against male warrant chiefs, that is native headmen who were recognized by the authorities and tasked with collecting taxes. In the end, the women who led the protest forced the authorities to concede in order to maintain stability in the colony's eastern regions. That European authority was so thin in places like Nigeria, the Belgian Congo, or India meant that many indigenous peoples exercised much autonomy, and that European agents were plagued by fears of disorder.

Education in the Colonies

Missionaries carried out much basic education, especially in sub-Saharan Africa and mainland southeast Asia. Access to more "advanced" or European-style education varied but generally was limited, for instance in India, where it was accessible only for the well-to-do, upper strata of Indian society. Education in Vietnam, for all its Eurocentrism, was extensive, and the number of public schools, the size of the teaching corps, and the number of school students increased significantly. Still, the goal was basic education and, like the British in India, the French restricted access to higher education, for example at the French-established Indochinese University at Hanoi. Thus there were some students of higher education, either in Vietnam or in France (where some went for study), but colonial authorities always feared the creation of an elite by means of education.

Because Europeans presumed their rule in Africa would be more or less permanent, they saw little need for higher education there, and invited very few Africans to Europe for study. In AOF, there were only some 15,000 students enrolled in primary education in French-run schools by 1910, which had only increased to 70,000 by 1938, and to 130,000 by 1949; the latter figure represented around 6 percent of the AOF school-age population. The most prestigious school in AOF was the École Normale William Ponty, founded in Gorée in 1918. The equivalent to a junior high school, it took in the smartest children, and from 1918–1945 graduated only 2,000 students. In British West Africa, Fourah Bay College, founded in 1827 in Freetown, Sierra Leone, was the only English-speaking college in Africa until World War II. At independence in 1960 there were only a handful of university graduates in the Belgian Congo from among a population of millions.

Despite being limited, European-style education transformed the lives of many of those who had access to it. In *The Dark Child* (1953), Camara Laye describes his upbringing in French Guinea in the 1930s. Camara went to a French school in the capital Conakry, and then departed for Paris for further education. In the semi-autobiographical novel *Climbié* (1956), Bernard Dadié from Côte d'Ivoire recounts the story of a young boy who focuses on his schoolwork, and fulfills the aspiration of many young Africans in AOF by passing his exams and attending the École Normale William Ponty. Climbié finds employment in Dakar, Senegal, AOF's capital, before returning home after World War II. Schools offered the possibility of advancement and the acquisition of new knowledge. As Ngũgĩ wa Thiong'o put it in his novel *The River Between*, "Schools grew up like mushrooms. Often a school was nothing more than a shed hurriedly thatched with grass. And there they stood, symbols of people's thirst for the white man's secret magic and power. Few wanted to live the white man's way, but all wanted this thing, this magic."

Education for colonial subjects was a tool of control that was highly Eurocentric and culturally disruptive. As Senegalese writer Cheikh Hamidou Kane (b. 1928) put it in his novel *Ambiguous Adventure* (1963), "The new school shares at the same time the characteristics of cannon and of magnet. Better than the cannon, it makes conquest permanent. The cannon compels the body, the school bewitches the soul." Many missionaries and teachers who left Europe to work in the colonies were rather condescending toward their students, and their teaching undervalued and often disparaged African and Asian culture. Rudyard Kipling's *Kim* is revealing of British attitudes toward the "oriental" mind: "My experience," says Reverend Arnold Bennett, an Anglican chaplain in the novel, "is that one can never fathom the oriental mind." Kipling trafficked in stereotypes not only of Indians but also of the Irish, the English, and Russians, among others. Still, Bennett's reference to "the oriental mind" is revealing of British stereotypes about non-European "others." Textbooks depicted white people, not Asians or Africans. History lessons for pupils in AOF or French Vietnam began, absurdly, with the same words spoken by children in metropolitan France, "Nos ancêtres les Gaulois …" – "our ancestors the Gauls …" In Hergé's *Tintin in the Congo* (1930–1931), the intrepid Belgian reporter Tintin visits a missionary outpost where he takes over a schoolroom for the day.

The Colonial Era, 1922–1931

Standing before a class of black African boys, he starts his lesson by declaring, "My friends, I'm going to talk to you today about your country: Belgium!"

Colonial rule was about power, and Europeans used symbols and other cultural tools, including language, to assert it. With the exception of linguists, the European denigration of Asian and African languages was general, and, while Europeans expected natives to learn their own language, they seldom returned the effort other than to learn words of command. In *A Passage to India*, Mrs. Turton, the Collector's wife, approaches a group of Indian women at a party: "Advancing, she shook hands with the group and said a few words of welcome in Urdu. She had learned the lingo, but only to speak to her servants, so she knew none of the politer forms and of the verbs only the imperative mood." Ngũgĩ wa Thiong'o recalls the harmony that reigned at home, raised in his native Gikuyu:

> And then I went to school, a colonial school, and this harmony was broken. The language of my education was no longer the language of my culture … English became the language of my formal education. In Kenya, English became more than a language: it was *the* language, and all the others had to bow before it in deference. Thus one of the most humiliating experiences was to be caught speaking Gikuyu in the vicinity of the school. The culprit was given corporal punishment … or was made to carry a metal plate around the neck with inscriptions such as I AM STUPID or I AM A DONKEY.

In *Climbié*, Bernard Dadié explains how French schools forbade the speaking of native tongues. Violators were given a small token they had to carry around, which they could be rid of only by passing it onto someone else who broke the rule, which students did as soon as they could.

Many have criticized this imposition of European languages on non-Europeans in the colonies. It is worthwhile remembering that Europeans imposed languages on other Europeans too. As noted in an earlier chapter, after Italian unification the Italian politician Massimo d'Azeglio said that "Italy is made. It remains to make Italians." This process included generalizing the use of Florentine Tuscan – what we call Italian today – across the Italian peninsula, beginning in the late nineteenth century, because most people spoke other languages like Friulian, Piedmontese, Sard, among others. Most French people did not speak French as a first language until the very end of the nineteenth century; instead they were native Breton, Flemish, Basque, Provençal, Catalan, or other speakers. German speakers divided up between High, Middle, and Low German. Today Spanish is still called Castilian in Spain because there are several Spanish languages, including not only Castilian but also Galician, Basque, Catalan, and Aranese. Centralization and nationalism in Europe imposed national languages among speakers of a diverse range of languages.

The Cold War

The Cold War did not begin in the immediate post-World War II years, with the Truman Doctrine, the Berlin Airlift, and the division of Germany but rather at the time of World War I. The Bolshevik withdrawal of Russia from the war in 1917 damaged east–west relations by allowing the German army to turn its full attention to the Western Front. The Bolsheviks published secret documents revealing antebellum diplomatic negotiations, airing the dirty laundry of their erstwhile allies, Britain and France. Lenin's anticolonialism and anticapitalism positioned Russia against the Western powers. At the time of the Paris Peace Conference, people the world over saw Woodrow Wilson and Lenin as offering distinct paths forward, reflecting a significant east–west divide.

The split between communist Russia and the Western powers deepened. To make a clean break with the past, the Bolsheviks disavowed all tsarist debts, hitting French and Belgian creditors especially hard. The Western powers supported the Whites against the Bolsheviks in Russia's Civil War, even sending troops to support them. With Stalin's rise to power and his launch of the first Five Year Plan in 1928, the Soviets confirmed a future different from the one proposed by the capitalist West, a contrast that became more stark with the onset of the Great Depression, which revealed capitalism's failures. Fascist parties came to power in Italy (1922) and Germany (1933) and sprang up across the Continent and Britain. Because fascism was virulently anti-Marxist and antisocialist, Russia felt threatened not only by capitalist democracies but also by Germany and Italy. When Adolf Hitler's National Socialist (Nazi) regime violated the Treaty of Versailles, announced unilateral rearmament (1935), reoccupied the Rhineland (1936), annexed Austria in the Anschluss (1938), and negotiated the 1938 Munich Agreement, it seemed to Stalin that the Western powers were appeasing Germany, perhaps in a bid to strengthen it against Bolshevik Russia. The Nazi–Soviet Non-Aggression Pact of 1939 and the German–Soviet invasion of Poland in September 1939 confirmed Bolshevik duplicity to the Western powers, widening the east–west gulf.

The Cold War extended to Europe's overseas possessions. Colonial authorities were highly suspicious of communist infiltration and went to great lengths to forestall communist-led uprisings. The plans of Sarraut, the French colonial minister, for the empire's *mise en valeur* can be read as an anticommunist tactic to develop the colonies and to keep Bolshevism at bay. Some communists linked their movement to anticolonialism. Dutch authority in the East Indies had assumed an increasingly oppressive nature by the 1920s because of growing nationalism, but it took the overt form of a violent suppression of a communist uprising in 1926. In 1927 the communist-backed Congress of Oppressed Nations met in Brussels, attended by numerous nationalists from Asia and Africa, including Jawaharlal Nehru. In Portugal, Salazar's intrinsically antisocialist and anticommunist (not to mention illiberal and antidemocratic) regime opposed the spread of communism and related ideologies to Portugal's overseas colonies.

Anticolonialism and Nationalism

To what degree did the interwar years lay the foundation for the demise of empire after 1945? Innumerable colonial subjects challenged European power, as in the case of India's 1920–1922 non-cooperation movement. Anticolonialism built on thought and agitation that predated World War I, for instance Japan's 1905 victory in the Russo-Japanese War, which showed that Europeans could indeed be defeated. World War I significantly affected the development of nationalism and independence movements. African, Asian, Caribbean, and other veterans who returned to their homes in the colonies reported that Europeans were no better or worse than they were – they bled and died just like everyone else – and four inward-looking years of combat had weakened Europe's hold on overseas territories.

In many places, colonial rule was made possible because Europeans and local elites struck deals. If local buy-in faltered, this threatened European rule. As noted earlier, the order for male warrant chiefs to raise taxes in Nigeria in 1929 was thwarted by the Aba Women's Riots. Everyday encounters reinforced opposition to colonialism. In many French colonies people suffered under the *code de l'indigénat*, a legal code enforcing punishments for natives without judicial process. It included categories of infractions and specific crimes of which only subjects could be accused or found guilty, not the French.

The emergence of organized anticolonial groups and leaders shook colonial authority. These included Ho Chi Minh's communist Vietnamese Workers' Party, the Indian National Congress, and South Africa's ANC. Hostility toward European regimes intensified after repeated attempts to extract concessions got nowhere, or following violent crackdowns like Amritsar. The All India Home Rule League emerged during World War I to achieve dominion status such as already existed for Canada, Australia, and New Zealand. Afro-Caribbeans and Africans founded the anticolonial Ligue de Défense de la Race Nègre, which had multiple branches. The Jamaican Dr. Harold Moody founded the League of Coloured Peoples in 1931. The Congolese war veteran Paul Panda Farnana mobilized for Congolese rights in Belgium. In response, Europeans often blamed outside communist meddling for disturbing the peace rather than facing up to imperialism's inherent inequalities and injustices.

The Great Depression's onset coincided with a number of violent revolts. In Libya, over which the Italians had only slowly reasserted control in the 1920s, Omar Mukhtar continued to fight for Arab independence. General Rodolfo Graziani waged punitive campaigns against Omar's forces into 1930–1931,

The Colonial Era, 1922–1931

Figure 5.2 Omar Mukhtar under arrest in Benghazi, Libya, September 1931. *Source*: Wikimedia Commons, https://commons.wikimedia.org/wiki/File:Omar_Mokhtar_arrested_by_Italian_Officials.jpg.

including building concentration camps in which thousands died, and Mukhtar was defeated, captured, and hanged in 1931 (Figure 5.2). The Kongo-Wara rose up in AEF between 1928 and 1931, the Vietnamese against the French in the 1930–1931 Yen Bay mutiny, and the Pende against foreign rule in the Belgian Congo in 1931. Clearly, colonial authorities were never completely in control.

By the 1930s Indian nationalism had assumed increasingly well-organized and clamorous forms. One result was the British Parliament's passage of the Government of India Act, or the India Act, of 1935 which granted India a new constitution, with changes. It attempted to balance the competing demands of nationalists, Indian princes, and the British, including the calls for greater local and regional autonomy, for extending the vote to more people, and for more Indian representatives in government. The India Act was, in some ways, designed to placate nationalists without making real concessions. At the same time, it could "be seen as an attempt to reassert British interests by reinforcing India's role within the imperial system … Consolidation rather than retreat seemed to be Britain's fundamental aim." It was shelved with the coming of war.

Gandhi remained the most prominent anticolonial leader in India. In some ways this was strange because, as noted earlier, he held certain beliefs that were at odds with those of other nationalists, as well as other rather eccentric views. In 1939–1940, as Germany and Italy unleashed war on Europe, Gandhi suggested that the British allow Hitler and Mussolini to do as they pleased: "If these gentlemen choose to occupy your homes, you will vacate them ... you will allow yourself man, woman and child, to be slaughtered." Later he asserted that "Roosevelt and Churchill are no less war criminals than Hitler and Mussolini." When negotiations over independence stalled in 1946–1947, Gandhi proposed installing the Muslim League leader Jinnah as prime minister of an independent India, an option that no one pursued.

As nationalism grew and spread, it became clear that anticolonial nationalists were anything but a monolithic bloc. Just as divisions existed between Nehru, Gandhi, and Jinnah in India, so were there differences between nationalists in Tunisia, Egypt, Syria, Nigeria, Vietnam, and elsewhere. In Algeria, Ferhat Abbas, an early leader for Algerian rights, was a liberal who doubted that an Algerian "nation" even existed. Ben Badis founded the Association of Ulamas in 1931 to push for more rights for indigenous Algerians, stopping short of demanding independence. Messali Hadj advocated independence from the start, and by the late 1930s his Paris-based Parti Populaire Algérien (PPA; Algerian Popular Party) was providing leadership for the Algerian pro-independence movement. Others also criticized the system directly from within. Herbert Macaulay, the "father" of Nigerian nationalism, formed Nigeria's first modern political party in 1923, the Nigerian National Democratic Party, composed of a small number of educated Nigerians, which was largely ignored by the British. A younger generation protesting limited education formed the Nigerian Youth Movement in 1933, and following World War II a number of other groups came into being under varied leadership, including that of journalist and nationalist Nnamdi "Zik" Azikiwe. At the same time, other subjects of empire embraced the system, while others held more ambivalent, shifting positions. In any case, that there was much more opposition to foreign rule, violence against empire, and varying reactions by the interwar years is unsurprising because, as noted, by the 1920s and 1930s European states ruled more territories and peoples than ever before.

Interwar anticolonial activity and discourse reveal one of the paradoxes of colonialism. The so-called civilizing mission necessitated the mobilization of colonial subjects, be it through education, proselytization, taxation, or other interference by the colonial state. More development meant more trade, greater movements of people, further interactions between colonial regime and subject, and more circulation of ideas within and between empires. Consider the example of the nationalist All India Home Rule League. Its "name, goals, and style were inspired by Irish nationalist agitation." Not only that, but the group was founded by an Englishwoman, Annie Besant. Just as African and Asian cultures influenced Europe and its cultures, peoples the world over were drawn to Europe's professed ideals of liberty and equality. Some were drawn to Lenin's anticolonial, anticapitalist rhetoric, and others to the promise held out in 1919 by Woodrow Wilson's worldview. Since European overseas rule was inherently repressive, this induced people to challenge systems that did not match up to the

The Colonial Era, 1922–1931

professed European ideals. The more successful the "civilizing mission," the more this dynamic undermined colonial authority.

Of course, European regimes have been criticized in retrospect for advocating the "civilizing mission" and denying democratization and equality. It should be noted that before World War I no European colonizing power was a democracy. Germany in the late nineteenth century was an authoritarian state. Women did not win the vote in Britain, the Netherlands, or in the United States until after World War I. Italy was a fascist, one-party state from 1922, and Portugal and Spain were dictatorships from the late 1920s and 1939, respectively. In Italy, Belgium, and France, women could not vote until after World War II. The fight for political rights was something that was taking place not "out there" against a more progressive Europe "back home," but rather simultaneously across both Western and colonial worlds.

Conclusion

After World War I, Europeans ruled more territories overseas than ever before, but these were empires that were never "complete" but always in a state of becoming. The scope of colonial control grew through the extension of education, increased missionary activity (particularly in sub-Saharan Africa), some health initiatives, trade, a growing settler presence in certain colonies, and limited infrastructure development. Nationalistic sentiment and organized anticolonial activity grew, and Europeans continued to rely on military force to counter resistance. The violence that resulted unveiled the tenuousness of Europe's control over its colonies, even if its military superiority prevailed for the time being, making successful acts of resistance rare. The resistance continued as colonial regimes and their subjects were put to the test by a massive global economic downturn, immediately followed by another world war.

Citations

Page   Source
109   "The political condition..." Munshi Premchand, "The Chess Players," in *The Chess-Players and Other Stories*, translated by Gurdial Malik (Bombay: Nalanda, 1946), 188.
109   "Not a single drop of blood..." Premchand, "The Chess Players," 189.
113   "during the worst years..." Martin Thomas, Bob Moore, and L. J. Butler, *Crises of Empire* (London: Hodder Education, 2008), 21.
113   "the maintenance, even intensification..." Stephen Constantine, "Migrants and Settlers," in *The Oxford History of the British Empire,* vol. 4: *The Twentieth Century*, edited by Judith M. Brown and Wm. Roger Louis (Oxford: Oxford University Press, 1999), 164–167 (quotation at 164).

The Colonial Era, 1922–1931

113 "The whole European colony…" Norman Leys, *Kenya* (1921), quoted in Raymond F. Betts, *Decolonization*, 2nd ed. (New York: Routledge, 1998), 3.

116 "a fatal attraction…" "España en Africa," *El Ejército Español*, July 24, 1909, quoted in Sebastian Balfour, *The End of the Spanish Empire 1898–1923* (Oxford: Clarendon Press, 1997), 185.

116 "new phase of French imperial expansion…" Martin Thomas, *The French Empire between the Wars* (Manchester: Manchester University Press, 2005), 46.

117 "From August 1925…" Martin Thomas, *Violence and Colonial Order: Police, Workers, and Protest in the European Colonial Empires, 1918–1940* (Cambridge: Cambridge University Press, 2012), 189 (emphasis added).

118 "After a long stay…" Georges Trial, *Dix ans de chasse au Gabon* [Ten Years of Hunting in Gabon] (Paris: Clépin-Leblond, 1955), 172, cited in Jeremy Rich, "'Tata otangani, oga njali, mbiambiè!' Hunting and Colonialism in Southern Gabon, ca. 1890–1940," *Journal of Colonialism and Colonial History* 10, no. 3 (2009), at http://muse.jhu.edu/article/368536, accessed October 2, 2017.

118 "crisscrossed with railroads…" Georges Trial, *Okoumé* (Paris: Albin Michel, 1939), 8, cited in Rich, "'Tata otangani.'"

118 "'We're not out here…'" E. M. Forster, *A Passage to India* (San Diego, CA: Harcourt Brace, 1924), 51.

119 "Twelve years ago…" Quoted in Guy Vanthemsche, "De Belgische socialisten en Congo 1895–1960" [Belgian Socialists and the Congo 1895–1960], *Brood & Rozen: Tijdschrift voor de geschiedenis van sociale bewegingen* 2 (1999), 35.

119 "colonial development…" Marc Frey, "Control, Legitimacy, and the Securing of Interests: European Development Policy in South-East Asia from the Late Colonial Period to the Early 1960s," *Contemporary European History* 12, no. 4 (2003), 397.

120 "Of the total capital…" B. Jewsiewicki, "Belgian Africa," in *The Cambridge History of Africa*, vol. 7, *From 1905 to 1940*, edited by A. D. Roberts (Cambridge: Cambridge University Press, 1986), 474.

122 "Schools grew up like mushrooms." Ngũgĩ wa Thiong'o, *The River Between* (Oxford: Heinemann, 1965), 68.

122 "The new school shares…" Cheikh Hamidou Kane, *Ambiguous Adventure* (Portsmouth, NH: Heinemann, 1963), 49.

122 "My experience…" Rudyard Kipling, *Kim* (1901) (London: Puffin, 2011), 129.

123 "Advancing, she shook hands…" Forster, *A Passage to India*, 42.

123 "And then I went to school…" Ngũgĩ wa Thiong'o, *Decolonising the Mind: The Politics of Language in African Literature* (London: James Currey, 1986), 11.

126 "be seen as an attempt…" Thomas, Moore, and Butler, *Crises of Empire*, 26–27.

126–7 "If these gentlemen choose…" Quoted in Stanley Wolpert, *Gandhi's Passion: The Life and Legacy of Mahatma Gandhi* (Oxford: Oxford University Press, 2001), 197.

127 "Roosevelt and Churchill…" Quoted in Wolpert, *Gandhi's Passion*, 213.

127 "name, goals, and style…" Barbara D. Metcalf and Thomas R. Metcalf, *A Concise History of Modern India*, 2nd ed. (Cambridge: Cambridge University Press, 2006), 164.

Bibliography

Bandeira Jerónimo, Miguel. *The "Civilising Mission" of Portuguese Colonialism, 1870–1930*. Translated by Stewart Lloyd-Jones. Basingstoke, UK: Palgrave Macmillan, 2015.

Conklin, Alice L. *A Mission to Civilize: The Republican Idea of Empire in France and West Africa, 1895–1930*. Stanford: Stanford University Press, 1997.

Gandhi, M. K. *Hind Swaraj and Other Writings*. Edited by Anthony J. Parel. New Delhi: Cambridge University Press, 1997.

Harper, Marjory, and Stephen Constantine. *Migration and Empire*. Oxford: Oxford University Press, 2010.

Jennings, Eric T. *Curing the Colonizers: Hydrotherapy, Climatology, and French Colonial Spas*. Durham, NC: Duke University Press, 2006.

Laye, Camara. *The Dark Child*. Translated by James Kirkup and Ernest Jones. New York: Noonday Press, 1954.

Manela, Erez. *The Wilsonian Moment: Self-Determination and the International Origins of Anticolonial Nationalism*. Oxford: Oxford University Press, 2009.

Orwell, George. *Burmese Days*. New York: Harper & Bros., 1934.

Thomas, Martin. *Violence and Colonial Order: Police, Workers, and Protest in the European Colonial Empires, 1918–1940*. Cambridge: Cambridge University Press, 2012.

Wolpert, Stanley. *Gandhi's Passion: The Life and Legacy of Mahatma Gandhi*. Oxford: Oxford University Press, 2001.

6
World War II, 1931–1945

"You're superior to them, anyway. Don't forget that. You're superior to everyone in India except one or two of the Ranis [wives of an Indian prince or king], and they're on an equality."

E. M. Forster, *A Passage to India* (1924)

Another major outbreak of resistance in Europe's interwar empires was an Arab rebellion against British rule in Palestine, including a strike and violent attacks, which started in the spring of 1936. Britain's wartime promises were coming back to haunt it. One such promise was the 1917 Balfour Declaration, whose support for a Jewish state became incorporated into the postwar mandate document on Palestine, encouraging more foreign Jewish nationalists to immigrate. Around 1919 Jews in Palestine numbered only 70,000, or about 10 percent of the area's population. Many more European Jews now arrived, 170,000 from 1933–1936 alone. Even though most settled in urban areas, many bought up massive swathes of land, and Jewish landholdings grew from 162,000 to nearly 300,000 acres by the end of the 1920s, increasing by another 175,000 acres before 1947. Thus did British promises aggravate tensions in Palestine. Another set of British wartime promises was to Arab nationalists, whom the British courted to bolster their efforts against the Turkish Ottomans. After 1919 the British did grant a greater degree of self-rule, even independence, to some Arab states – if only nominal – including Egypt and Iraq. Arabs in Palestine saw no such advances.

The 1936 strike and revolt prompted the British to institute the Peel Commission in 1937 to investigate grievances, the very establishment of which dampened

European Overseas Empire, 1879–1999: A Short History, First Edition. Matthew G. Stanard.
© 2018 John Wiley & Sons, Inc. Published 2018 by John Wiley & Sons, Inc.

down the revolt, though only temporarily. When the commission recommended a partition of the mandate and transfers of population numbering in the hundreds of thousands, the rebellion resumed, this time including attacks on Jewish property; lasting until 1939, it required tens of thousands of British troops to suppress it.

The 1936–1939 Arab revolt in Palestine was one of the most serious uprisings ever against British overseas rule, and it illustrates several of this chapter's themes. First, the revolt revealed the impact of settler colonialism. Whether it was French *colons* in Algeria, English war veterans settling in Kenya, or Jews buying up land in British Palestine, foreign settlers expropriated the best agricultural lands at the expense of the local people. Second, it was clear by the interwar era that colonial rule had stimulated indigenous nationalism. When white explorers and their guides traipsed around central Africa or in small parties up the Mekong, they elicited little notice. But when Europeans supplanted local rulers, confiscated land, and otherwise intruded into people's lives in heavy-handed ways, this provoked reactions, including the development of nationalism. Thus, the 1936–1939 revolt signaled increasing opposition to foreign oppression.

Naturally, colonized peoples pursued their own agendas, which seldom matched the priorities of colonizing powers. One tool used by colonial regimes to assert their power was the management of colonial difference, that is, delimiting and controlling social, racial, political, sexual, and other frontiers between colonizer and colonized to better control the latter. Still, as the colonial era moved into full swing, situations arose that revealed how colonial situations shaped and constrained the colonizer as much as the colonized. Complicating all this was a worldwide economic downturn starting in 1929, another battle between Italy and Ethiopia beginning in 1935, and a second world war of empire.

The Great Depression

A second global war and the massive economic downturn that preceded it profoundly affected European states and their colonies. Post-World War I economic dislocations, the US stock market crash, and a lack of confidence and cooperation between political leaders and bankers contributed to an economic depression beginning in 1929. By 1931 even more self-sufficient or insulated economies, for instance that of France, were affected. The depression hit more industrialized countries the hardest, and by 1932 unemployment in Germany and the United States was running at 30 percent. Governments implemented higher tariffs, global trade dropped, and nonindustrialized regions that were dependent on exporting raw materials saw prices plummet. The global price of wheat had declined by about 50 percent by mid-1930 and that of rice by more than 50 percent by January 1931. Although this benefited consumers, it was terrible for farmers. India, like many other colonies, remained overwhelmingly rural and agricultural, and the depression and the abrupt drop in prices halved the value of crops there.

Worse still, colonial policies foisted the costs of the Great Depression onto workers as authorities continued to demand that colonies pay for themselves. The authorities collected taxes but cut outlays. Colonial administrations and their business allies lowered wages and expenditures on workers to squeeze as much as possible out of overseas territories at the lowest possible cost. This led to terribly low wages, abysmal working conditions, and layoffs in those zones that had been incorporated into colonial economies. The results were often dreadful, for example on the large rubber plantations in British Malaya, in southeast Asia, which were often worked by imported Indian laborers. Management pursued profit despite declining rubber prices, and working and living conditions became so bad and wages so low that some laborers chose death instead: in 1929 alone there were 45 suicides.

The Great Depression waylaid economic development plans, meaning the *mise en valeur* of the colonies remained a dead letter. Developments in the Belgian Congo, where mining had become central to the colonial economy, illustrate the depression's effects. In the southern Katanga region, where copper was king, the mining giant Union Minière du Haut-Katanga (UMHK) and the colonial authorities had "stabilized" the worker population by the late 1920s. To ensure a regular labor supply rather than recruiting new workers every year, UMHK built housing for workers, who now lived at the mines. When the depression hit, UMHK tried to stay profitable by imposing the costs of low world copper prices on African mine workers through lower wages or dismissals. But the decline in agricultural prices meant that workers no longer had the option of returning to the land. The dismissal of workers from the mines increased to the extent that the countryside could absorb no more. Worker dissatisfaction exploded into unrest in 1931. UMHK tried to reassert control over the mines by introducing African educators and monitors who reported on African social activity.

Labor unrest and strikes by plantation workers, dock workers, or mine workers concerned all colonial authorities from the Caribbean to west Africa to south Asia. Which raw materials were extracted and how they were produced shaped colonial policing. Thus, in Sierra Leone colonial policing supported diamond mining, whereas in Malaya it oversaw rubber production. "Police operations reflected not just the colonial political order but its economic structures as well."

Thus, colonial subjects did not remain passive victims of heavy-handed policies. Africans resisted mandatory cultivation schemes by resorting to what James Scott calls "weapons of the weak," including non-cooperation, choosing infertile ground for compulsory planting or cutting the roots of trees underground. Flight or suicide (as in British Malaya) were acts of resistance. The Congolese in Belgium's colony gave whites facetious nicknames, drawing attention to humorous physical traits. In British West Africa, where the colonial system had induced

Africans to produce export crops for the world market, cocoa growers in the Gold Coast protested low prices in 1937 by withholding cocoa deliveries. It worked to a degree: European buyers raised prices somewhat, and that they could do so shows that, despite the depression, there was money out there. Indeed, even if, all things considered, colonialism might not have been profitable, some enterprises and individuals made fortunes. The global and diverse company Lever Brothers, for example, *expanded* overseas operations during the 1930s, including its plantations in sub-Saharan Africa.

Managing Colonial Difference

Colonial authority was based on the premise, establishment, and maintenance of difference. Europeans cultivated the idea of white superiority and predicated their right to rule on the inferiority of the governed. As we have seen, nineteenth-century scientific racism undermined Enlightenment ideals of a shared humanity. Because Europeans also came to equate industrial and technological know-how with racial and cultural advancement, they lost respect for sophisticated cultures in the Islamic world and Asia, a loss that events like the 1857 Indian mutiny only reinforced. By the interwar era, the belief that whites were superior was general among Europeans and their descendants in the United States. E. M. Forster captured this in his novel *A Passage to India*, set in the fictional Indian city of Chandrapore, in which the city's head official, the Collector, and his wife, Mrs. Turton, arrange a bridge party for the recently arrived Mrs. Moore and Miss Quested to meet some Indians. As quoted in this chapter's epigraph, Mrs. Turton confidently reassures the two Englishwomen not to be nervous because they are superior to *everyone* in India.

Imperial experiences shaped not only what it meant to be "black" or "Asian," but also "white" or "mixed." The action in *A Passage to India* centers around a purported attack by a Muslim Indian doctor against an Englishwoman. When one Englishman stands up for the doctor at the British club in town, his lack of racial solidarity outrages his fellow whites: "The Collector looked at him sternly ... he had not rallied to the banner of race. He was still after facts, though the herd had decided on emotion ... All over Chandrapore that day the Europeans were putting aside their normal personalities and sinking themselves in their community." In this way, colonial rule induced white solidarity.

Creating "whiteness" necessitated the policing of racial boundaries. "Children of empire," or mixed-race children, were troublesome. Many Europeans urged women to move to the colonies to prevent men from taking concubines, which produced mixed-race children who blurred the dividing line between colonizer and colonized. *Métissage*, or race mixing, led to people caught in between societies and cultures, who in the end found themselves excluded from both. One of the characters in *A Passage to India*, Mr. Harris, is a Eurasian of mixed descent: "When English and Indians were both present, he grew self-conscious, because he did not know to whom he belonged. For a little he was vexed by opposite currents in his blood, then they blended, and he belonged to no one but himself." In V. S. Naipaul's *A Bend in the River* (1979), set in postindependence Congo, one of the main characters, Ali, changes his name to "Metty," from the French *méti*, reflecting his mixed-race background.

Paradoxes of Colonial Power

Whereas imperialism oppressed colonized peoples variously, the colonial situation also bound those ostensibly "in charge," that is, white Europeans. George Orwell learned this firsthand. Born in India in 1903, Orwell was raised in England, then began a career as a policeman in Burma. On a visit to England after different postings in Burma, he quit the colonial police to take up writing, drawing on his Burmese experiences to write works criticizing empire, in particular *Burmese Days* (1934) and the essays "A Hanging" (1931) and "Shooting an Elephant" (1936). "A Hanging," which depicts the horrific scene of the execution of a man in Burma, is a scathing indictment of the death penalty. *Burmese Days*, a quasi-autobiographical novel whose protagonist, Flory, is stationed in Burma, highlights empire's corrupting effects. Flory lays bare the lie "that we're here to uplift our poor black brothers instead of to rob them. I suppose it's a natural lie enough. But it corrupts us, it corrupts us in ways you can't imagine."

In "Shooting an Elephant," Orwell reveals how the colonial situation controlled the colonizer as much as the colonized. In the story, a domesticated elephant goes wild, and the unnamed protagonist and narrator, a colonial policeman, reluctantly calls for a gun. He recognizes the elephant's value as a living being and as a work animal. To kill it was "comparable to destroying a huge and costly piece of machinery … As soon as I saw the elephant I knew with perfect certainty that I ought not to shoot him." With a growing crowd of Burmese about him, and recognizing the need to appear in control, he realizes that he will have to shoot the elephant anyway:

> The people expected it of me and I had got to do it; I could feel their two thousand wills pressing me forward, irresistibly. And it was at this moment, as I stood there with the rifle in my hands, that I first grasped the hollowness, the futility of the white man's domination in the East. Here was I, the white man with his gun, standing in front of the unarmed crowd – seemingly the leading actor of the piece; but in reality I was only an absurd puppet pushed to and fro by the will of those yellow faces behind. I perceived in this moment that when the white man turns tyrant it is his own freedom that he destroys … For it is the condition of his rule

that he shall spend his life in trying to impress the "natives," and so in every crisis he has got to do what the "natives" expect of him.

The white man was as much a captive of the situation as the native, except, of course, that it was the Europeans who had decided to send the white man to Burma in the first place.

Orwell's fiction also reveals how people, however progressive, remained products of their era. The unnamed narrator of "Shooting an Elephant" deplores the colonial situation but also hates the Burmese. The protagonist of *Burmese Days*, Flory – and by extension Orwell – is typical of racist colonial officials in that Burmese people are absent from his life even though they are all around him. With the exception of one or two prominent characters in the novel, the Burmese simply pass by unremarked upon, like scenery. Flory has a local concubine but wants to marry a white woman, which complicates his situation when an Englishwoman arrives in his remote area. Indeed, European colonials in Africa and Asia often had local "wives" and children, but it was the rare man who recognized them as legitimate or brought them home when returning to Europe.

Bernard Dadié's novel *Climbié* picked up on the displacement Europeans suffered as a result of either depression or their own cruelty toward natives: the character N'zima knows that whites in Africa are often unhappy and unstable. When a white police commissioner dies and the reason is not immediately known, suicide is suspected. Upon hearing the news, a citizen of Grand-Bassam, Côte d'Ivoire, says, "He must have killed himself ... the Europeans, you know, often put a revolver to their heads." Returning home did not resolve such unease:

> When in Africa, these men would always think of their home town. And once returned to their own country, they would hurry to get back to Africa, because, at home, their attitudes were out of place, and often hurt people's feelings ... Africa catches up with them, claws them, marks them for ever. They have the blues in Africa. They have nostalgia in Europe. They are no longer men of one continent, but a hybrid species.

While much has been made of critics of empire like Orwell, or insights into *mentalités* like those in *Climbié*, they hardly reflected universal sentiments. Indeed, it was only because so many others accepted and invested in imperialism that Orwell's or Dadié's critiques today appear prescient. Contrast "Shooting an Elephant" with the colonial administrator J.-M. Domont's account of an event in Belgium's colony in 1941:

> The monotony of office work was sometimes broken by a fortuitous incident, characteristic of tropical countries. It is thus that one morning it suddenly happened a great, unusual tumult in the area around the offices of the *Territoire*. Was it a protest? The start of a riot? The cries of rage increased in volume as the group of bawlers grew in size ... And I heard the cries of "nioka nene" (big snake) several

times ... I headed toward the route followed by the snake to cut his path. While running I grabbed a stone as a weapon of defense or attack ... [I] found myself a meter in front of him. Right away he attacked me ... Our confrontation was enveloped by a heavy silence. Not a shout. The Blacks assembled at a prudent distance asked themselves with a certain anxiety what their White was going to do; as soon as the snake lifted itself up I understood that I was dealing with a spitting cobra ... As soon as I heard a gentle hiss, I saw at the same moment, spurt out the milky jet of venom directed toward my eyes ... I congratulated myself on having the stone because, well aimed, it broke the hinge joint of the snake that had allowed it to lift itself up to confront me and that was vital to its crawling ... It was a mortal blow. The yelling redoubled, joyous this time. "The White wasn't afraid," "the White has killed the snake," "the White is the smartest and the strongest," "the cobra is dead."

Domont believed that his success showed fortitude, but his first thought upon hearing noises outside his office was that there might be a riot underway, suggesting nervousness. Nonetheless, in contrast to Orwell's embarrassment, Domont relished the moment, showing that some were comfortable with and even enthusiastic about colonial rule.

Domont's snake story reveals another aspect of colonial administration: boredom. His story begins with the monotony of office work. Boredom translated into pastimes – to pass time – such as card playing, hunting, and drinking. Graham Greene based his novel *The Heart of the Matter* (1948) on his wartime sojourn in Sierra Leone. The novel opens with the colonial official Edward Wilson on his hotel room balcony in an unnamed west African colony. "A black boy brought Wilson's gin and he sipped it very slowly because he had nothing else to do except to return to his hot and squalid room and read a novel – or a poem." Later, Wilson and a colleague in a neighboring apartment are so bored that they compete to see who can kill the most cockroaches. The drinking of alcohol recurs throughout the novel: whiskey, beer, wine, pink gins, and more gin. In Forster's *A Passage to India*, Mrs. Moore and Adela Quested, recently arrived from England, are at Chandrapore's whites-only club. When Quested complains about not seeing the "real" India, the Collector tries to placate them, suggesting, "Have a drink, Mrs. Moore – Miss Quested – have a drink, have two drinks." In the semi-autobiographical novel *Gangrene*, by the former Belgian colonial administrator Jef Geeraerts, the protagonist stumbles through a number of sexual and other adventures, often blind drunk after having indulged to excess with either fellow Belgians or Africans.

Culture and Empire

Empire had cultural ramifications across the colonial world. As we have seen, imperialism reshaped cultures, including colonial influences on African art; a decline in Indian artistic production as a consequence of the undermining of

Indian princes, who were traditional patrons of the arts; and subtle Anglo-Indian controls over information, language, even dress in India. In Vietnam the promotion of French culture led to investment in primary education and to changes in mentalities, literature, music, the fine arts, and religion. Vietnam's Catholic minority was one example of how different people reacted to foreign intrusions variously across mainland southeast Asia. Catholic missionaries had arrived in Indochina as early as the seventeenth century, and by 1931 there were some 1.3 million Vietnamese Catholics out of a population of 15 million. Although the French saw the civilizing mission as part and parcel of colonial rule, the longer their presence endured, the greater their skepticism about the projection of French civilization because of growing awareness of the richness, sophistication, and endurance of Asian cultures. When colonial rule undercut Vietnamese arts and crafts production by undermining local powers, and by extension their spending as patrons of the arts, some of the French, particularly those in Vietnam, began to champion Vietnamese art in order to save it, an irony that was repeated across the colonial world.

Whereas people long believed that empire's cultural effects were largely a one-way affair as European culture spread outward, recent research has revealed profound effects on the colonizer. By the mid-nineteenth century, Europe had already been profoundly reshaped as a result of fifteenth- and sixteenth-century voyages of exploration and the Columbian Exchange of diseases, plants, animals, peoples, products, and ideas between Africa and Eurasia on the one hand and the Americas on the other. A mania for all things Egyptian swept western Europe in the early nineteenth century, which one can see in the paintings of the Frenchman Eugène Delacroix, inspired as he was by his 1830s voyage to north Africa. Even if respect for China and its culture waned in the nineteenth century, as reflected in the decline of popularity of chinoiserie, fascination with Japanese art (*japonisme*) bloomed in the latter half of the nineteenth century, as seen in the Japanese influence on paintings by the Dutch artist Vincent van Gogh. India had long influenced British trade and politics as well as the English language, poetry, theater, and art. As noted, Spain's traumatic loss of its colonies to the United States in the Spanish–American War led to the soul-searching literary movement called the Generación del '98. By the early twentieth century, so-called primitive art, or *art nègre*, was influencing artists in Paris and beyond. Pablo Picasso's encounter with African masks during a visit to a 1907 ethnographic exhibit in Paris led him to paint the famous *Les Demoiselles d'Avignon* (1907), in which two of the women appear with mask-like faces. Such fundamental reshaping of culture disproves the idea that Europe was a fixed "thing" that projected itself outward, or that colonization affected only non-European cultures.

As early as the eighteenth century, Orientalists studying the Islamic world and south and east Asia influenced Europeans' self-identity and how they saw themselves in relation to the rest of the world. The "Orient" was not a place but rather a European idea created in texts and discussion; it was a discursive production. Scholars of the Orient conceived of it as irrational, passive, undesirable, and "other," while Europeans by contrast were rational, active, and good. In this way the Orient acted as a foil for the Occident: for Europeans, knowing the Orient was a way in which they could produce and know "Europe" and what it meant to be European. In a similar way, explorations and eventually imperialism reinforced the idea of the nation-state both by making the nation-state the actor that carried out conquest and colonial rule, and by setting off "nations" and citizens in Europe against non-European others. This could be seen most clearly in the colonies themselves; for example, Frenchmen in Algeria were more French than their compatriots across the Mediterranean, and the British in India were more British than those back home.

Nowhere are empire's effects on Europe better seen than in the British Raj where, by the mid-nineteenth century, India had already shaped British culture and Britain India's in turn. The British appropriated cultural practices and made them their own, for instance Indian durbars (traditional princely processions or festivals). At a psychic level, India became a source of British pride. To break the Chinese monopoly on tea production, the British encouraged tea cultivation in India, which resulted in a huge increase in exports from India to Britain and a growth in British tea consumption. India pale ale developed as a distinctive drink for the Anglo-Indian market, which was then introduced into Britain. Exposure to India enriched the English language. For example, the word "punch," which originally referred to a drink composed of five ingredients, comes from the Hindi–Urdu word *păc*, meaning five; "jungle" derives from the Hindi–Urdu *jangal*; "thug," meaning ruffian or gangster, originates from the Hindi–Urdu *thag* (thief); the term for an Indian soldier of the Raj, "sepoy," comes from *sipāhī* (soldier) in Persian. (The latter term spread to Turkey and north Africa, and the French later raised colonial *spahi* units in the colonies, which fought during both world wars and still march in Bastille Day parades today.)

There was no simple spread of European "modernity" outward to backward parts of the world. The development of what many call "modernity" in Europe emerged in many ways out of interactions with non-Europeans. "Far from modernity 'happening' in Europe and then being transplanted to a country like India," write Barbara and Thomas Metcalf, "many of these changes took place in relation to each other." Many British "modern" practices, technologies, or institutions emerged in tandem with developments in or experiences with India, including municipal cemeteries, English literature as a curricular subject, state-sponsored surveying, and scientific study and institutions. The expansion of state bureaucracies in Europe, a hallmark of the late nineteenth-century state, had its parallel in the growth of colonial bureaucracies, perhaps nowhere more so than in British India. Urban redesign in Europe developed simultaneously with colonial urban development.

World War II, 1931–1945

One can not only trace the ongoing influence of the colonies on European culture in the interwar era; in many ways the influences were so pervasive and commonplace as to go unnoticed. Many things that we consider fully "European" were shaped, or were wholly created, by the world beyond, such as tea drinking in England or couscous in French cuisine. The Nazi Party's *Sturmabteilung* members adopted the khaki uniforms (*khaki* itself being an Urdu word) in the 1920s that gave them the nickname of "brownshirts" because the uniforms were colonial military surplus, and therefore inexpensive.

The imperial experience helped create "Europeans," who, as noted, defined themselves against the other, that is supposedly weaker, inferior colonized peoples. As Catherine Hall puts it in regard to the British, "the colonies provided the many benchmarks which allowed the English to determine what they did not want to be and who they thought they were." British influence in nineteenth-century Egypt is illustrative. It extended to reordering schools, housing, and the military, working from the premise that Europeans were logical, advanced, and orderly whereas Egyptians were backward, disordered, and illogical. "Egypt was to be ordered up as something object-like … Colonial power required the country to become readable, like a book." Egypt's new, British-inspired army disciplined bodies. The new colonial school system was designed to a conceptual framework, in contrast to the madrassas, which appeared relatively disordered and undisciplined. Egyptian learning had been based on interpretations of interpretations going back eventually to fundamental texts including the Koran. "Education, as an isolated process in which children acquire a set of instructions and self-discipline, was born in Egypt in the nineteenth century. Before that, there was no distinct location or institution where such a process was carried on, no body of adults for whom it was a profession, and no word for it in language." The duality of the world was extended to the person, which was to be understood as divided into physical and nonphysical parts. All of these "tended to produce the effect of a structure, which seemed to stand apart as something conceptual and prior." This conceptualization of order created the "oriental" because, without the contrast with the oriental, "order" as such could not exist. This opposition, "Oriental" versus Western, penetrated Egyptian discourse in textbooks, among teachers, and in novels.

The insinuation of empire into European cultures suggested that empire had a long future. The 1924–1925 British Empire Exhibition at Wembley Park and Belgium's 1930 Exposition Internationale Coloniale, Maritime, et d'Art Flamand in Antwerp had been large shows, and were followed by Glasgow's Empire Exhibition of 1938 and Portugal's Exposição do Mundo Português in 1940. Colonial exhibits at world's fairs and elsewhere set apart representations of colonial things both from the reality they represented and from the mind of the viewer, turning the colonial into an imaged other. The 1931 Paris Colonial Exposition in the Parc de Vincennes was a huge such celebration of empire. The

French naturally took pride of place, but also present were the Portuguese, Dutch, and Belgians. A "counterexposition" by the Surrealists and others tried to dissuade people from visiting, declaring in one pamphlet, "Do not visit the Exposition!" But that only some 5,000 saw the counterexposition as compared to eight million who visited the colonial fair reveals the appeal of empire.

Of major import in the francophone African diaspora was the Négritude movement. René Maran, Aimé Césaire, Léopold Sédar Senghor, Léon Damas, and other black writers from different regions were united by the French language and the colonial experience; "people of color," they melded French language, art, and literature with local culture in the colonies and in France. Maran, for example, won the Prix Goncourt for his novel *Batouala* (1921). Consider Senghor's wonderful retort to the idea of Africans being colored in his work "Poème à Mon Frère Blanc" (Poem to My White Brother):

> Dear white brother,
> When I was born, I was black,
> When I grew up, I was black,
> When I am in the sun, I am black,
> When I am sick, I am black,
> When I die, I will be black.
> While you, white man,
> When you were born, you were pink,
> When you grew up, you were white,
> When you go in the sun, you are red,
> When you are cold, you are blue,
> When you are scared, you are green,
> When you are sick, you are yellow,
> When you die, you will be gray.
> So, between you and me,
> Who is the colored man?

Thus did the new wave of empire building of the last decades of the nineteenth century bring with it new or intensified effects for both Europeans and non-Europeans, the latter in particular in south Asia and Africa, the main targets of the New Imperialism.

World War II

By the time the Japanese bombed Pearl Harbor on December 7, 1941, war had been underway for more than a decade. Imperialistic expansion led to its outbreak. Japan, an entente ally during World War I, had seen its territorial expansionism sanctioned at the Peace of Paris as it took over several territories. While

Japan had selectively adopted quasi-democratic forms from Western countries during the Meiji Restoration era, it veered away from parliamentary democracy from the 1920s, a development that accelerated during the Great Depression. Japan's military leadership adopted an expansionistic policy to secure resources to safeguard the country's future. In September 1931 Japanese forces in Manchuria, in northwest China, staged an explosion along a railway line in a Japanese concession area, and the government used this Mukden Incident as pretext to attack China in what became an undeclared war. Following its success, Japan created the puppet state of Manchukuo in Manchuria and installed the last Chinese emperor, the Xuantong emperor – better known as Puyi – who had abdicated in 1912.

Japan declared open war against China in 1937, inaugurating a second Sino-Japanese War. Its forces racked up gains against a China that was divided between a Nationalist government under Chiang Kai-shek and a communist movement led by Mao Zedong. The Chinese suffered terribly at the hands of vicious Japanese attacks premised on Japan's racial superiority, for instance Japan's assault on the Nationalist capital, Nanjing, which led to a massive loss of life.

From our present vantage point, it is easy to condemn the Japanese for their aggression and antidemocratic tendencies. At the time, Japan was following the lead of the world's industrial powers as it competed for markets, territories, resources, and influence. This included the rhetoric it used to cloak its ambitions. Just as Europeans and Americans claimed that they were engaged in an altruistic "civilizing mission," Japan claimed that it was building a "Greater East Asia Co-Prosperity Sphere," within which Asian peoples could be free of Western dominance. In truth, the Japanese were building their own oppressive, racially based empire in which foreign peoples were to serve their interests.

Italy's War on Ethiopia

Western reactions to Japan's war against China were muted because of both the Nazi accession to power in Germany in January 1933 and fascist Italy's war against Ethiopia. Economic and political crises in postwar Italy resulted in the fascist party leader Benito Mussolini forming a government in 1922. Once in power, fascists dismantled Italy's liberal democratic state piecemeal. In their search for legitimacy, they not only tried to remake Italy at home but also planned colonial expansion. Italian leaders had long used empire building to legitimize the young state and its liberal parliamentary regime. Where Mussolini's regime took things to a new level was in its seeking of revenge for Adowa, Italy's defeat at the hands of Menelik II and Ethiopia in 1896.

Italy attacked Ethiopia beginning in October 1935 from its Red Sea colony of Eritrea, waging an atrociously brutal war. As one scholar puts it, "the full force of a relatively modern industrial society was brought to bear on a still semi-feudal and agricultural one. Half a million Italian men made the trip to the Horn of Africa and vast quantities of up-to-date ordinance, including mustard gas bombs ... were shipped through the Suez canal ... The Italian military were effectively granted a blank cheque." Hundreds of thousands of Ethiopians died before the conflict drew to a close in May 1936, and the Italian occupation that followed included massacres of Ethiopians that killed untold numbers.

Mussolini gained a colony for Italy at a huge cost, and in the process helped set the stage for a postcolonial order. Italy's aggression provoked international condemnation, although the League of Nations, of which Ethiopia was a member, took no direct action. Still, League of Nations members, some of them colonial powers themselves, did speak out against Italy's actions – this meant that they spoke out in support of the rights of an African nation, a precedent not lost on many contemporaries.

The Bolsheviks' Russian Empire

Not just Japan and Italy but also the Soviet Union under the Bolsheviks was colonizing new lands, continuing a Russian expansionism that dated back centuries. Although the Bolsheviks had proclaimed a break with Russia's tsarist past, in many ways theirs was a regime of continuation, from the extensive use of a secret police to political repression to the privileging of an elite. Expansion and colonialism also continued.

Much internal colonialism was carried out by means of the gulag, the state's extensive prison and labor camp system. Consider what happened on the island of Nazino. In May 1933 peasants who had been exiled internally were sent to the island of Nazino in the Ob River, in remote north-central Russia. Two convoys from western Russia, with a total of 6,114 prisoners, took many days to get to the Ob River and Nazino Island. Food rations were so restricted and traveling conditions so deplorable that by the end some 35 to 40 people were dying daily. The prisoners arrived on May 19, only to find the island uninhabited and barren, with no shelter, no tools, no food, and no grain. The next day, it started snowing. The wind blew so hard that they could not light fires. After the first day, they buried 295 people. When on the fifth day authorities reached the island by boat with some flour, the prisoners were so hungry that they ate it raw. By August, some 4,000 had died. Those who were still alive subsisted on the dead. Survivors were later rearrested, charged with cannibalism.

World War II, 1931–1945

The island of Nazino was just one corner of a massive communist gulag system that continued the russification of much of the central Eurasian landmass. The size of the Russian empire of the Bolsheviks is mind boggling. Maps representing the 1941 Nazi invasion of Russia place emphasis on rapid German army advances across hundreds of miles, deep into Soviet territory. Yet Germany, even at the height of its invasion, never controlled more than 10 percent of the Soviet Union, so vast were its lands. Whether through the gulag or through deliberate settlement schemes, the Bolsheviks continued the internal colonization of Russia's Eurasian empire.

Global War of Empires

War in east Asia was followed by war in Europe. While the causes of World War I are much debated, those of World War II are not: historians locate the latter in the aggressive expansionism of Germany and Japan. The leader of the Nazi Party, Adolf Hitler, took power as chancellor in 1933, promising not only to remake Germany domestically but also to overthrow the postwar order of the Versailles Treaty. There was an irredentist movement in Germany among those desiring to reclaim the lost colonies. Some went further, arguing for the creation of a German Mittelafrika at the expense of the Belgians, the Portuguese, and others. Hitler, too, spoke of regaining the country's lost overseas empire.

Hitler's true ambition, however, was an east-central European land empire that would transform Germany into a continental power rivaling the sea-based British empire and the land-based United States. Such an empire meant the destruction of the Soviet Union. The Nazis paid lip service to colonial irredentism, supported Italy's overseas ambitions, and even fought in north Africa, but remained focused on the East. This was clear as the 1930s unfolded and Nazi Germany took over, first, Austria, then Czechoslovakia, and finally Poland. It was headed eastward, even if it also attacked westward, taking Norway, Denmark, the Netherlands, Belgium, France, and Luxembourg by mid-1940.

Franco-British and Franco-French rivalries

Although France and Britain are close allies today, they were rivals for centuries. The 1904 Franco-British entente and four years as allies in World War I drew the two countries closer together. A common enemy united them again in the 1930s. The two declared war against Germany in September 1939 and fought side by side in France in May–June 1940. Their famous June 1940 joint evacuation of troops at Dunkirk saved the Allied war effort. It was from London that the Free French leader Charles de Gaulle made his famous appeal to the French people to continue fighting, and the British initially financed de Gaulle's Free

French government. France and Britain emerged from the war as allies and founding members of the United Nations Security Council.

Considering this, many are surprised to learn that the British and French fought each other during World War II. Following Germany's defeat of France in 1940, Britain remained unconquered, de Gaulle decamped to London, and a collaborationist regime came to power in south-central France, at Vichy. France's naval fleet, based at Mers-el-Kébir in French Algeria, remained in limbo, and the British did not want it to revert to Vichy French control. After trying and failing to secure its surrender, British naval forces attacked Mers-el-Kébir on July 3, 1940, killing nearly 1,300 French sailors. Other British attacks on French overseas positions followed, and Free French and Vichy French forces jockeyed for control of the empire. World War II was not only fought in Europe and the Pacific but also across the globe, and it was not just a war against fascism but also one of empire.

For the French, defeat gave the colonial empire a renewed importance. In July 1940 leaders of the Third Republic turned over authority to the World War I hero Marshal Philippe Pétain. Germany occupied northern France and its Atlantic coast, and the remainder came under the authority of Pétain's new Vichy-based government. Being a rump, collaborationist state, Vichy needed the empire to prove its relevance in a Nazi-dominated Europe. De Gaulle also saw the colonies as a way to confirm his authority. The Free French were dependent on others for financing and even troops, and de Gaulle was at the mercy of his allies. The colonies offered the resources needed for the Free French to stand on their own.

What followed was a protracted competition for empire between French forces. When de Gaulle announced from London in 1940 that France would continue to fight, the response among those in the colonies was hesitant. The Mers-el-Kébir attack drove the French navy into the Vichy camp, and the AEF governor-general Pierre Boisson sided with Vichy and was promoted head of French Africa. When Chad's governor, the Martinican Félix Éboué, brought his territory over to de Gaulle, the British tried to leverage the move, attacking Vichy-loyal Dakar in Senegal in September 1940. The French repelled the assault, placing west Africa firmly in the hands of Vichy-loyal Boisson.

There followed Allied attacks on French-held Syria in June–July 1941 and on the French-held protectorate of Morocco and French Algeria in 1942, at which point the United States were involved. Operation Torch in November 1942 took the Maghreb, and the Free French established their Committee of National Liberation in Algiers, de Gaulle thus returning Free French leadership to French soil. By January 1943 the British had taken Madagascar. In 1944 many thousands of Algerian soldiers figured among those who liberated France. Officials that year held a major conference in Brazzaville, then the capital of AEF. Led by de Gaulle, the conference concluded with the Brazzaville Declaration, which called for a renewed relationship between France and its colonies that, however vague, signaled the potential for change.

In east Asia, Japan enjoyed victories from the late 1930s to the early 1940s at the expense of the Chinese and then European and American powers and their colonial subjects. When the Japanese advanced on Indonesia, the Dutch colonial state folded. Japanese victories at Singapore and in the Philippines humiliated the British and the Americans. After France's 1940 defeat, the governor of Indochina, Jean Decoux, remained loyal to Vichy but was threatened by Japan. As long as Decoux's administration accommodated Japan, it was allowed to run its own affairs. For the British and Americans, dealing with their own problems, the possibility of taking French Indochina was remote. Only in late 1944, when the outcome of the war was becoming clear, did the French in Indochina begin to resist; this induced the Japanese to overrun Indochina and to unseat the colonial government in March 1945. Within weeks, however, Japan was retreating, and as its forces withdrew it granted Indochina and the Dutch East Indies their independence.

Colonies and the conflict

As the competition for empire between Vichy and Free French forces suggests, the colonies and colonial subjects played important roles during the war. Britain also mobilized its empire. Some 140,000 Nigerians enlisted for military service, for instance, and the dominions rallied: Australia, New Zealand, South Africa, and Canada made great sacrifices. Workers from overseas territories again played a major role, as did colonial raw materials. The Congo provided uranium for the first atomic bombs, for instance, in addition to helping preserve Belgium's sovereignty and paying its government-in-exile's wartime bills.

World War II was crucial to what followed. Britain's fight for empire helped lead to its demise. "We mean to hold our own. I have not become the King's First Minister in order to preside over the liquidation of the British Empire," Winston Churchill said in 1942. The war took care of it for him. In the late 1930s nationalists made clear that India would not fully back Britain unless there were real moves toward home rule. Britain then hauled India into World War II without consultation, and Congress members who had been elected under the 1935 Constitution resigned. Some Indians derided or even attacked the Indian Army, while others, like S. C. Bose, exploited the situation to try to break free; Bose even traveled to Germany and Japan. Muslim and Hindu leaders rejected the 1942 Cripps mission with its promises of dominion status and elections in exchange for India's full cooperation in the war effort, and Congress launched the nonviolent "Quit India" movement. The British government outlawed Congress, at least technically. Japanese forces took Singapore in February 1942, and by mid-year had occupied Burma's capital,

Rangoon. When they sank ships in the Bay of Bengal, threatening India, the British agreed to independence to keep India loyal. British inaction in the face of famine in Bengal in 1943 gave the lie to the idea that they were there for the benefit of the Indians. Bengal's minister for civil supplies, Huseyn Shaheed Suhrawardy, said that there was enough grain but that hoarding was the problem. The British secretary of state for India, Leo Amery, agreed, and although Viceroy Lord Linlithgow saw problems he made missteps. In short, the British government prioritized the war effort rather than furnishing food for Indians, and more than two million people perished. When Congress was made legal again in 1945, everyone understood that independence was a question not of if but of when.

The Japanese attack on one US outpost of empire, Hawai'i, in December 1941 brought the United States into the war. No one but the Japanese bought into the Greater East Asia Co-Prosperity Sphere as the conflict dragged on in China, Burma, and elsewhere. By 1942–1943 the Battle of Midway had turned the tide in the Pacific, as did the 1942–1943 Battle of Stalingrad in Europe, where the Soviets began to push back the German forces. British and US action against Italian positions in north and east Africa brought an end to Italy's overseas empire: Ethiopia (1941); Eritrea (to Ethiopia, independent in 1993); Italian Somaliland (1941); Tunisia (1943); Libya (1943); and the Dodecanese islands (united with Greece by 1947). Facing imminent collapse, King Victor Emmanuel III dismissed Mussolini in July 1943, and Mussolini was arrested. Rescued from prison, Mussolini was set up by the Nazis in a northern Italian state called the Italian Social Republic, or Salò regime, which now had no colonies. However, continued Red Army advances in eastern Europe and the opening of another front in France in June 1944 doomed Nazi empire building in Europe.

By the late summer of 1945, World War II was over. Germany lay in ruins, completely occupied and flooded with millions of displaced people. Britain, although victorious, was broke – rationing for some staples did not end for years. France was liberated but was severely compromised by defeat and collaboration. Italy, which had switched sides, was disgraced. Eastern Europe was shattered, nowhere more so than Poland. At the war's end, according to the US presidential adviser George Kennan, Europe was "teetering on the edge." Both Japan and China were devastated, having suffered massive losses. By the time the United States dropped a second atomic bomb on Nagasaki in August 1945, China had been at war with Japan (declared or undeclared) for 14 years. The lives of millions of Chinese had been snuffed out by the conflict. Much of southeast Asia had been subject to brazen Japanese military aggression and occupation, followed by the return of colonial powers: the United States to the Philippines, France to Indochina, and the Dutch to the East Indies. Even areas that had escaped direct hostilities, for example British India, AEF, and the Belgian Congo, had faced intense wartime demands. The service terms of colonial administrators were extended for years, and authorities placed intense pressure on indigenous laborers and farmers to produce for the war effort. Such pressures led to revolts such as the 1944 uprising at Luluabourg in the Belgian Congo, and the 1945 protest at Sétif in Algeria (see Chapter 7).

Overseas imperialism and the Holocaust

It took a surprisingly long time for the world to acknowledge that one aspect of Nazi empire building in Europe was an attempt to kill all of Europe's Jews. Following recognition of this some years ago, historians, other scholars, and people the world over have asked themselves how this could have happened. One line of explanation has pinpointed overseas imperialism as an underlying cause. Some argue that it is possible to trace a line from Windhoek to Auschwitz, that is, from the German genocide of the Herero and Nama in German South West Africa in 1904–1907 to the death camps in eastern Europe. Some aver that the genocide of the Herero and San laid the basis of the Holocaust, and that there is a connection between Lothar von Trotha's *Vernichtungsbefehl* in South West Africa and the war of destruction and extermination that the Germans waged in eastern Europe from 1939. Some see Nazi dreams of a massive eastern empire – of *Lebensraum* – as being rooted in the desire for compensation for overseas losses suffered as a result of the Treaty of Versailles. After the war, with newly emergent states to the east, German attitudes hardened, and the land switched from being open, friendly, and potentially open to colonization to being a hostile land of nations that had to be conquered and its peoples subjugated or eliminated.

Nonetheless, a consensus has emerged that there was no causal connection between overseas colonial wars and Nazi Germany's race war in Europe. Other regimes carried out colonial atrocities, from those of concessionary companies in the French Congo and the Belgian Congo to the British killing of thousands at Omdurman in 1898, yet those countries did not develop exterminationist ideologies. What is more, Hitler's and the Nazis' east-oriented ideology was *sui generis*, based more on a racial worldview in which competition was everything rather than being rooted in specific actions in overseas colonies.

The attack on Europe's Jews and the failure of so many states to accept Jewish refugees gave impetus to the foundation of a Jewish state. Britain, which could no longer control its Palestine mandate, ceded authority there after the war to the nascent United Nations. Although the United Nations disappointed Palestinian Arabs, the organization held out hope for many in the years after its establishment in 1945, and it developed into a forum for intensified opposition to colonial rule. Founded with 51 member states, the United Nations boasted 99 member states by 1960, one-third of whom were recently independent former colonies or protectorates.

World War II, 1931–1945

The World in 1945

The United Nations developed into a major site to contest colonial rule as a "British world" ceded to a bipolar one split between two powers that emerged from the war stronger than ever. The United States was supreme in the Pacific, and had millions of soldiers stationed in Europe and Japan. Americans, protected by two oceans, enjoyed a massively expanded industrial base and a mainland that had remained untouched by hostilities. It was the only country with nuclear weapons and had proven that it could and would use them. The Soviets suffered unthinkable losses in the war, yet, paradoxically, emerged in an even stronger position. In the autumn of 1941, following the initial Nazi onslaught against Russia, more Soviet prisoners of war perished each day than British and US prisoners of war died *during the entire war*. One million people died in Leningrad alone. Still, the Soviet Union emerged as the war's greatest victor. Whereas the Western democracies had failed to halt fascism in the 1930s, the Soviets' communist system had been tested and had prevailed, and many thus believed that communism had defeated fascism. The Soviet Union's open anticolonialism garnered it support from many quarters. Victory reinforced Stalin's hold on power, and millions of Red Army soldiers were spread across eastern Europe, a result of their defeat of Nazism. In short, a war waged to defeat fascism had made the world safe for communism.

European metropoles could expect neither the capitalist West nor the communist East to support their overseas colonial ventures. The United States and the Soviet Union advocated different ideologies, but both were overtly anticolonial, even if both were empires in their own right. One lesson Stalin had learned from the war was never to be threatened by Germany or any other Western power again, and he therefore created eastern European satellite states. Early in the war, in August 1941, Churchill and the US president Franklin Roosevelt had signed the Atlantic Charter, which made US anticolonialism plain. That the United States granted the Philippines independence in 1946 signaled to many that it was uninterested in formal overseas control. Nonetheless, the United States increasingly acted like an imperial power. Americans referenced ancient Rome's dominion to justify the exercise of control over other places and peoples. The way they did so paralleled Britain's "informal empire" of the nineteenth century and arguably the Roman empire's means of control, dating back nearly 2,000 years. The United States rejected the label of "imperialist," yet US conceptions of global power matched Rome's idea of *imperium*, that is hegemony through power, not territorial control.

In practice, the United States often supported or at least tolerated Portuguese, French, Spanish, Belgian, and British overseas rule in order to advance the United States' larger goal of promoting democracy, capitalism, and free markets – in the northern hemisphere. A heightened Cold War aroused dread among many Americans and Europeans, as fears about communism's influence in the colonies intensified, based both on reality and on paranoia. The United States needed its allies to be strong in order to fight communism. Put simply, in practice the United States prioritized anticommunism over anticolonialism or self-determination.

This was not apparent at the time, and many were excited by postwar prospects. World War II was a fight not only against fascism but also against racism. Because both Nazi Germany and fascist Japan were guided by race-based ideologies, their defeat gave hope to those suffering at the hands of racist colonial regimes. What is more, colonial troops had played major roles in bringing about victory, which meant that many in north and sub-Saharan Africa, south Asia, and elsewhere in the colonial world believed that a significant change was due to the status quo.

Moreover Japan's retreat was a boon to indigenous nationalism. As defeat approached, Japan granted Vietnam independence. When the French (with British and American help) tried to reassert their influence, it sparked a full-scale war. The Japanese had cultivated anti-Dutch feeling and Indonesian nationalism in the Dutch East Indies after defeating the Dutch there early in the war. As they retreated, the Japanese released Indonesian nationalists from detention, and in 1945 Sukarno and Mohammad Hatta declared an Indonesian republic, independent from the Netherlands.

Although it was ultimately vanquished, Japan's cascade of victories from 1937 to 1942 had smashed lingering notions of white superiority, sapped the influence of colonial powers over subject territories, and further diminished what remained of any aura of European supremacy. As we have seen, Japan's defeat of Russia in 1904–1905 had already led many to wonder who else might be able to defeat a European power. World War I catalyzed anticolonial sentiment, left many colonial veterans disillusioned, distanced colonial powers from their overseas territories, and left Europe weakened by four inward-looking years of combat. Then, in another world war, for the second time in two decades German occupation – this time of the Netherlands, Belgium, and France – separated metropoles from colonies for years and tarnished the reputation of Europeans. Colonial rivalry between Vichy and the Free French sowed confusion and diminished respect for French authorities. Japanese control over Indochina laid bare French weakness. The war's costs undermined Europe's economies and ability to hold onto far distant territories. During the war's last years, colonial subjects were exposed to American power and wealth as US forces used different territories as staging grounds for combat. The contrast between feeble European resources and the abundance of US goods was striking. The world in 1945 was one of great hope for the world's colonized peoples.

World War II, 1931–1945

Conclusion

The Great Depression contorted the dynamics of empire as Europeans pursued empire on the cheap in a time of diminished resources. Even if officials, settlers, businessmen, missionaries, and others continued to enjoy colonial systems designed to benefit them, the interwar era revealed that empire was never a simple story of European states projecting their power outwards as colonizers discovered themselves to be, in many ways, as much subject to imperialism's dynamics as the colonized. A key difference, of course, was that it was Europeans who had gone out to the colonies, not the other way around. George Orwell, for instance, could (and did) make the decision to quit Burma's colonial police while on a home leave. The Burmese, by contrast, could not "quit" Burma's colonial situation without ejecting the British. Imperialism's impact was greatest in places that became settler colonies, where people suffered as the best lands were snapped up by privileged foreign settlers. In the face of determined foreign rule, anticolonial sentiment grew, and peoples from west Africa to Tunisia to India to Indonesia became more nationalistic.

As colonial regimes endeavored to endure – in part by establishing and sustaining colonial difference – another global war erupted. World War II, like the Great War before it, was a conflict of empire that redirected the trajectory of European overseas rule. Many Europeans emerged from the conflict more convinced than ever of the importance of colonies, yet, as administrators drew up plans to adapt to changed circumstances, events regularly overtook them.

Citations

Page	Source
133	"Police operations reflected..." Martin Thomas, *Violence and Colonial Order: Police, Workers, and Protest in the European Colonial Empires, 1918–1940* (Cambridge: Cambridge University Press, 2012), 25.
134	"The Collector looked at him..." E. M. Forster, *A Passage to India* (San Diego, CA: Harcourt Brace, 1924), 183.
135	"When English and Indians..." Forster, *A Passage to India*, 98.
135	"that we're here to uplift..." George Orwell, *Burmese Days* (New York: New American Library, 1950), 36.
136–7	"comparable to destroying..." and "The people expected it of me..." George Orwell, *Shooting an Elephant and Other Essays* (New York: Harcourt, Brace & World, 1950), 8.
136	"He must have killed himself..." and "When in Africa..." Bernard B. Dadié, *Climbié*, translated by Karen C. Chapman (London: Heinemann, 1971), 42–43, 129–130.
137–8	"The monotony of office work..." J.-M. Domont, "Un territorial au pays des sectes politico-religieuses au Bas-Congo pendant les années 1939–1945" [A Colonial Administrator in the Land of the Political-Religious Sects of the Lower Congo during the Years 1939–1945], *Académie Royale des Sciences d'Outre-Mer* 50, no. 3 (1988), 58–59 (my translation).

137 "A black boy..." Graham Greene, *The Heart of the Matter* (New York: Penguin, 1971), 12.
137 "Have a drink..." Forster, *A Passage to India*, 23.
137 "In the semi-autobiographical novel..." Jef Geeraerts, *Gangrene*, translated by Jon Swan (New York: Viking Press, 1975).
139 "Far from modernity..." Barbara D. Metcalf and Thomas R. Metcalf, *A Concise History of Modern India*, 2nd ed. (Cambridge: Cambridge University Press, 2006), 92.
140 "the colonies provided..." Catherine Hall, "Gender, Nations, and Nationalism," in *People, Nation and State: The Meaning of Ethnicity and Nationalism*, edited by Edward Mortimer, with Robert Fine (London: I. B. Tauris, 2011), 47.
140 "Egypt was to be ordered..." Timothy Mitchell, *Colonising Egypt* (Berkeley: University of California Press, 1988), 33, 85, 149.
143 "the full force..." Giuseppe Finaldi, *Mussolini and Italian Fascism* (Harlow, UK: Pearson Longman, 2008), 82.
146 "We mean to hold our own." Quoted in *Churchill by Himself: The Definitive Collection of Quotations*, edited by Richard Langworth (New York: PublicAffairs, 2011), 93.
147 "teetering on the edge." Quoted in Tony Judt, *Postwar: A History of Europe Since 1945* (New York: Penguin, 2005), 88.
149 "imperialist." Ali Parchami, "The Echoes of Rome in British and American Hegemonic Ideology," in *Echoes of Empire: Memory, Identity and Colonial Legacies*, edited by Kalypso Nicolaïdis, Berny Sèbe, and Gabrielle Maas (London: I. B. Tauris, 2015), 119.

Bibliography

Baranowski, Shelley. *Nazi Empire: German Colonialism and Imperialism from Bismarck to Hitler*. Cambridge: Cambridge University Press, 2010.
Bayly, Christopher, and Tim Harper. *Forgotten Armies: The Fall of British Asia, 1941–1945*. Cambridge, MA: Belknap Press, 2005.
Ginio, Ruth. *Vichy Unmasked: The Vichy Years in French West Africa*. Lincoln: University of Nebraska Press, 2006.
Louis, Wm. Roger. *Imperialism at Bay: The United States and the Decolonization of the British Empire, 1941–1945*. Oxford: Clarendon Press, 1977.
Mann, Gregory. *Native Sons: West African Veterans and France in the Twentieth Century*. Durham, NC: Duke University Press, 2006.
Mitchell, Timothy. *Colonising Egypt*. Cambridge: Cambridge University Press, 1988.
Saada, Emmanuelle. *Empire's Children: Race, Filiation, and Citizenship in the French Colonies*. Translated by Arthur Goldhammer. Chicago: University of Chicago Press, 2012.
Scott, James C. *Weapons of the Weak: Everyday Forms of Peasant Resistance*. New Haven: Yale University Press, 1985.
Thomas, Martin. *The French Empire at War 1940–1945*. Manchester: Manchester University Press, 1998.
Thomas, Martin, Bob Moore, and L. J. Butler. *Crises of Empire: Decolonization and Europe's Imperial States, 1918–1975*. London: Hodder Education, 2008.

7

Unfinished and Finished Empires, 1945–1958

If we want things to stay as they are, things will have to change.
Giuseppe di Lampedusa, *The Leopard* (1960)

Gérard De Boe's short documentary *Bakouba* (1952) is about the Bakuba kingdom, located in an east-central region of the enormous Belgian Congo. It ends with a scene of the Bakuba *nyimi* (king), Mbop Mabiinc maMbeky (r. 1939–1969), clad in his awesome royal regalia made of innumerable finely interwoven cowrie shells. The costume is so heavy that, once donned, it immobilizes its wearer. Alongside the king sit several fine baskets and drums. The narrator, speaking in French, interprets the scene:

> The king has a whole wardrobe of sumptuous costumes. This one, the most sumptuous – and the heaviest, too – weighs 80 kilograms. He will wear it but two times: the day he ascends the throne when he is presented to his people, and when he has breathed his last breath … In the past, upon the death of the king, all his wives would have been sacrificed and buried with him. Today only these drums and these baskets will accompany him to his final rest. They have a ritual form, decorated with pearls and shells, and their contents are secret. According to popular belief, he would thus be able to continue in the afterlife with the prestigious life to which his legendary origin destined him.

At first hearing, the description seems straightforward: the narrator is providing insights into Bakuba symbols of authority and ideas about the afterlife. The

European Overseas Empire, 1879–1999: A Short History, First Edition. Matthew G. Stanard.
© 2018 John Wiley & Sons, Inc. Published 2018 by John Wiley & Sons, Inc.

accompanying images seem to present a direct and unmediated representation of reality.

Further reflection raises doubts about the documentary. Not only the narrator but the entire film crew was European. How reliable is this outsider's perspective? Why were these Europeans making the film in the first place, and would the Bakuba have made such a film? The documentary not only represents Bakuba culture, but it also stresses the benefits of colonial rule: as the narrator points out, the Bakuba no longer sacrifice a king's wives upon his death as they did in the past. What is more, the narration includes a blatant falsehood, that the king wears the costume only twice, once upon his ascent to the throne and again at his death. As the film shows, the king was still very much alive in 1952, which means that the king would have worn the outfit at least three times. It is not that the narrator is incorrect, but that the film deliberately tells an untruth. What other untruths does the documentary include?

De Boe's *Bakouba* underscores several aspects of the post-1945 colonial situation. Filmed with a Belgian audience in mind, the film reveals Europeans' continued interest in the colonies overseas. The documentary also highlights the difficulty of interpreting historical sources, and how an interpretation of what was going on at the time – on the ground in the colonies – often depended on one's perspective. *Bakouba* also suggests that imperialism was a cultural project that included the creation and control of "colonial knowledge," as well as an enduring power imbalance in the colonial situation. For all the autonomy of colonized peoples and their resistance to foreign rule, it was after all Belgians who were making ethnographic films in their colony about Africans in the 1950s, not Congolese in Belgium making a documentary about Europe for African audiences. Hundreds of films were made in central Africa in the 1950s, but not one of them was directed by a Congolese director.

Even in colonial situations that were apparently well under control, such as the Belgian Congo, changes were afoot. There remained a broad consensus in postwar Europe, from Portugal to the Netherlands, that overseas empire was not only good but necessary. Many British people even viewed the loss of India in 1947 not as the death knell of colonialism but as a strategic streamlining of the empire. Nevertheless, many recognized that, as the Italian writer Giuseppe di Lampedusa put it in another context, "If we want things to stay as they are, things will have to change." The impetus to give empire a new lease on life led to reforms in many cases and to long, drawn-out wars in others. A crisis in Suez in 1956 revealed Britain and France's reduced scope of action in the colonial world; Ghana's independence in 1957 – the first for a black African country – was a milestone; and in 1958 an anticolonial war in Algeria brought down France's Fourth Republic. By the second half of the 1950s, fundamental change had taken place.

Unfinished and Finished Empires, 1945–1958

Sustaining Empire After the War

As the postwar years unfolded, even if many Europeans believed that they remained colonial masters – an impression that films like De Boe's documentary reinforced – developments across the globe belied the reality again and again. "Imperial sway by 1939 derived mainly from profit-sharing with business and power-sharing with indigenous elites overseas." After World War II, more and more elites in the colonies – whether traditional leaders like the Bakuba *nyimi* or new nationalist leaders – demanded their freedom. And they began to win it. It has been said that Britain fought World War II to save the empire but that, in winning the war, Britain lost it. Earlier, a hands-off attitude by the United States and others had facilitated colonialism on the cheap so that empire did not cost European taxpayers much, if anything. The costs of World War II created severe financial pressures, and overseas territories remained expensive to administer. When after 1945 local power brokers decided that empire was no longer worth it, Europeans did not have the wherewithal to resist. Still, some powers hung on to their colonies for years, despite sometimes fierce anticolonial resistance and, in the ensuant struggles between rulers and ruled, the outcome was anything but predetermined.

European commitment to empire revealed itself in outbursts of repressive violence like the Sétif massacre, in Algeria. The war's effects on Algeria had been many, including hardships like food scarcity. Axis forces got close (Germany and Italy held Tunisia for a spell) and a large American presence, beginning with Operation Torch in November 1942, impressed many Algerians. Defeat of the racist Nazi regime and Algerian participation in France's liberation raised expectations. When on May 8, 1945, people took to the streets to celebrate Victory in Europe Day, PPA members in Sétif waved placards expressing nationalist sentiment, some of which demanded independence. The celebration degenerated into a vicious confrontation in which 102 Europeans were killed, including women and children, which only validated settlers' worst fears of being overwhelmed by natives. French forces retaliated with an air and naval bombardment that massacred thousands of Algerians, a repression that was particularly hamhanded and brutal because the country's best military units were stationed in recently liberated mainland France. Sétif hardened settler attitudes and pushed more Algerians into the pro-independence camp.

Such a willingness to use force was seen elsewhere. France (with British assistance) returned to Indochina in 1945–1946, sparking a years-long war. French forces savagely suppressed a 1947 uprising in Madagascar, killing some 80,000–100,000 Malagasy. The post-1948 "apartheid" regime in the British dominion of South Africa was backed up by the use of force. In Kenya, British colonial authorities crushed the Mau Mau uprising (1952–1960), as they did a communist-inspired uprising in Malaya where they declared an emergency and fought a years-long conflict.

India's Independence and Partition

The British did not resort to force in India, where postwar developments revealed the contingency of decolonization. By 1945 all major actors could envision what independence would look like. Muhammad Ali Jinnah, the Muslim League leader, saw all Muslims united in one state, Gandhi wished for one India, and even the British hatched a new plan for the Raj as late as March 1946. None of these visions transpired. As late as the early 1940s virtually no one was talking about partition, but that is exactly what happened in 1947.

Britain's exit from India "was messy, hasty, and clumsily improvised." The first postwar election in Britain, in 1945, led to the Labour leader, Clement Atlee, ousting the Conservative prime minister, Winston Churchill. Although India achieved its independence under a Labour government, politicians across the spectrum recognized the need for independence. There was no public will to hang onto India at any price, and the costs were outweighing the benefits. British annual expenditures on military and diplomatic activity from 1934–1938 were £6 million. In 1947 alone Britain budgeted £209 million for military spending. That same year, the year of India's independence, Britain's financial situation was so severe that it faced a sterling convertibility crisis. The US president Harry Truman announced the Truman Doctrine in 1947 to aid free countries that resisted outside (for which read "communist") interference, precipitated in part by Britain's disengagement from a postwar Greek civil conflict between royalists and communists. Britain, which had supported the royalists against the communists, announced that it simply did not have the funds to do so anymore.

It was not that Britain "gave up" India, but rather that Indians won their liberation. By World War II, Congress, joined by Jinnah's Muslim League, had made clear its wish for independence. Without local buy-in, the British Raj could not function, illustrating again how profit and power sharing with local business and political elites made empire work. But there were more than just two "sides," one British and the other Indian. Innumerable personalities and interests were involved in negotiations, protests, resistance, and clashes, from Anglo-Indians to politicians in London, to the Indian Army, to prominent anticolonial leaders. Many Indians advocated for "national" interests, others for more narrowly or locally defined constituencies. Religious belief often shaped identity, but sometimes only indirectly. The Muslim League leader Jinnah, who used Islam as an organizing force, himself lived a secular life, dressed in Western suits, and married a Parsi convert to Islam. He backed a nation-state uniting all Muslims but opposed an Islamic state.

Unfinished and Finished Empires, 1945–1958

An inability among the British to understand the political divisions among the Indians made the interminable negotiations leading up to independence more tortured. The penultimate viceroy, Archibald Wavell, revealed in his journal that he simply could not grasp why Congress leaders might be thinking along political lines rather than just as "Indians." Jinnah argued that India must be divided so that Muslim Indians would not be trading a British Raj for a Hindu one. Gandhi conceived of independence differently not only from Jinnah but also from his fellow Congress leader Nehru. As we have seen, Gandhi had some ideas that made him an outlier, even if his charisma and nonviolent approach of *satyagraha* propelled him to preeminent leadership. He envisioned a united India exercising self-rule – the British could become Indians and stay if they wished – whereas Nehru prioritized socialist development. The British were divided as well. Wavell agreed with his prime minister, Churchill, on many things, and they shared a profound dislike of Gandhi: Churchill famously referred to him as a "half-naked fakir," and Wavell referred to him as a "malevolent old politician." But, just as often, Wavell and Churchill disagreed.

Improvisation and negotiations initially led the British to announce that independence would come no later than June 1948. The last viceroy, Lord Mountbatten, declared in June 1947 that independence would arrive that August. As evening fell on August 14, 1947, India was a colony; at midnight Nehru declared the birth of a new nation-state. The Indian Independence Act of 1947 partitioned the colony into two states: a Hindu-majority India, and a Muslim-majority Pakistan with eastern (Bengal) and western (the Sind) regions. After the Indo-Pakistani War of 1971, East Pakistan gained independence as Bangladesh.

Partition reflected both intractable divisions between Hindus and Muslims and poor planning. Religious divisions had taken root as early as the turn of the century and had grown by World War II. Communal violence escalated as independence approached, consuming numerous lives, including one victim of a 1946 attack whose perpetrators tied him down and drilled a small hole in his skull, "so that he would bleed to death as slowly as possible." Partition led to one of the largest and deadliest migrations in history. Some 10 million to 15 million people changed lands, Muslims moving from India into East or West Pakistan and Hindus departing Pakistan for India. A frenzy of aggression occurred, including rape, disfigurement, dismemberment, and murder. The British claimed that some 200,000 people died, but historians have shown that one to two million of those who were uprooted in 1947 did not survive.

India's fate determined much else in south Asia. After wars to take Burma in the mid-nineteenth century, the British had annexed it to India, making it a separate colony only in the 1930s. Burma's invasion by Japan, its reoccupation by British forces, and rising anticolonial sentiment led to negotiations, and in 1948 Burma achieved independence. Britain had become involved in Ceylon after supplanting the Dutch there at the same time as it took over the South African Cape Colony from the Netherlands during the Napoleonic Wars. At the time of the Burmese and Indian negotiations, opposition to foreign rule in Ceylon culminated in talks on the future of that British colony, and it emerged as the independent Dominion of Ceylon in 1948, becoming the republic of Sri Lanka in 1972. In subsequent years, India took over the remaining French-held enclaves of Pondicherry, Karikal, Yanaon, Mahé, and Chandernagore and the Portuguese-held territories of Dadra and Nagar Haveli, leaving only Portuguese Goa, Daman, and Diu as the last European possessions on the Indian subcontinent by 1955.

East and Southeast Asia

The United States granted the Philippines independence in 1946 but retained significant influence over the archipelago's affairs, which were important in the Cold War context. A communist insurgency in Malaya, which started in 1948, provoked a British-declared "Malayan Emergency." British and Malaysian anti-communist forces were victorious over the communists, who were always in the minority, by 1960, during the course of which Malaysia gained its independence in 1957.

Post-World War II Dutch yearning for southeast Asian territories, which were to be ultimately frustrated, had been intensified by defeat and occupation by Nazi Germany and the need to rebuild after the war: "The return of peace brought with it a Dutch political system that produced a recalcitrant state policy pitted against decolonization or even compromise ... Dutch public opinion, although not unanimous, by and large endorsed the stance of political elites who prioritized maintaining the Indies and fighting the Republic [of Indonesia]." Indonesian nationalists fought a war of independence simultaneous with the Chinese communists' fight against Chiang Kai-shek's Western-backed Nationalist government, with the same result: they ended decades of direct foreign interference.

Several things drove Indonesian independence. Growing access to higher education and limited entrance into the Dutch colonial establishment encouraged political ambitions and led to calls for constitutional changes. The East Indies then felt the aftereffects of Japanese conquest. The Japanese dismantled the Dutch administration, disseminated anti-Dutch propaganda, and then released nationalists from prison as they retreated. When the Dutch prepared to resume control in 1945, a young nationalist movement led by Sukarno declared self-rule. The Dutch miscalculated the degree to which the nationalists embodied the people's desire for self-determination, which led to a fruitless four-year-long war, to which the Dutch dispatched some 135,000 soldiers to join the 70,000-strong Royal Netherlands East Indies Army. In a bid to salvage the situation, some of the Dutch called for the creation of "Netherlands–Indonesian Union," which would be linked by the monarchy. As fighting continued, a consensus emerged that independence was inevitable, and large numbers of colonials who had relocated to, or who had been born and raised in, Indonesia began to relocate to the Netherlands.

Thus the war was fought over the form independence would take. A Dutch priority was safeguarding business interests. It is telling that a major Dutch military operation was called "Operation Product." As it was for the French in Vietnam, a crucial factor was the US position. The lack of American support pushed the Netherlands to negotiate, as did nationalist sentiment, postwar financial weakness, distance, an untenable military situation, and pressure from the United Nations, and the Dutch East Indies became Indonesia at the end of 1949. The country's freedom spurred further nationalist activity when it played host to the 1955 Bandung Conference of leaders of newly independent countries and of anticolonial movements in places that were not yet independent.

By 1949 Mao Zedong's communist forces were victorious in China's civil war. Chiang Kai-shek's Nationalists retreated to Taiwan, which the communists considered a province in rebellion, and from which Chiang Kai-shek believed that Nationalists would one day retake the mainland. Although this civil conflict formed a battlefront in the capitalist–communist Cold War, its outcome also represented China seizing its destiny and expelling foreign interference. The communist victory led to a kind of "decolonization" of China, ending decades of external meddling, symbolized by an exodus of foreigners from China around 1949. Following the communists' victory, opponents of the US president Truman claimed that he had "lost" China. Truman vowed to make no such mistake in Korea after the communist North attacked southward in 1950 to unify that country. The Korean War, which lasted until 1953, stoked Cold War fires. It also led to a rise in commodity prices, making colonial territories all the more valuable.

War in French Indochina

Indochina was to France as India was to Britain: an imagined crown jewel of empire. However, the contrast between British and French postwar goals and actions in their respective colonies was important. A priority of France's Fourth Republic was restoring the country's glory and rightful place as a great power, which had been tarnished by defeat and occupation. Many believed that empire was essential in the task. Because Japan's occupation had to all intents and purposes removed the French from power in mainland southeast Asia – in a similar way to the situation in the Dutch East Indies – this meant reoccupying Laos, Cambodia, and most importantly Vietnam, where the British, French, Chinese, and indigenous forces controlled different parts of the country in 1945.

The Vietnamese nationalists felt otherwise. The Indochinese Communist Party controlled much of Tonkin, and assiduously courted foreign support. The opening of the communist leader Ho Chi Minh's Vietnamese declaration of independence of 1945 echoed that of the United States:

> All men are created equal. They are endowed by their Creator with certain inalienable rights, among them are Life, Liberty, and the pursuit of Happiness ...

It continued quite differently, however.

> Nevertheless, for more than eighty years, the French imperialists ... have deprived our people of every democratic liberty ... have enforced inhuman laws ... they have drowned our uprisings in rivers of blood ... they have forced us to use opium and alcohol ... They have robbed us of our rice fields, our mines, our forests, and our raw materials ... they have mercilessly exploited our workers.

The United States looked askance on colonialism but needed a strong France to counter communism in Europe and consequently remained aloof while the British assisted the French in reoccupying Vietnam in 1945–1946 and as the French negotiated China's withdrawal from the country's north. This reassertion of colonial rule sparked a war.

France's war efforts suggest how empire induced exchanges and migrations. French troops in Vietnam included *spahi* regiments from Algeria. So, into the 1950s, *spahi* regiments of Maghrebi soldiers and French officers fought in mainland southeast Asia under a name of southwest Asian origin. Many other "French" combat soldiers fought in Vietnam as well, and their varied backgrounds underscore how empire moved people around. France sent nearly a half million soldiers, all professionals, to Indochina during the war, only 233,467 of whom were French nationals; the rest were Legionnaires (72,833), north Africans (122,920), and Africans (60,340); this does not include the hundreds of thousands of native Indochinese who fought on the French side.

Although at no time did France control all of Vietnam, Ho's forces were always in a precarious position because of France's superior firepower and control of the skies. After the communist victory in China, first Mao's government, then the Soviet Union, and then North Korea recognized Ho's government. The French persuaded US officials that the conflict was not a colonial one but a fight against communism. From the early 1950s the Eisenhower administration stepped in, providing crucial support for the French and committing the United States to a prolonged involvement there.

But France lost the war on the ground, ceding independence to Laos and Cambodia in 1953, and then to Vietnam after suffering ignominious defeat in the 1954 Battle of Dien Bien Phu. The makeup of French forces at Dien Bien

Figure 7.1 Vietnamese refugees leaving a French ship for USS *Montague*, August 1954. Source: Photo by Par PH1 H.S. Hemphill (Navy), Wikimedia Commons, https://commons.wikimedia.org/wiki/File:HD-SN-99-02045.JPEG.

Phu underscores the degree to which colonial rule depended on mobilizing resources across the empire, including people. Among the roughly 4,000 "French" soldiers at the battle's end were Foreign Legion and Vietnamese paratroopers, Moroccan Rifles, Arab and African gunners, Algerians, Tai (ethnic minority Vietnamese), and French paratrooper battalions, half of whom were Vietnamese. By the time of the 1954 Geneva Conference that ended French rule, some 110,000 French colonial soldiers had been killed in the conflict or were presumed dead.

Vietnam divided into North and South, and the United States stepped in with full support for South Vietnam against the communist North (Figure 7.1). The early 1950s witnessed a transformation of US policy. During the 1954 Geneva negotiations, the Eisenhower administration decided to "salvage something" in Indochina that was "free of the taint of French colonialism." The secretary of state,

John Foster Dulles, averred that the United States would "hold this area and fight subversion within with all the strength we have," using economic and military assistance. As Fredrik Logevall writes, "It was a monumental decision, as important as any made by an American administration on Indochina, from Franklin Roosevelt's to Gerald Ford's." Whereas in 1945 Vietnamese had been hopeful for US support, in 1954 the Central Committee of the Vietnamese Workers' Party declared the United States the "main and direct enemy."

Planning for Empire

India's independence and Ho Chi Minh's success against France did not mean that people saw decolonization as inevitable. Following Japan's retreat, the British authorities kept to their planned reconstruction of empire in the East, many of them viewing Indian independence and partition not as a retreat but as a strategic move to streamline empire. Peoples across the colonial world struggled against foreign rule as most foreign occupying regimes showed no signs of retreat.

How could Europeans continue to believe in colonialism in an era when events seemed to be working against it? Consider one on-campus exchange in 1950 at Lincoln University in Pennsylvania, a historically black university and the alma mater of the US Supreme Court justice Thurgood Marshall, the poet Langston Hughes, and the first presidents of Nigeria (Zik Azikiwe) and of Ghana (Kwame Nkrumah). The university president Horace Mann Bond encouraged Lincoln to enroll students from west Africa, and in 1950 the school founded an Institute for African Studies. Numerous delegates spoke at the institute's inauguration, including representatives from Belgium, Britain, and the US State Department. Many attendees were from current or former colonies including Sudan, Egypt, and Nigeria. Students "attacked" the speakers, for example peppering the Belgian representative with questions about the meager presence of Congolese in institutions of higher learning, or about how much Belgium profited from its colony. But students reserved their greatest criticism for the British delegate, Mr. Cook. After Cook used the term "native" to refer to Africans, a Nigerian student protested. Cook replied that he himself was a "native of Scotland, also an oppressed nation," a comment that drew laughs. "Empire" remained the status quo in many places, despite much change.

Still, some were planning for a future beyond empire. By the late 1940s some Christian churches in Africa were engaging in the "Africanization" of their clergy. The first southern Sudanese priests of the Anglican Church were ordained as early as 1941. This was not uniform: there remained differences of opinion within and between Protestant and Catholic denominations, and within the Catholic Church between the Vatican and local clergy. Moreover, although Catholic and Protestant churches were influential in sub-Saharan African – and the Catholic Church in Vietnam – they had little influence in north Africa, the Middle East, India, and other areas of southeast Asia, where Islam or Buddhism prevailed and where, in many cases, missionary activity was less significant.

Cold War context

Whereas China, Korea, and mainland southeast Asia assumed center stage in the heated-up post-1945 Cold War, not so sub-Saharan Africa, where US and Soviet actions were impeded by ignorance. The US State Department formed an Office of African Affairs very late, which issued its first country policy statements only in 1950. When French Guinea broke free of France in 1958, the Soviets sent assistance: snow plows. Although the Soviet Union preached anticolonialism and brought some African nationalist leaders to Russia for education, support, and grooming, it did comparatively little else, and its influence was hampered by a boycott of the United Nations for most of 1950 to protest the lack of recognition of the communist government of mainland China. The United States was torn between anticolonialism and its support for colonial peoples on the one hand, and its European allies on the other. But the United States was not a passive observer. The well-being of France and Britain mattered much to the United States because of the threat of communism and the need for Europe's economic recovery, so the United States supported them. "Post-war US government might pay lip service to America's proud anticolonial tradition, but, in practice, there was no sustained pressure on France, Britain or the smaller European imperial nations to quit Africa." As African nationalism developed and disorder threatened, and as anticommunism intensified during the Eisenhower administration, the picture became more unclear.

Attempted reforms in sub-Saharan Africa

Many in Europe continued to believe that overseas rule, especially in Africa, was normal and necessary and that many regions needed decades to prepare for self-rule. Thus empire remained respectable, even popular. This was not just a question of perspective but also of money. Colonies were more economically significant than ever as activity picked up post-1945 and as Europe faced ongoing shortages. Britain rationed some foodstuffs for years after the war, including sugar into 1953. Colonial exports brought in US dollars, which European states needed to balance their current accounts. Over time, immigrants from colonies helped to meet labor shortages in Europe.

All the same, colonial powers recognized that these were different times, and that, if they wanted to keep things the same, things would have to change. Thus the era of the "late colonial state" witnessed extensive new development plans; in contrast to the interwar era, the postwar years were more prosperous, which meant that many of these plans were actually carried out. Britain's Colonial Development and Welfare Act of 1940, sidelined by the war, was followed by another in 1945, which included development grants. In southern Africa such funds created agricultural research stations and investment in new technologies. Nigeria had a 10-year development plan starting in 1945. France launched its Fonds d'Investissement pour le Développement Économique et Social (Investment Fund for Economic and Social Development) as of 1946, and Belgium enacted a 10-year plan for investment in the Congo beginning in 1949. The 1955 Soustelle Plan called for more funding for Algeria from Paris. There were exceptions. António Salazar, who had been in power at the head of Portugal's Estado Novo (New State) since 1932, made the colonies central to Portugal's self-image as a world power and to the Estado Novo's fight to combat degeneration. Portugal's problem was that it was poor: the per capita income in 1960 was just $160 compared to $219 in Turkey and $1,453 in the United States. Because the British had long supported and influenced Portugal, some called Portugal "a colony with colonies." Portugal's overseas territories remained underdeveloped and dependent on forced labor.

Postwar development schemes exemplify how overseas empires were never fixed but were always in the process of becoming, as do the new or reformed administrative structures that emerged after 1945. In 1951, to counter opposition to colonial rule and to forestall any outside intervention, Portugal declared its colonies integral parts of Portugal itself. The Cape Verde islands, Portuguese Guinea, São Tomé and Príncipe, Angola, Mozambique, Timor-Leste, and Goa, Daman, and Diu in India became Portuguese provinces that just happened to be located thousands of miles overseas. Some provinces dwarfed the home country: Mozambique is nearly nine times the size of Portugal, and Angola is even larger. Spain likewise declared some of its overseas territories to be provinces in the 1950s, including Ifni on Africa's northwestern coast. As discussed earlier, there were calls in the Netherlands for a Netherlands–Indonesian Union linked by the monarchy. Belgian officials floated the idea of a Belgo-Congolese Community with the monarchy forming its linchpin. Belgium never transformed the Congo into an overseas province, but there was talk of it, and many referred to it as the "tenth province" (Belgium had nine). As King Baudouin wrote during a 1955 trip to the Congo: "People talk about the Congo being Belgium's 10th province. It would be wonderful to have our residence here and to come from time to time to Belgium, which would not be more than a little district of the Congo." One goal of all this was to preempt outside interference. If overseas territories were integrated into the metropole, colonial issues became domestic ones, beyond the purview of international bodies like the United Nations.

The postwar situation spurred France to adopt major changes, including a new constitution in 1946, which ditched the term "empire" for the "French Union" and turned "old colonies" in the Caribbean into *départements* within France. Rhetoric about *La Plus Grande France* resonated both as a sign of strength and as a recognition that overseas subjects and citizens were unified in some sense with French of the metropole. People began to speak of a confederation or other structure to meld metropole and colonies. The French Union allowed for greater representation in Paris without ceding real control, yet Africans seized the opportunity of negotiating the union to be heard, and more Africans joined the National Assembly. Trade unions, which were legal after World War II, led a railway strike in 1947 on the ground in AOF, in part to push for more equitable salaries. In short, colonial subjects worked within the system and used European rhetoric as political tools to achieve rights. When authorities thwarted this, it undermined their legitimacy.

The issue of citizenship was central. The French wanted their "hundred million Frenchmen" but did not want those millions to overwhelm the metropolitan population. While the French saw it more narrowly, some Africans argued for a more heterogeneous conception of citizenship. A number of people across France's west African federation already had formed the Rassemblement Démocratique Africain (RDA; African Democratic Rally) party to exercise political rights. Lamine Guèye, a citizen from Senegal elected to France's National Assembly in 1945, proposed a law extending citizenship to all inhabitants of the empire. Up until then, only some inhabitants of Martinique and Guadaloupe and specific communes in Senegal had been able to obtain citizenship. To show how open-ended developments were, from 1945 colonial subjects could travel freely to France to work or visit, an arrangement that ended only in 1974.

Thus there was a fundamental debate over what it meant to be French and what citizenship was. Many if not most French people never believed that the African, Algerian, or Vietnamese people in their colonies were truly "French," but for years after World War II, the situation remained in flux. Rather than empire being Europe *here* colonizing overseas lands *out there* – a center and a periphery – it was more about the making of imperial "formations." France and the colonies, Portugal and its empire, Belgium and the Congo: these were not distinct entities but parts of a whole. Thus, rather than view the French empire as contradicting the ideals of the French Republic, for example, we need to reconsider France and the colonies as forming one imperial nation-state.

A step in the protracted debate as to what was to be was the *loi-cadre* or "framework law" of 1956, to establish new rules in the French Union, which, now that France's possessions in Indochina were independent, centered on AOF, AEF, and Madagascar. (It did not apply to Algeria or to the protectorates Tunisia and Morocco, which won independence in 1956.) To craft the law, the minister of overseas France, Gaston Defferre, worked with Félix Houphouët-Boigny, a National Assembly member from Côte d'Ivoire and a proponent of more autonomy for west Africa. Although the *loi-cadre* transferred key powers from Paris to the colonies, it did not signal that decolonization was inevitable. It was a kind of divide-and-rule approach that dealt with individual colonies rather than the federations of AOF and AEF, allowing French officials to play nationalist leaders and economic interests against each other. Similar to the India Act of 1935, France's *loi-cadre* was not a retreat from imperialism but an attempt to redesign the country's relationship with its overseas territories for changing times.

The *loi-cadre* was not a one-way imposition of a cynical colonial power. Just as the fight for Indian independence revealed fissures among Indians, so did the *loi-cadre* reveal differences between Africans and, once again, how colonialism was anything but a simple two-sided relationship. Some leading Africans embraced France's one-on-one dealings with individual colonies, first and foremost Côte d'Ivoire's Houphouët-Boigny, because doing so gave local leaders like himself a bigger role. The Senegalese leader Léopold Sédar Senghor opposed the *loi-cadre* exactly because it threatened to split up AOF, and many others joined him in this opposition. Senghor saw France as the nation and his local people as the *patrie*, perhaps analogous to how one can be both a fervent *valenciano* but also Spanish, or a Latina and Angeleno but also a proud American.

British colonials likewise planned for a future with empire, illustrated by the reorganization of Northern Rhodesia, Southern Rhodesia, and Nyasaland into a Central African Federation (CAF) in 1953, an ambitious plan that suggested a great deal of self-assurance. This affected millions of Africans and thousands of white settlers across vast territories: Southern Rhodesia (present-day Zimbabwe) is about the size of Montana, the fourth largest state in the United States, while Northern Rhodesia (present-day Zambia) is nearly twice as large. The CAF's administrative structure was byzantine. In addition to a federal government, each member of the federation had its own government. Officials had to manage relations not only between these four governments, but also between themselves and London. The CAF's governor-general reported to Britain's Commonwealth Relations Office, as did Southern Rhodesia's governor, the latter having been granted responsible government in 1923. Northern Rhodesia's and Nyasaland's governments, by contrast, reported to London's Colonial Office.

The British Commonwealth also developed. It had its origins in periodic conferences of Britain and the dominions, that is, colonies that had become self-governing, as formalized by the 1931 Statute of Westminster. But most British dominions remained "colonial" in a more general sense. Between 1948 and 1957, one million British left Britain to settle in the dominions, and most whites in them identified as "British." Dominion governments remained agents of colonialism into the post-World War II era, which began to change only from the 1960s, as dominions began to achieve greater cultural, political, and economic independence, putting some distance between themselves and Britain and drawing closer to other countries like the United States.

At its heart, the colonial "project" remained a race-based discriminatory system. Colonial regimes refused to recognize nonwhites as equals, espousing

European culture and values but ignoring ideals of equality and liberty. The CAF, for instance, was designed to maintain white rule, and the French Union did not accord equal rights to colonial subjects. Reforms in Algeria in the 1950s included half-hearted changes crafted to sustain settler domination. Consider the case of the Belgian Congo, where abuses continued despite administrative reforms, contrasting with the rosy picture authorities projected at home and abroad. Authorities banned whipping as a penalty for Africans only in 1951, and even then it continued. A *carte de mérite civique* (card of civic merit) granted qualified Congolese what was called *évolué* status and equal rights, but the process privileged only European norms: one had to endure intrusive inspections into one's personal life, and ultimately very few Congolese ever obtained one. Belgian authoritarianism created a "soft" apartheid regime, including urban segregation in Congo's booming cities and an unofficial but real color bar in employment and in public life. Some white *colons* subjected the Congolese to terrible abuses. In 1953, at Kaponde in Kasaï Province, a white settler who suspected his *boy* of theft locked the young man in his car to force him to confess. When he tried to flee, the settler tied him to a table leg by his neck, killing him by strangulation. When a dozen or so *évolué* Congolese ordered drinks at a bar at the Elisabethville airport in 1957, the owner refused, saying "he would not serve monkeys." In 1958 a European worker on a coffee plantation tied an African he suspected of theft behind his truck and dragged him through the plantation. The European was fired and left the colony, escaping prosecution. Europeans proved remarkably incapable of recognizing a central contradiction of colonial rule: it proclaimed that all peoples were worthy of advancement and development, yet was predicated on racial discrimination and domination.

Exchanges and Migrations

Greater development meant intensified interventions into people's everyday lives. Colonial states continued to tax. Although postwar regimes largely eschewed forced labor – except Portugal – infrastructure projects and other development schemes ramped up their recruitment of local laborers. Other interventions were highly personal. One Belgian initiative of the 1950s addressed proper birth spacing. In Usumbura (present-day Bujumbura) in the United Nations Trust Territories of Ruanda–Urundi, authorities implemented a *foyer social* program from 1946 to teach native women the "proper" way to keep a home, as part of an attempt to stabilize urban populations. House visits by instructors checking participants' progress gathered information about African households, redefined the African family as a nuclear one, and prescribed what it meant to be a proper mother and wife. Some women participated in order to be empowered, especially in relation to their husbands, others for the sake of benefits including prenatal care. But only 15 percent of women participated in the program, which meant that Usumbura's women were in no sense unanimous in their opinions about it.

Empire kept on putting people on the move. Europeans continued to recruit subjects as soldiers, which was especially irksome to nationalists when they were employed to sustain colonial regimes. Indian troops staffed large parts of the Indian Army, the Royal Netherlands East Indies Army, and the Congo's Force Publique. As discussed, France recruited and deployed tens of thousands of colonial subjects including Vietnamese in Vietnam to keep it French, and Algerian *harkis* who fought to keep Algeria French. The Portuguese deployed African soldiers to Goa in India, and British troops from different colonies and the Commonwealth fought in Malaya and in Kenya through much of the 1950s. It is unsurprising the 1958 Resolution of the All-African People's Conference at Accra, Ghana, bemoaned "the militarization of Africans and the use of African soldiers in a nefarious global game against their brethren as in Algeria, Kenya, South Africa, Cameroons, Côte d'Ivoire, Rhodesia and in the Suez Canal invasions." The transport of convicts to overseas penal colonies, a practice dating back centuries – by 1976 France's penal archipelago had held 600,000 to 800,000 men – did wind down in the post-World War II era.

By the late 1940s, immigration to western European countries from colonies and other parts of the non-European world picked up, meeting labor demand as Europe rebuilt after 1945. People from the West Indies emigrated to Britain in large numbers in the 1950s, encouraged by the labor demand and the Nationality Act of 1948 granting the right to settle there. Political developments also played a role. Many departed Indonesia in the late 1940s and early 1950s as the country neared independence. Vietnamese immigration into France spiked in 1954 at the time of the Vietnamese victory at Dien Bien Phu, as it did again in the mid-1970s after North Vietnam united the whole country, leading many to flee the country by boat, tens of thousands of whom perished before reaching their destination. Emigration out of north Africa also picked up around 1954, as the French–Algerian war began.

Apartheid South Africa

White minority rule intensified in South Africa with the advent of apartheid in 1948. Apartheid, meaning "apartness" or "separateness," was a social and legal system designed to benefit the white minority by separating South Africa's peoples according to so-called races. Its implementation did not come out of nowhere. As we saw in Chapter 5, black African resistance had had a negligible effect on heightened white domination in South Africa between the wars. In the 1930s the more pro-British South African Party led by Jan Smuts and the pro-Afrikaner Nationalist Party began working together as the United Party. The Nationalist Party re-emerged under D. F. Malan as the Afrikaner-dominated Purified Nationalist Party, which scored a major publicity coup in 1938 when it took charge of centenary celebrations of the Great Trek. Smuts's United Party continued to rule, but faced growing dissatisfaction. It brought South Africa into World War II on the side of Britain and against Nazi Germany, in spite of support among some Afrikaners for Germany. Also, the government eased restrictions on black workers to meet wartime exigencies, for example allowing the wages of black workers to rise faster than those of whites.

The (Purified) Nationalist Party won the 1948 elections, launching the apartheid era. Apartheid was based on four principles, the first being that there were four races in South Africa, each with its own culture: white, Coloured (those of mixed descent), Indian, and African. Second, of the four races, whites were the most civilized and therefore should be in control. Third, white interests were paramount. And, finally, whites – Afrikaners and British – comprised one nation, whereas Africans were members of several nations or groups, each with its own culture. By this reasoning whites constituted the largest "nation" in South Africa, whereas in 1936 2 percent of the population was Indian, 8 percent Coloured, 69 percent African, and only 21 percent white. Coloureds were mainly centered in the Cape Province in and around Cape Town, and Indians lived in Cape Town as well as along the eastern coast. Africans were officially relegated to ten "homelands" by 1951.

A host of legislation created apartheid's infrastructure. The 1949 Mixed Marriages Act and 1951 Immorality Act legally prohibited different races from marrying or having sexual relations. The open-ended 1950 Suppression of Communism Act gave the state broad powers to suppress groups connected to communism, and in practice the government used it to attack groups threatening apartheid. The 1950 Group Areas Act zoned urban areas by race, leading to population displacement. An example is the destruction of Sophiatown, an enormous black suburb of Johannesburg. Adding insult to injury, the white neighborhood that replaced Sophiatown was named Triomf (Triumph). Other legislation further separated the races: the Population Registration Act, which put everyone into racial categories and required identification cards (1950), the Native Laws Amendment Act (1952), the Bantu Education Act (1953), the Criminal Laws Amendment Act (1953), and the Reservation of Separate Amenities Act (1953). All such legislation not only separated white, black, Coloured, and Indian, but also impoverished black Africans, creating a cheap supply of labor for white farming and industrial operations. The Nationalist Party's electoral support grew, including among non-Afrikaner whites.

How could a white minority government sustain such an inherently repressive regime? Diamonds and especially gold had shifted the colony's economy from pastoralism to mining. Gold mining was labor-intensive and dangerous work. Between 1933 and 1966, 19,000 South African gold miners died, 93 percent of whom were black. Wealth extracted from the ground, and at the cost of so many lives, gave the white-dominated state the means to sustain its domination. South Africa's white government also cast itself as a bulwark against communism's spread, garnering support from Western powers like the United States and Britain.

Mining also wrought changes in culture and put people on the move. Female agency had played a key role in women's migration in the first half of the twentieth century. Women even migrated away from the prosperous community of Phokeng, for instance, which was late to suffer the privations imposed by white dominion. The residents of Phokeng had not even had their land dispossessed as a result of the 1913 Land Act. It was primarily noneconomic factors, such as the draw of city life and the desire to escape oppressive parental and tribal controls, that led them to migrate. So, while there clearly were larger economic and political forces at work in southern Africa, the pull of city life coupled with the push of rural African society played a significant role in determining the migration of African women.

Men, too, were attracted by city life and wage work. In Peter Abrahams's novel *Mine Boy* (1946), the novel's protagonist, Xuma, arrives in Johannesburg, which was built on gold wealth. Xuma explores the city as a naive newcomer, seeing women carving out their own place and autonomy through beer brewing. He witnesses accidents and labor conflict in the mines, and becomes caught up in his own visions of a color-free society. Although certain people of European descent, like the character Paddy, give him hope, Xuma's experiences in the city and the mines reveal to him the bald discrimination that exists. To Paddy's claim that he understands Xuma's situation, Xuma counters, "You say you understand ... but how can you? You are a white man. You do not carry a pass. You do not know how it feels to be stopped by a policeman in the street. You go where you like. You do not know how it feels when they say 'Get out! White people only.' ... You understand with your head. I understand with pain."

Such pain translated into tough defiance. The ANC Youth League had already formed by 1944 to mobilize against white rule, pushing the ANC in the early 1950s to confront the regime with the need for change. People of all races who opposed apartheid joined to launch the Defiance Campaign in 1952. As elsewhere, however, this was not a story with only two sides: a split developed within the multiracial ANC, some arguing for an African-centered group. Thus did the Pan-Africanist Congress (PAC) emerge.

North Africa and the Middle East

The immediate postwar years led to political change in the Middle East. France's hold on the former Ottoman territories of Lebanon and Syria ended in 1946, Oman gained nominal independence from Britain in 1951, and that same year

Unfinished and Finished Empires, 1945–1958

Libya, a site of fighting during the war, emerged independent under King Idris. Defeat in Indochina, a war in Algeria, rising anticolonialism such as that seen at Bandung in 1955, and pressure from Neo Destour nationalists in Tunisia and from the nationalist Istiqlal Party in Morocco forced France's hand. France ended its protectorates over Tunisia and, along with Spain, over Morocco in 1956. Tunisia emerged independent under the nationalist Habib Bourguiba of the Neo Destour party, while in Morocco power reverted not to the independence Istiqlal Party but to Sultan Mohammed V.

On the eastern fringe of the Mediterranean, the state of Israel emerged in a land of religious significance. The Jewish presence in the Levant, dating back some 3,000 years, had dwindled to where there were almost no Jews there by the mid-nineteenth century. Jewish settlement in Palestine coincided with the era of the New Imperialism and increased with growing attacks on Jews, especially in eastern Europe, which was home to most of the world's Jews. Still, in 1900 almost all people in Ottoman Palestine were Arab Muslims. By 1919 Jews numbered some 76,000 in Palestine compared to more than half a million Muslims.

Some nationalists mobilized for a Jewish state and, as we have seen, received encouragement from the 1917 Balfour Declaration, which stated that Britain looked "with favor" on the possibility of a Jewish homeland in the Near East. The interwar years witnessed further Jewish immigration, and both Arabs and Jews chafed under postwar British Mandate rule. World War II and the Holocaust gave urgency to the formation of a Jewish state, and Britain, facing growing Arab and Jewish resistance, ceded authority in Palestine to the United Nations. Jewish nationalists, spurred on by the United Nations' plan to partition Palestine, declared Israel's foundation in 1948, and war ensued as Arabs took up arms against the newly declared state. The new Jewish state, victorious in battle, seized the initiative and established its independence.

The Suez Crisis

Of growing interest to not only the French and British but also the United States and the Soviet Union were the oil-producing regions of the Near East where nationalist sentiment created an unstable situation. Take Iran, for instance, long a nominally independent buffer state between British and Russian spheres of influence. Britain and Russia jointly occupied Iran during World War II to forestall German action there, deposed Reza Shah Pahlavi, and installed his son Mohammad Reza Pahlavi as shah. The British controlled oil production but the Iranian prime minister, Mohammad Mossadegh, who was elected in 1951, nationalized the oil companies. The US Central Intelligence Agency instigated a coup deposing Mossadegh in 1953, and returned the shah to what was called the Peacock Throne.

In Egypt, too, nationalist sentiment blossomed. An army officers' coup in 1952 overthrew the king and pushed the British out, and the coup's main architect,

Gamal Abdel Nasser, seized power. This paved the way for a crisis in 1956, which not only was the greatest crisis in Egypt since the 1882 British takeover, but also indicated the changed postwar situation of European overseas empire.

From the point of view of Washington and the European capitals, Nasser was dangerous because many people were drawn to his anticolonialist, pro-liberation pan-Arabism. The Egyptians' loathing of continued foreign interference is captured in *Palace Walk* (1956), by the Nobel Prize winner Naguib Mahfouz. The novel is set in Cairo during World War I at a time when the British occupying presence was heavy. Although *Palace Walk* is not explicitly about the occupation, an undercurrent of discontent with the British runs through the novel. At one point, "The capital appeared sad, angry, desolate. There was good news that attorneys and civil servants were about to strike. The heart of the nation was throbbing. It was alive and in rebellion ... A self-conscious awakening had rocked the Nile Valley." The novel says less about the era in which it is set than about the time at which it was written.

As Nasser's popularity and power grew, it became obvious that Washington, London, and Egypt were working toward different futures. Things came to a head over the Suez Canal, which had been internationalized, with special British privileges. When the United States withdrew funds that had been promised for the construction of the Aswan High Dam on the Nile (to generate electricity), Nasser nationalized the canal to pay for it. Britain and France, in coordination with Israel, launched an invasion that was successful but that provoked the US president Dwight Eisenhower's ire because it had been plotted in secret without advance notice to the United States. When both the United States and the Soviets pressured France and Britain to leave, it showed that the latter had both miscalculated badly. The final result – withdrawal – signaled the end of Britain's and France's ability to act independently in the region, and only boosted Nasser's prestige.

The outcome of Suez also revealed how much the post-1945 situation differed from the post-World War I era, when the United States and Russia had retreated into isolationism. After World War II the Red Army had hundreds of thousands of troops stationed across eastern Europe, and showed that it was willing to intervene, as it did when it suppressed a 1956 uprising in Hungary. In the Middle East, Syria became an important Soviet client state. The United States was interventionist as well, taking down the independent Mossadegh regime in 1953 and sponsoring the shah. A sign of US willingness to flex its muscle was its role in forming the Baghdad Pact between the United Kingdom, Turkey, Iran, Iraq, and Pakistan in 1955. In response, and under Nasser's leadership, Egypt and Syria formed the United Arab Republic (UAR) that same year, and when revolt broke out in Lebanon against its pro-Western government, some Muslim Lebanese called for joining the UAR. In 1958 Eisenhower ordered troops to the area to sustain the government of the pro-Western

Lebanese president Camille Chamoun, confirming a US willingness to act abroad. Whereas from the nineteenth century to as late as the 1940s, western European powers were able to act independently in a world dominated by Britain and its navy, this was no longer the case by the 1950s, by which time a "British world" had ceded to a bipolar Cold War world.

War in Algeria

On November 1, 1954 – All Saint's Day – nationalists in French Algeria launched a series of attacks, the opening salvo of a war for an *Algérie algérienne*. The conflict became one of the most vicious chapters of decolonization.

France had begun its conquest of Algeria in 1830 and dominated there by the 1870s. It became France's only true settler colony, its European population increasing from 37,000 in 1840 to 500,000 by 1890 and to 1.2 million by 1954. By comparison, a mere 30,000 to 35,000 French lived in Vietnam by World War II, and just a few thousand across all of AOF. Settlers in Algeria came from France and elsewhere in Europe; for example, the Algerian-born philosopher, writer, and Nobel Prize winner Albert Camus had a French father and a Spanish mother. By the 1950s many Europeans in Algeria were like Camus in that they had not immigrated but been born there, for example designer Yves Saint Laurent (1936–2008) and actor Daniel Auteuil (b. 1950). Still, the Algerian population dwarfed that of the settlers, or *colons*: 8.5 million to just 1.2 million *colons* in 1954. Keeping Algeria French was essential for the settlers, who would otherwise be overwhelmed by the Algerian majority. Absent so many settlers, France would not have engaged in a bloody, long-drawn-out war.

French rule overwhelmingly advantaged Europeans, giving them access to the best terrain through the appropriation of agricultural lands. Discrimination and segregation were basic components of the legal system and of everyday life. Intermarriage or children of mixed parentage were rare; people interacted only as economic relations necessitated. By 1950, 80 percent of Europeans lived in urban areas, half of them in Oran and Algiers. Although Algeria was part of the French Republic, with few exceptions Algerians were not citizens but subjects. They had to abide by the hated *code de l'indigénat*, which imposed punishments for crimes that did not even exist for Europeans. And the *mission civilisatrice* was not working. Land holdings by 1954 were, on average, 306 acres for French farms with annual earnings of £2,800 (approximately US$91,200 in 2017 terms) compared to a mere 29 acres for Algerian farms, with annual earnings of £100.

World War II raised expectations. The fight against fascism in Europe led some Algerians to believe that reform would happen. Instead, the gap between indigenous Arabs and Berbers and the French only grew as tensions rose and conflicts erupted, such as at Sétif in 1945. The French enacted reforms, but in such a way as not to cede real power. The government extended the franchise to Algerians, for example, but maintained effective control through a voting system that thwarted majority rule and kept real power in the hands of settlers.

Despite the lack of real change, pro-Algerian groups like Messali Hadj's PPA remained resolutely within the law, prompting diehard nationalists to form a number of secret pro-independence groups that emerged in 1954 as the unified Front de Libération Nationale (FLN; National Liberation Front). The FLN did not view the world with a particular political ideology, as anticolonial communists did in Malaysia, for example. Rather, the FLN's unifying ideology was liberation, period.

It was the FLN that attacked in November 1954. Although the All Saints' Day violence unnerved settlers, reactions across the Mediterranean were muted. During the conflict's first few years, it looked as if France would prevail. Paris reaffirmed that Algeria was part of France and that it would remain so. As attacks continued into 1955, concern grew, and the Paris government named Jacques Soustelle as governor-general. He developed the Soustelle Plan to integrate Algeria by ceding some political rights to the Algerian majority, increasing its apparent participation without compromising French rule. The plan also called for more funding for Algeria and defeating the rebels with force. The FLN intensified its attacks and carried out civilian bombings in Algiers and other cities. In August 1955 it carried out a massacre at Philippeville that left dozens dead and many mutilated. Like Sétif in 1945, Philippeville widened the gap between Algerians and settlers.

Although it is easy to think of the war as a two-sided affair, French against Algerian, it was extraordinarily complex, with innumerable sides. Some of the French sympathized with Algerian nationalists, while others embraced their cause because they saw it as a class struggle against oppressive Western capitalism. Many settlers were diehard *colons*, convinced that they were not going anywhere, which for them meant that the FLN had to be destroyed. Many Algerians embraced the FLN while others detested it. Some Algerians were largely assimilated, others not at all, and innumerable individuals occupied intermediary positions. Consider again Albert Camus, a resistance fighter who had struggled against oppression and authoritarianism during World War II, editing the underground newspaper *Combat*, but who criticized Algerian freedom fighters for using terrorism to achieve political ends. He responded to one reporter's question on the subject in 1957 by saying, "People are now planting bombs in the tramways of Algiers. My mother might be on one of those tramways. If that is justice, then I prefer my mother." Eventually he fell silent on the war, a silence that he kept until his death in an automobile accident in 1960.

Another illustrative figure is Mouloud Feraoun, a Berber (Kabyle) French-language teacher in Algeria. Feraoun was a learned, humane observer who kept a penetrating diary that reveals the war's pain and anguish. He saw the conflict from multiple vantage points:

> It is extremely cruel that France should lose Algeria where it has done so much, given so much, to the point that the country has become part of France itself. But it is inhuman to massacre the indigenous people who know that Algeria belongs to them and that they have nothing in common with the French, nothing but this servile relationship that has been going on for a century. It is inhuman to send one's own children, descendants of free men, to die or to kill other children who themselves want to be free.

Even though Feraoun decried the violence inflicted by France, he remained ambivalent about the FLN, not believing that it represented Algeria. He feared its dictatorial tendencies:

> The brutal executions, the arbitrary ransoms, the arrogance of a brand-new, narrow-minded, and scornful authority will, little by little, look like a yoke that will become more unbearable than the one from which we claim to be breaking free ... we are allowing ourselves to be led by men with neither scruples nor education. They are bandits who should go back to jail, not leaders or guides for a people suffering and thirsting for dignity.

Both French and FLN forces escalated atrocities. The FLN attacked not only the French but also Algerians, sowing terror in a ploy to make people like Feraoun choose sides. French and FLN forces tortured and maimed, stuffing victims' severed genitals into their mouths or inflicting *le grand sourire* (the big smile) by slitting their throats from ear to ear. The FLN seemed to be following the lead of Frantz Fanon, a Martinican doctor who worked in Algeria beginning in 1954, and who argued that violence bound people together. In *The Wretched of the Earth* (1961) Fanon wrote that the people had to use violence to know the real social truths of the colonial situation. Without violence, independence could be achieved in name only. Fanon advocated a politics of anticolonialism that eliminated any middle ground between colonizer and colonized.

The French parliament's 1956 Special Powers Law, comparable to the 1964 Tonkin Gulf Resolution or the 2002 Iraq War resolution in the United States, authorized the military to do whatever was necessary to win, with little oversight. Because the conflict was being waged within France, soldiers were not technically fighting a war but conducting "operations for the maintenance of order," and combat fell beyond the purview of international organizations like the United Nations. Rebels were not enemy soldiers but outlaws, outside the law but subject to it. More than 500,000 soldiers were deployed to Algeria by 1958, a number equaling that of American troops stationed in Vietnam at the height of the US war there and drawn from a much smaller population. (This figure, of course, excludes FLN fighters.) Paris began recalling reservists and started drafting men into the army.

The military remained committed. Many officers suffered from *le mal jaune* (yellow evil), with its roots in France's 1940 defeat and more immediately in the loss of Indochina following Dien Bien Phu. Officers tended to interpret Algeria in light of their Asian experience, many of them believing that their efforts in Indochina had been sabotaged by political treachery at home. They were estranged from France, feared betrayal, and were willing to forgo the chain of command to prevail, believing that they could no longer remain politically neutral. Defeat was not an option, certainly not in Algeria, which was part of France. Settler resolve encouraged the officers' determination.

One result of the extended powers of the military was the 1956–1957 Battle of Algiers, during which the army took control of the city and, by using informants, detention, and torture, and by "disappearing people" (extrajudicial killings), dismantled the FLN leadership and its Algiers-based network. The army arrested untold numbers, including Frenchman Henri Alleg, a communist newspaper publisher who wrote in *La Question* (*Torture*) (1958) about the repeated torture he endured in prison, including waterboarding and electric shocks to his ears, chest, and penis. The Battle of Algiers succeeded, and as 1958 dawned the French were winning. But news of torture and summary executions provoked opposition. Paul Teitgen, secretary-general of the Algiers police, resigned over the issue, and many others spoke out. In response the government suppressed unfavorable information, pressurized the press, and banned books like Alleg's. Many could not believe that France, historic champion of human rights, self-styled liberator of oppressed peoples, and recent victim of Nazi brutalities, was betraying its most noble traditions.

British "Success" at Decolonization?

Another nationalist movement developed in the Gold Coast, which became Ghana, the first sub-Saharan African colony to gain self-rule. Kwame Nkrumah, a leading figure of the movement, returned to the Gold Coast in 1947 after obtaining a college degree in the United States and pursuing graduate work in the United Kingdom. A new colonial constitution had been implemented in 1946, offering greater room for political activity. Nkrumah immediately embarked on political organization, developing the United Gold Coast Convention (UGCC), a party dedicated to nonviolence and political autonomy. In the face of British inaction and conservatism among the UGCC membership, Nkrumah struck out on his own in the early 1950s to form the Convention People's Party. Growing anticolonial violence forced the British to allow for limited elections. When resistance continued and Nkrumah's party won 90 percent of the vote, the British saw no option but to ask Nkrumah to form a government, which led to an independent Ghanaian state by 1957. This success fueled movements elsewhere, contributing to the British government policy of ceding independence to colonies in sub-Saharan Africa one by one.

It is often said that Britain did a comparatively good and enlightened job of granting independence compared to other countries. After all, the French fought long, bloody wars of decolonization first in Vietnam, then in Algeria. Portugal's wars of decolonization were long and destructive. Belgian decolonization in 1960 was a fiasco. But were the British really "better" at winding down empire? Indian partition in 1947 was deadly and disastrous. As we shall see, Southern Rhodesia's settlers declared white rule through a Unilateral Declaration of Independence in 1965, which resulted in a years-long civil war. South Africa's apartheid regime lasted decades, and South Africa in turn ruled South West Africa as a mandate, denying it independence until 1990. In Kenya, Britain had prevailed against the Mau Mau rebellion (1952–1960) but, in order to win, its forces had tortured untold numbers of Kikuyu people and had built concentration camps that held hundreds of thousands. One former settler and member of the Kenya Regiment described part of the operations:

> We would be given word that we were needed at, say, the camps out in Lake Victoria, and we would go and pick up a few of the filthy pigs and bring them to one of the interrogation centers set up by the CID [Criminal Investigation Department]. These were the hard-core scum, the ones who wouldn't listen to anyone and [were] causing trouble. So we would give them a good thrashing. It would be a bloody awful mess by the time we were done ... Never knew a Kuke [Kikuyu] had so many brains until we cracked open a few heads.

Worse still, Britain engaged in a cover-up that has only very recently come to light. Such evidence suggests that the British were not as enlightened as some claim.

Conclusion

Aside from isolated cases such as Rhodesia, apartheid South Africa, and Portugal's colonies, by the late 1950s it seemed that formal empire and white rule were in serious jeopardy. Colonial administrators might draw up new plans for reformed colonial regimes, but anticolonial nationalists were making and pursuing their own plans and driving the course of events. The postwar consensus in many parts of Europe that colonialism remained a good thing could not be sustained when confronted with the facts or with the costs of maintaining an empire in the face of growing opposition. As indigenous collaboration with or accommodation to foreign rule withered, Europeans faced the prospect of fighting or ceding. When they fought, they lost. That said, it remained to be determined what specific forms that independence would take and what the world would look like after decolonization.

Citations

Page   *Source*
153   "If we want things to stay..." Translated by Archibald Colquhuon.
153   "The king has a whole..." Gérard De Boe, *Bakouba* (1952). (my translation).
155   "Imperial sway..." Wm. Roger Louis and Ronald Robinson, "The Imperialism of Decolonization," in *Ends of British Imperialism: The Scramble for Empire, Suez and Decolonization* (London: I. B. Tauris, 2006), 453.
156   "was messy, hasty..." William Dalrymple, "The Great Divide: The Violent Legacy of Indian Partition," *New Yorker* (June 29, 2015), 65.
157   "malevolent old politician." Penderel Moon, *Wavell: The Viceroy's Journal* (Karachi: Oxford University Press, 1974), 236.
157   "so that he would bleed..." Dalrymple, "The Great Divide," 68.
158   "The return of peace..." Elizabeth Buettner, *Europe After Empire: Decolonization, Society, and Culture* (Cambridge: Cambridge University Press, 2016), 90.
162   "hold this area..." Quoted in Fredrik Logevall, *Embers of War: The Fall of an Empire and the Making of America's Vietnam* (New York: Random House, 2012), 593.
162   "It was a monumental decision..." Logevall, *Embers of War*, 593.
162   "native of Scotland..." Jan-Albert Goris to Paul van Zeeland, no. 415, November 20, 1950, Archives Africaines, Ministry of Foreign Affairs, Brussels, Belgium.
163   "Post-war US government..." Martin C. Thomas, "Innocent Abroad? Decolonisation and US Engagement with French West Africa, 1945–1956," *Journal of Imperial and Commonwealth History* 36, no. 1 (2008), 50.
164   "People talk about the Congo..." Baudouin to Leopold III, May 29, 1955, quoted in Olivier Mouton, "Lettres de Baudouin," *Le Soir* (June 19, 2010) (my translation).
167   "banned whipping." Dibwe Dia Mwembu, "La Peine du Fouet au Congo Belge 1885–1960" [Punishment by Whipping in the Belgian Congo 1885–1960], *Les Cahiers de Tunisie* 135–136 (1986), 137.
167   "In 1953, at Kaponde." Bulletin d'Information, no. 11 (3e trimestre 1957), 18, Portefeuille AI 4733, AI, Archives Africaines, Ministry of Foreign Affairs, Brussels, Belgium.
167   "he would not serve monkeys." Bulletin d'Information, no. 11 (3e trimestre 1957), 36, Portefeuille AI 4733, AI, Archives Africaines, Ministry of Foreign Affairs, Brussels, Belgium.
167   "In 1958 a European worker." Bulletin d'Information, no. 14 (2ème trimestre 1958), 34–35, Portefeuille AI 4734, AI, Archives africaines, Ministry of Foreign Affairs, Brussels, Belgium.

168 "the militarization of Africans..." "Resolution of the All-African People's Conference at Accra, Ghana, on Imperialism and Colonialism, 1958," in *The Imperialism Reader: Documents and Readings on Modern Expansionism,* edited by Louis L. Snyder (Princeton: D.Van Nostrand, 1962), 172–173.
170 "You say you understand..." Peter Abrahams, *Mine Boy* (Oxford: Heinemann, 1946), 172.
172 "The capital appeared sad..." Naguib Mahfouz, *Palace Walk,* translated by William Maynard Hutchins and Olive E. Kenny (New York: Anchor Books, 1991), 360.
175 "It is extremely cruel..." Mouloud Feraoun, *Journal 1955–1962: Reflections on the French–Algerian War,* edited by James D. Le Sueur, translated by Mary Ellen Wolf and Claude Fouillade (Lincoln: University of Nebraska Press, 2000), 93.
175 "The brutal executions..." Feraoun, *Journal 1955–1962,* 118–119.
177 "We would be given word..." Anonymous interview, Naivasha, Kenya, January 14, 1999, quoted in Caroline Elkins, *Imperial Reckoning: The Untold Story of Britain's Gulag in Kenya* (New York: Henry Holt, 2005), 193.

Bibliography

Betts, Raymond F. *Decolonization.* 2nd ed. New York: Routledge, 1998.
Elkins, Caroline. *Imperial Reckoning: The Untold Story of Britain's Gulag in Kenya.* New York: Henry Holt, 2005.
Fanon, Frantz. *The Wretched of the Earth* (1961). Translated by Constance Farrington. New York: Grove Press, 1963.
Feraoun, Mouloud. *Journal 1955–1962: Reflections on the French–Algerian War.* Lincoln: University of Nebraska Press, 2000.
Logevall, Fredrik. *Embers of War: The Fall of an Empire and the Making of America's Vietnam.* New York: Random House, 2012.
Louis, Wm. Roger. *Ends of British Imperialism: The Scramble for Empire, Suez and Decolonization.* London: I. B. Tauris, 2006.
Manning, Patrick. *Francophone Sub-Saharan Africa 1880–1995.* 2nd ed. Cambridge: Cambridge University Press, 1998.
Moon, Penderel. *Wavell: The Viceroy's Journal.* Karachi: Oxford University Press, 1974.
Schwarz, Bill. *Memories of Empire: The White Man's World.* Oxford: Oxford University Press, 2011.
Turnbull, Colin M. *The Lonely African.* New York: Simon & Schuster, 1962.

8
Decolonization's Second Wave, 1958–1975

> "I too used to live in Algeria. In Tlemcen. It's near Oran. Do you know it?"
> "No, M'sieur. I've never been to Algeria."
> "So, let's see. I am French, but I was born in Algeria, and you were born in Lyon, but you're Algerian."
>
> Azouz Begag, *Shantytown Kid* (2007)

In the spring of 1960, people in the Congo voted in their first country-wide elections. Patrice Lumumba, leader of the Mouvement National Congolais (MNC), a national political party, became the country's first prime minister. Newly born on June 30, 1960, the Democratic Republic of the Congo was one of the world's largest states, larger even than Greenland. It was rich in natural resources and had a growing population.

Within days of independence the situation unraveled. The army mutinied. Riots broke out. Resource-rich Katanga, the country's southernmost province, seceded, followed by the South Kasai region. The former colonial power, Belgium, sent in troops, threatening the country's independence. Desperate for aid, yet rebuffed by both the United States and the United Nations, Lumumba turned to Nikita Khrushchev's Soviet Union. The United Nations intervened, and communist China threatened to do so. Many foreigners, including Belgians, considered Lumumba dangerous, and he had fierce domestic opponents whose narrower regional or ethnic interests clashed with the MNC's nationalist agenda. The United States, paranoid about Lumumba's possible communist leanings, decided that he must be eliminated. He was captured, delivered to political opponents in Katanga, and murdered in January 1961. So as to leave no traces of

European Overseas Empire, 1879–1999: A Short History, First Edition. Matthew G. Stanard.
© 2018 John Wiley & Sons, Inc. Published 2018 by John Wiley & Sons, Inc.

his assassination or a martyr's resting site for remembrance, his killers disinterred Lumumba's body after burial to rebury him at another site. Finally two men, both Belgians, were ordered to unearth his corpse a second time and to eliminate all traces of it, which they did by cutting it into pieces that were then burned or dissolved in acid. Lumumba's death and destruction did not end the Congo Crisis, and the world watched it unfold until army chief Joseph-Désiré Mobutu (later Mobutu Sese Seko) seized power in a 1965 coup.

The Congo Crisis was one of several during the tumultuous era from the late 1950s through the mid-1970s, years that represented a second wave of decolonization, in contrast to a first wave between India's independence in 1947 and a slew of countries becoming independent in 1960. Several themes run through this second wave. First, there was a qualitative difference between this later era and the one that witnessed India, Pakistan, Indonesia, and China's independence from foreign meddling in the late 1940s. The Suez Crisis revealed the changed situation. Unlike after World War I, the United States and the Soviet Union did not retreat into isolationism after 1945, and their Cold War rivalry dominated international affairs by the late 1950s. The Chinese communists' 1949 victory and the 1960–1961 Sino-Soviet split added a third pole of influence: Mao's China. The United Nations, while still young, was by the late 1950s already proving itself more resilient than the ineffective League of Nations and a site for anticolonial mobilization.

Most important was the increased strength of anticolonial movements, some of long standing, others of which developed only at this late stage, for example in Portuguese Africa. Across the colonial world, nationalist leaders propelled independence movements. Europeans rejected the idea that empire was on the way out, seeking to continue it formally or informally. The result was the peaceful transfer of power in some places, such as in most of France's sub-Saharan African colonies; violent anticolonial wars elsewhere; and ongoing informal European, US, and sometimes Soviet influence across much of the formerly colonial world, which raised question as to the real meaning of decolonization.

The Nature of Decolonization

People used to think of the concept of decolonization as a straightforward one: political independence meant independence. The British used the phrase "transfer of power" as if sovereignty could be placed in a box and handed from one person to another. Ceremony only reinforced this idea. The Indian prime minister, Jawaharhal Nehru, declared India independent in a national broadcast at midnight on August 14, 1947. In the course of a single night, India switched from being a colony to an independent state. The last colonial governor in Mauritius lowered the Union Jack in 1968 and the prime minister of the newly

Decolonization's Second Wave, 1958–1975

independent state raised the new national flag, a scene that was repeated many times elsewhere as decolonization became "complete."

In reality, decolonization was more complex, and it was never finished. Independence was often political and formal at best, with continuing economic, social, cultural, and other factors working against true self-determination. The French continued to influence former colonies in west and central Africa through military agreements, development aid, and banking and currency controls, including having African currencies pegged to the French franc. Jacques Foccart, the French secretary for African and Malagasy affairs, was a key administration figure under both presidents Charles de Gaulle (in office 1958–1969) and Georges Pompidou (in office 1969–1974) in a country whose neocolonial ambitions in Africa were so blatant that there was a term for it, *Françafrique*.

Colonialism continued to shape even the largest, most stable, and economically significant states like India in fundamental ways. One simple fact was that such states owed their very existence to the fight *against* colonial rule; another was that they emerged at the height of the Cold War, which meant that, like it or not, the struggle between the capitalist West and the communist East molded them and their international relations. Some newly formed countries joined India in the Non-Aligned Movement (NAM), in part to escape the confines of the bipolar Cold War framework. Yet the fact that the NAM defined itself against former colonial masters and against the Eastern and Western blocs meant that countries in the NAM were fundamentally defined by them.

In other cases independence came late or not at all. After Indonesia's independence in 1949, the Netherlands kept control over Western New Guinea until 1962, and over Caribbean possessions including the Dutch Antilles and Dutch Guiana for even longer, the latter of which achieved independence only in 1975, when it became Suriname. Other colonies became juridically and politically incorporated directly into European countries, including the Dutch islands of Aruba, Curaçao, Sint Maarten, Bonaire, Saba, and Sint Eustatius; French Guiana in South America; several of France's Caribbean islands; Mayotte and Réunion in the Indian Ocean; and the north African exclaves of Ceuta and Melilla, which today remain part of Spain. European states continued to administer numerous tiny territories, such as the Falkland Islands in the South Atlantic, Saint Pierre and Miquelon off Canada's northeastern coast, and French Polynesia. The United States kept the Virgin Islands, Puerto Rico, and Guam as territories without granting their denizens full citizenship.

Colonial legacies, infrastructure, mentalities, and relations did not vanish overnight. Memories of empire remained, and new configurations developed from former connections. After the conclusion of Algeria's war against France in 1962, many French people of Algerian descent either emigrated to France or were born there. Among them was Azouz Begag, a son of immigrants who was born in Lyon, France, and who went on to become a government minister and successful author.

Hundreds of thousands of *pieds noirs* – those of European descent born or raised in Algeria – relocated to France beginning in 1962, including one of Begag's teachers. This chapter's epigraph relates an exchange between Begag and his teacher, who was ethnically French. Born in Algeria, his teacher spoke Arabic and knew the country better than Begag, an "Algerian" who had never been there.

Contingency and Decolonization

1958: Brussels and Accra

It is easy to think that decolonization was inevitable. After all, essentially all the major colonies achieved independence in fewer than three decades, from India in 1947 to Angola, Portuguese Guinea, and Mozambique in 1975. But there was nothing certain about the timing, unfolding, or outcome of developments, as shown by two events in 1958: the Brussels World's Fair, and Accra's All-African People's Conference.

The Brussels universal exposition that opened in April 1958 was the first since the New York World's Fair of 1939–1940, a remarkable gap considering that, since the first universal expositions of the mid-nineteenth century, rarely had a year gone by without one – in this case, World War II intervened. The 1958 exposition showcased the promise of technology and modernity, its massive Atomium representing an iron molecule magnified 150 billion times. In the atomic age, the fair was saying that advanced technologies needed to be used for good.

Also on display was Belgian confidence in the future of colonial rule, and one of the exposition's four sections showcased Belgium's colony. The Congo section's high-tech pavilions called attention to achievements in central Africa, and there was a tropical garden with a *village indigène*, or "native village." Such "villages" had been part of many international or colonial fairs since the nineteenth century. This one in 1958 housed African artisans behind fences, where they were to be seen going about their crafts daily from April until the fair's close in October. By the end of July, though, the village was empty. The Congolese artisans had asked to depart early because of the abuse they received at the hands of visitors. Some of the visitors who had peered at them from across the fence had asked if they could inspect their teeth or see the color of the palms of their hands; some had even thrown food at them.

Also taking place in 1958 was the All-African People's Conference in Accra, the capital of Ghana (formerly the Gold Coast), the first independent country in black Africa. The Ghanaian president, Kwame Nkrumah, took a leadership role, and delegates from independent countries like Morocco and Guinea joined anticolonial leaders. The conference's declaration was a clarion call to halt the manipulation and abuse of colonial peoples the world over, for example the recruiting of African and Asian soldiers to fight wars for colonial powers. Delegates called for the end of empire:

> The All-African People's Conference in Accra declares its full support to all fighters for freedom in Africa, to all those who resort to peaceful means of non-violence and civil disobedience, as well as to all those who are compelled to retaliate against violence to attain national independence and freedom for the people.

The countervailing motivations and forces at work at Brussels and Accra in 1958 show how the outcome of the struggle between imperial oppression and independence was anything but preordained.

So what made decolonization happen? It was above all particular circumstances, individuals, and events that determined what happened in each specific area of the colonial world. As we have seen, defeat led to Italy's loss of its overseas colonies, which Britain largely took over during the war, converting them into United Nations trust territories, which soon achieved independence. Half a world away, the United States granted independence to its largest colony, the Philippines, as promised in 1946, although the United States maintained an outsized influence there. The Vietnamese had achieved victory against the French in 1954, yet faced more than 20 years of war before it could fully expel all Western influence. Some colonies became independent almost overnight. The Belgian Congo, like its neighbor Portuguese Angola, seemed well under the control of the colonizing power as late as 1959. The Congo then became independent within months, whereas Angolans had to fight a 15-year war to break free of European control. Traditional authorities assumed power in some newly independent countries, for example the Ngwato chief, Seretse Khama, became Botswana's first president, and Sultan Mohammed V assumed power in Morocco. In other cases nationalist leaders came to power, for example the Neo Destour leader, Habib Bourguiba, in Tunisia. Some colonies achieved independence peacefully, for instance Niger and Australia. Others endured long-drawn-out wars of independence, for example Rhodesia (present-day Zimbabwe) and Algeria.

Algeria's Independence from France

Before Lumumba's assassination and the Congo Crisis of 1960–1965, events in another part of Africa – Algeria – had captured world headlines. As we saw in Chapter 7, by 1958 France had won the Battle of Algiers and dismantled the FLN leadership. Yet the Battle of Algiers could not turn the war around because the growth of Algerian nationalism and the conflict's fevered pitch made compromise impossible. France maintained that it was engaged in a domestic police operation, a fiction that few outsiders believed. Unlike the wars in Indochina, which were fought by professional soldiers, it was mainly conscripts who fought in Algeria, and conscription took its toll. As French people learned of the methods used to win the Battle of Algiers – torture, imprisonment, summary executions, the "disappearing" of people – they turned against it. Alleg's book *The Question* revealed an inescapable truth, namely that a people who were recently victim to occupation and torture at the hands of a foreign power, Germany, had themselves become occupiers and torturers.

The army and *colons* saw things otherwise and held out as the war continued. Another governing coalition in Paris fell in early 1958, and President René Coty asked Pierre Pflimlin of the center-right Mouvement Républicain Populaire to form a new one. Some *pieds noirs* feared that Pflimlin would appease the Algerian rebels, and they rioted in Algiers. The situation deteriorated. Army leaders in Algeria initiated Operation Resurrection, a plan to take Paris – a military putsch. General Jacques Massu, a veteran of World War II and French Indochina, led the operation. Into the picture stepped Charles de Gaulle: military officer, Free French leader, and head of the country's provisional government after the Libération in 1944. De Gaulle had withdrawn from politics because of disagreements over the form the new Fourth Republic should take, retiring to write his memoirs, a time he called his "years in the desert." With time, he had achieved almost mythical status. Now, in 1958, his country on the verge of a coup or worse, he re-emerged to, as he put it, "make himself available" to France and to take control.

De Gaulle's return ended the threat of invasion and civil war. Because he had always staunchly supported empire, and because his Free French had depended on the colonies for resources, revenue, and legitimacy, Massu and other putschists trusted him. De Gaulle now exploited the situation to assume broad powers and write a new constitution, ending the Fourth Republic (1946–1958) and inaugurating the Fifth (1958 to the present). In short, the Algerian crisis led to a coup that brought in a new regime under de Gaulle, supported by the military.

De Gaulle's assumption of power did not end the war right away, and it ground on with terrible consequences. There was French–Algerian, Algerian–Algerian, and French–French violence. The war spread from Algeria to metropolitan France where, between 1956 and 1961, 3,889 Algerians were killed and another 7,678 wounded in Algerian–Algerian attacks. A police crackdown on a peaceful protest in Paris in 1961 killed dozens of Algerians, and bodies were fished out of the Seine for days.

As time passed, *pieds noirs* and the army in Algeria began to fear that de Gaulle's views were evolving, and for good reason. De Gaulle's changing views underscored how decolonization was a history of interconnected stories. After World War II, like all French leaders of the time, de Gaulle believed that empire was necessary. As he put it, "France cannot be France without greatness." But he did not merely reference French history. He also thought of Portugal when trying to envisage his country's future in an era of decolonization, at one point wondering about France, "Va-t-elle se portugaliser?" Would France, like Portugal, become a second-rate power? In 1960 the British prime minister, Harold Macmillan, made a famous speech before South Africa's parliament, saying that "The wind of change is blowing through this continent. Whether we like it or not, this growth of national consciousness is a political fact." De Gaulle shared Macmillan's view, and developed a plan for changed relations with the remaining sub-Saharan colonies and a different approach toward Algeria. To restore France's *grandeur*, de Gaulle concluded that it was necessary for the country, as he put it, to "marry the century" – that is, to abandon an outdated colonialism and embrace the future, one without formal overseas colonies. France could be great without its colonies by means of its global influence, a *force de frappe*, or "strike force" (France detonated its first nuclear weapon in 1960), and power in Europe. To ensure French influence in Europe, de Gaulle eventually vetoed Britain's application to join the European Economic Community not once, but twice. He spoke of decolonization, then self-determination, and finally of an *Algérie algérienne* (Algerian independence).

In the context of the war, which by 1960 was in its sixth year, de Gaulle decided on an *Algérie algérienne*. His recall of a prominent army general in January 1960 formed the pretext for yet another rebellion by army officers in Algeria, which ended only after de Gaulle personally addressed the nation by television – one of the first such dramatic televised moments in history – and called on them to stop. In January 1961 he put his position to voters in a referendum, and the results were overwhelming: 75.2 percent voted in favor of an *Algérie algérienne* (Algeria for the Algerians), and only 24.7 percent against. This set the stage for negotiations. April 1961 witnessed yet another putsch by army generals in Algiers. When de Gaulle condemned it, it collapsed. This drove settler and French army extremists in Algeria underground, and as the Évian accords on Algerian independence were negotiated, the FLN continued its attacks. The extremist *colon* Organisation Armée Secrète (OAS; Secret Army Organization) carried out terrorist actions in both Algeria and France. Whereas the FLN sought independence and control over Algeria, the OAS sought to impose its now minority vision of the future on Algeria and France, a vision that just recently had been that of the majority of French men and women. De Gaulle himself became a target, and an August 1962 assassination attempt left the presidential Citroën riddled with bullets. When de Gaulle and his wife escaped unharmed, it only added to his mystique.

By mid-1962 the FLN had won a war that had reshaped Algeria and France. Fighting was followed by postwar reprisals in Algeria. The FLN, OAS, and others killed vast numbers of suspected collaborators, *harkis*, and innocents – at least tens of thousands – in the weeks and months around independence. One of the hundreds of thousands of war victims was the teacher Mouloud Feraoun, who was assassinated by the OAS three days before the signing of the Évian accords. Tens of thousands of *pieds noirs* left for metropolitan France, as did thousands of Muslim Algerians, seeking refuge. The moment transformed French notions of citizenship. The French state recognized Algerian refugees of European or Jewish descent as "repatriates," but those of Muslim descent as "refugees." Many of the latter, even *harkis* who had fought for France, ended up in "temporary" camps, sometimes for years, their loyalty rewarded with suspicion, poor living conditions, and racist treatment.

The United Nations and Decolonization

The United Nations was into its second decade as France's war in Algeria reached fever pitch and the Congo Crisis hit, by which time it had become a conduit for anticolonial sentiment and a means to internationalize conflicts. Whereas both France and the Viet Minh had sought to internationalize the war in Vietnam after 1946, France tried to prevent interference in Algeria by casting the conflict as a domestic issue. The FLN made a case on the world stage for intervention in its war of liberation. The United Nations was initially a Western club, reflected in the five permanent members with veto power: the United States, Britain, France, Nationalist China (Taiwan), and the Soviet Union. Some joining members were former colonial or mandate countries, including Ethiopia, Iraq, the Philippines, India, Pakistan, Burma, and Indonesia. By 1958 members included Libya, Ghana (formerly the Gold Coast), Sri Lanka (Ceylon), Laos, Cambodia, and Guinea. Because the legitimacy of these newly independent nation-states was tied up with the fate of colonialism, they used the United Nations as a platform to denounce foreign rule, especially at the United Nations' Special Committee on Non-Self-Governing Territories.

Portugal, Britain, Spain, France, and Belgium feared that anticolonialism at the United Nations would give impetus to nationalist movements. Even though Britain and France were permanent members of the Security Council, they were also United Nations trust territory powers, which meant that they were subject to its Trust Territories Commission, where they were exposed to anticolonial attacks. They countered these with specific political changes, arguments, and public relations efforts. As noted, Spain and Portugal transformed some colonies into provinces in the 1950s (see Chapter 7), arguing that this made any disputes there domestic affairs and beyond the United Nations' reach. Even though Belgium never made the Congo its "tenth province," Belgians consistently refused outside interference. The minister of colonies, André Dequae, declared that his country would "never accept any control whatsoever over her activities in the Congo on the part of UN unless this control is extended to all underdeveloped peoples, whatever their political status might be." This was the "Belgian thesis," according to which the United Nations had to supervise the well-being of "dependent" peoples anywhere, whether in colonies or in independent countries. The idea was to threaten the Soviet Union, the United States, and even newly independent countries that had minority or "underdeveloped" populations to get them to back off. The Soviet Union contained numerous minorities, and Belgian pamphlets alluded to the problems of African Americans, Native Americans, and underdevelopment "in the Americas," implicating its US ally without naming it.

Wars in Vietnam

In south Asia and Oceania, decolonization proceeded apace in the 1960s. As noted, the Dutch were forced to hand over New Guinea to Indonesia by 1962. Although Australia and New Zealand were nominally independent, both maintained important ties with Britain and remained within the Commonwealth, and it was not until the 1960s that they started to develop strong national identities. Both drew closer to the United States in terms of trade and diplomacy.

Most of Asia was politically independent by the late 1950s, with a glaring exception: Vietnam. The French had left by 1954, granting independence to Laos and Cambodia and leaving Vietnam divided between a communist North and a French- and US-backed South. By the mid-1960s, US military personnel had arrived in mainland southeast Asia in significant numbers to defend South Vietnam. To Americans, the anticolonial war of 1945–1954 had morphed into an anticommunist one, and US leaders saw Vietnam as a Cold War front against the Soviet Union and China. The mindset took hold among many in the United States that leaving would cause South Vietnam to fall to the North, leading to a loss of face in the Cold War and across the globe. Then there was the "domino theory," according to which Vietnam's "fall" to communism would be followed by other such losses in southeast Asia. First China, then North Korea, and now Vietnam: communism appeared to be on the march.

The United States got directly involved in South Vietnamese affairs under the Kennedy and Johnson administrations, and ramped up its presence there. By 1968 there were half a million US service personnel in the former French colony. To halt supply and personnel lines running through Laos and Cambodia, the United States and its few allies launched a years-long punishing bombing campaign. Laos suffered nearly 600,000 bombing runs, or 2,000 pounds of explosives for each person in the country as the US and South Vietnamese air forces dropped more bombs on Laos than the United States dropped on both Germany and Japan during World War II.

North Vietnam, led by Ho Chi Minh, pressed on, motivated by nationalism and the desire to rid Vietnam of foreign influence and to unify the country under communist control. President Richard Nixon, after continuing the war for his entire first term, finally withdrew US troops in favor of the "Vietnamization" of the South Vietnamese military. Following the US military drawdown and departure, the North overran the South in a matter of months. When Saigon fell in 1975, Vietnam was finally independent from foreign rule, though it fought Cambodia from 1975 to 1978 and then a war with China in 1979. By the latter's conclusion, Vietnam had been at war for more than three decades.

The Middle East

The Suez Crisis signaled a shift in French and British influence in the Middle East and confirmed Gamel Abdel Nasser as a pan-Arab and anticolonial leader. There was a Cold War competition for influence: as the French and British receded, while retaining some influence, the United States sought to fill the void, as did the Soviet Union. Of course a major driver of foreign involvement was access to oil, the region's top export. The enduring presence of the state of Israel and the growing number of Jewish settlers were another issue, leading to wars in 1967 and 1973.

As events in the 1950s suggest, although Muslim-majority states in north Africa, the Near East, and southwest Asia were independent, their independence had developed in the shadow of the Cold War and of postcolonial relations. Foreign control, both formal and informal, continued over domestic oil industries, as did cultural influence, for instance the promotion of the French language in Syria, Lebanon, and elsewhere. Colonialism's heritage shaped politics at a profound level because conceptualizations of the future across the political spectrum developed in response to a century of foreign domination. Some Arab and Iranian thinkers, writers, and leaders sought to shape the future by returning to a (mythical) precolonial past and by supporting fundamentalist Islam. Others looked to Europe and the United States for inspiration, embracing modernization along Western lines. Others embraced reformism, still others (for example the shah of Iran) clientelism.

African Nationalism and Independence

Ghana's independence in 1957 did not mean that others would necessarily follow. The French engaged in a kind of decolonization divide-and-rule by dividing up AOF and AEF into colonies so as to negotiate with them individually rather than with larger, potentially more powerful, federations. President de Gaulle's changing views, along with the ongoing conflict in Algeria, led him to offer France's sub-Saharan colonies three options in 1958: remain a territory as part of a decentralized French Community to replace the French Union, with the option of later independence; become fully integrated into France as an overseas *département*; or become independent. Almost all voted to become territories in the French-led "community," before in 1960 exercising the option of complete independence. This caused a cascade of assertions of independence in 1960.

An exception was French Guinea, which, spurred on by nationalist leader Ahmed Sékou Touré, voted for full independence in 1958. Sékou Touré's leadership of Guinea's pro-independence vote is instructive. Touré made his name in the AOF trade union movement after France legalized unions in west Africa at the end of World War II. Union leaders like Touré used French rhetoric regarding equality and rights to make demands on the colonial system, for example for higher wages and benefits matching those of French employees. Africans had formed the RDA to exercise political rights, and its French Guinea section was called the Parti Démocratique de Guinée (PDG; Democratic Party of Guinea). A key turning point was a strike in 1953. Colonial authorities cut the working week to 48 hours, and workers demanded corresponding wage increases to maintain their total income. Their demand was not met, and rail workers went on strike for 71 days, led by Touré, who took over leadership of the PDG and developed it into a powerful party combining political with trade union organization. When de Gaulle presented colonies with three choices in 1958, Touré said that Guinea would accept membership in the new community only if it provided for real equality among members. De Gaulle sidestepped the issue, expecting that economic underdevelopment and ongoing dependency would give France the upper hand in dealings with individual colonies. Saying that he preferred "poverty in liberty to riches in slavery," Touré argued for a no vote when the question was put to a 1958 referendum.

The result was an overwhelming no vote followed by independence, which turned Guinea into an intransigent troublemaker for the French. Other leaders were much closer to the French position, for instance Côte d'Ivoire's Houphouët-Boigny, who used French support to his advantage by portraying himself as capable of bringing benefits to Côte d'Ivoire's peoples. Guinea's independence vote provoked French retaliation. Administrators emptied their offices and cleared out, supposedly even yanking telephones by their cords out of the walls. When the United Nations voted to approve Guinea's membership, France abstained and also refused the new country bilateral assistance. The message was clear: former colonies needed to cooperate.

Despite French vindictiveness, there was optimism in Guinea, just as there was across many former colonies in the 1950s and 1960s. Touré enjoyed great support, and took on a leadership role within the international community, where he was viewed as a leader not only of African independence movements but of rights throughout the African diaspora. But as the 1960s unfolded into the 1970s, Touré's rule turned authoritarian as his one-party state suppressed any opposition, and ironically even trade unions. Touré argued that a strike against colonial employers was progressive, but against an African government it was "historically unthinkable … The trade union movement is obligated to reconvert itself to remain in the same line of emancipation." The government arrested union leaders, put down strikes, suppressed political dissent, and either imprisoned or exiled potential regime opponents.

Unlike the French, who treated sub-Saharan colonies with a centralized approach — de Gaulle offered only *three* choices to *all* the French sub-Saharan colonies — the British dealt with each colony on an individual basis, of course with larger considerations in mind. In the postwar period, the British were not averse to moves toward greater autonomy. Ghana won its independence in 1957. Nigeria had its origins in the clumping together of very different peoples. Africans pushed for more rights based on the basic British principles of self-rule, constitutionalism, autonomy, and citizenship rights. Nigerian nationalists achieved a constitution by the early 1950s through negotiations over the form of government, and the stage was set, through ongoing negotiations, for greater self-rule in Nigeria's three regions, and finally independence in 1960. Nigeria emerged as a federal state with a constitution that devolved a great deal of power to the country's three regions: southeast, southwest, and north.

Events elsewhere, for example in the Belgian Congo, further suggest the contingency of decolonization. As late as 1955, "not a single indigenous organization was even dreaming about an independent Congo." The Belgians thought that independence lay in the distant future. When a Belgian professor published a "thirty-year plan" in 1955 for the Congo's independence, some thought the publication unwise; others laughed it off as a ridiculous notion. As we have seen, the 1958 Brussels World's Fair revealed Belgium's confidence in its accomplishments, and the belief that the Congolese remained in need of European tutelage.

A small and growing nationalist movement emerged, and political activity increased. In January 1959 riots broke out in the colony's capital, alarming the administration. Having seen what was going on in Algeria at the time, the Belgian government hastily entered into discussions with Congolese leaders, wagering that the Congolese were so ill prepared that they would lean on the Belgians into the postcolonial period, allowing the latter to keep control.

Independence ceremonies on June 30, 1960, revealed that the Belgians were mistaken on many fronts. The contrasting speeches of those representing the outgoing and incoming powers said much about how differently Europeans and Africans viewed the nature of colonialism. When Belgium's King Baudouin condescendingly addressed the gathered plenipotentiaries that June day, he praised his infamous predecessor Leopold II:

> The independence of the Congo is the crowning of the work conceived by the genius of King Leopold II, undertaken by him with firm courage, and continued by Belgium with perseverance ... For eighty years Belgium has sent your land the best of her sons, first to deliver the Congo basin from the odious slave trade which was

decimating its population. Later to bring together the different tribes which, though former enemies, are now preparing to form the greatest of the Independent states of Africa ... It is your job, gentlemen, to show that we were right in trusting you.

The freshly elected prime minister, Patrice Lumumba, who had not originally been scheduled to speak, rose to deliver a stinging rebuke: "Men and women of the Congo, victorious fighters for independence ... We are proud of this struggle, of tears, of fire, and of blood, to the depths of our being, for it was a noble and just struggle, and indispensable to put an end to the humiliating slavery which was imposed upon us by force."

As noted, the young country descended into chaos within days. Katanga and South Kasai provinces seceded and Lumumba was murdered. Events demonstrated the inter-imperial webs that shaped the form of decolonization. One could say that the Belgians helped "disappear" Lumumba in January 1961, in a similar way to how French forces "disappeared" FLN fighters in Algeria. Some of the same French soldiers, who had been schooled in the 1946–1954 Indochina War and who had suffered *le mal jaune*, left Algeria to become mercenaries in service of the short-lived Katanga breakaway state, fighting the "good fight" where it could still be fought.

The problem of borders

To some, Lumumba was a martyr for the nationalist cause. In retrospect, it has become clearer that nationalist movements in the Congo and elsewhere represented "nations" only to a limited degree. Decolonization did not just have two "sides," colonialist and nationalist. As there were differences between Léopold Sedhar Senghor, Houphouet-Boigny, and Sékou Touré, and among Algerian or Indian nationalists, anticolonial leaders differed as to their means and goals. Men dominated political parties that purported to represent entire nations, including their women. Such movements often served as vehicles for the ambitions of narrow ethnic or regional interests. New national governments oppressed minorities, or were themselves minority-dominated, ruling over majority populations that were underrepresented.

Independent states in the Middle East also suffered the problem of borders that only dated back to the nineteenth century or to the post-World War I settlement. In their efforts to control as much land as possible, Arab leaders grabbed what they could, helping to establish states of great ethnic, national, and religious diversity. Iraq, for instance, was divided between Shia Arabs, Sunni Arabs, and Sunni Kurds. All newly independent states were kingdoms or republics run by a small elite, be it Saudi Arabia under the Saud ruling house, or the kingdom of Jordan under the Hashemites. Arab nationalism revealed itself in revolts against minorities and foreign influence.

States elsewhere grappled with the consequences of colonial borders and the challenge of minority populations. Kenya encompasses peoples of numerous ethnicities, including speakers of Nilotic, Afro-Asiatic, Bantu, and Indo-European languages. There are ethnic tensions between African, creole, and Indian-descended populations in the Caribbean region. India's partition, creating the nations of India and Pakistan, entailed deadly population transfers, and then Bangladesh emerged in a bloody 1971 war between Pakistan's eastern and western halves. Not everyone moved, which means that today India, which is overwhelmingly Hindu, is the world's fourth largest Muslim country by population because of its large Muslim minority. There continues a decades-long dispute between India and Pakistan over the disputed Kashmir region, which has included four wars – a clash between two countries that have been nuclear powers since the 1990s.

The problem of borders plagued sub-Saharan African states. Nigeria is divided not only between a Muslim north and a Christian and animist south, but also by hundreds of languages (from three different language families) and by numerous ethnicities and groups of diverse social, political, and cultural origins. All this was manifest after oil production took off in the mid-1960s. Nigeria sits on one of the world's largest oil reserves. In 1966 a rebellion of young military officers overthrew the constitutional government. This was followed in 1967 by the secession of the Ibo-dominated southeastern region, which called itself the Republic of Biafra. Civil war ensued (1967–1970) and regional tensions have existed ever since.

Apartheid South Africa

In 1960, the same year that numerous black African countries achieved independence, police in white-ruled South Africa fired on peaceful demonstrators, killing 69 people. It was a sign that South Africa's apartheid regime was not going anywhere anytime soon. In the years following the Nationalist Party's 1948 victory at the polls, that party put apartheid into place to "separate" the country's races in order to benefit the country's white minority. Continued oppression, including the 1956 extension of pass laws, provoked growing opposition, some of it violent. Laws requiring workers to carry passes to be stamped by (white) employers had existed as early as the eighteenth century in order to control the African population. The apartheid government regularized the practice – for men – and in 1956 extended the laws to cover women. By 1958 the PAC was organizing demonstrations to oppose these laws, and at Sharpeville in 1960, police opened fire on a peaceful march, killing 69. The government banned both the PAC and the ANC. South Africa became a republic and left the Commonwealth. Also in 1961, Nelson Mandela and others launched Umkhonto we Sizwe, or "Spear of the Nation," a militant branch of the ANC

Figure 8.1 Nelson Mandela burning his pass in front of press photographers, 1960. Source: Photographer unknown, Wikimedia Commons, https://commons.wikimedia.org/wiki/File:Mandela_burn_pass_1960.jpg.

that committed sabotage and bombed police stations, post offices, and power stations (Figure 8.1). The government tracked down and arrested Umkhonto we Sizwe leaders, including Mandela, and in 1964 held what came to be known as the Rivonia Trial, at which Mandela was sentenced to life imprisonment. The court allowed Mandela to make a lengthy statement. Only recently recovered in an audio version, Mandela's explanation of the situation and his motivations is a model of defiance and rectitude in the face of oppression. A black man under arrest and on trial in an apartheid state, before a white court and a white judge, Mandela concluded by saying:

> During my lifetime I have dedicated myself to this struggle of the African people. I have fought against White domination, and I have fought against Black domination. I have cherished the ideal of a democratic and free society in which all persons live together in harmony and with equal opportunities. It is an ideal which I hope to live for and to achieve. But if needs be, it is an ideal for which I am prepared to die.

South Africa's apartheid state dominated the region and interfered in neighboring countries. South Africa had taken over German South West Africa following World War I as a League of Nations mandate, but treated the territory as a colony and, at one point, even tried to annex it. South Africa aided Rhodesia after its unilateral break with the British in 1965, helped Portugal in its colonial wars by funneling men and money to uphold white rule in Angola and Mozambique, and launched military interventions into neighboring states in pursuit of its agenda.

The End of the Portuguese Empire

Assistance from South Africa was not going to save Portuguese rule anywhere in Africa. Overseas colonialism had become a central facet of Portuguese identity and a basis of the Salazar regime's legitimacy, and nationalist movements arrived late to Portugal's African territories. By 1961 anticolonial wars had broken out in Angola, Mozambique, and Portuguese Guinea. Taking advantage of Portuguese weakness, India's military marched on Portuguese Goa, Daman, and Diu in 1961, all of which fell after a brief fight. The Portuguese government viewed this as an attack on its own territory, Portugal having converted these outposts from colonies to overseas provinces. What is more, the Portuguese had ruled these territories for more than 400 years. People around the world applauded India's victory, while Portugal refused to recognize the outcome.

Portugal's wars in Africa dragged on as Amílcar Cabral and the African Party for the Independence of Guinea and Cape Verde, the Frente de Libertação de Moçambique (FRELIMO; Mozambique Liberation Front) and Resistência Nacional Moçambicana (RENAMO) in Mozambique, and several nationalist groups in Angola fought for freedom. The conflicts inflicted heavy losses on all sides. By the mid-1960s, one in every four Portuguese men of military age was being conscripted for four years' mandatory military service, and by 1973 11,000 people had died in the fighting, 122 per 100,000 of the population. (In comparison, during the contemporaneous Vietnam War, 58,000 Americans died out of a population of 212,000,000, or 27 per 100,000.) Many more Africans died or were wounded. No one knew better than the armed forces that the colonial wars were expensive and hopeless. After Salazar died in 1970, his successor, Marcello Caetano, continued his policies. The 1973 international oil crisis led to strikes and domestic discontent. African nationalists' continued success brought about the overthrow of Caetano's government by the Armed Forces Movement, ushering in democratic reforms. Thus not only did Mozambique, Angola, Guinea-Bissau, and Cape Verde achieve independence, but these developments led to the advent of democracy in Portugal in 1975, and in the same year the country's new government recognized the legitimacy of India's takeover of its former subcontinental exclaves.

Migration and Immigration

The independence of Portugal's colonies led to an exodus from Africa. The nearly 500,000 so-called *retornados* who "returned" to Portugal – many of whom had never lived there – increased Portugal's total population by an astonishing 5 percent.

Indeed, the decolonization era witnessed large, sustained movements of people. At the time of Indonesia's independence in 1949 some 300,000 Europeans and people of European descent left Indonesia and New Guinea to settle in the Netherlands, many of whom had been born in the Dutch East Indies and were arriving there for the first time. Several thousands of political refugees later fled Indonesia for the Netherlands in the tumultuous years following General Suharto's accession to power in 1965. The 1960s witnessed growing emigration from the Caribbean to Europe, and today there are almost as many Surinamese in the Netherlands as there are in Suriname. Within a month of the Congo's independence 38,000 of the approximately 88,000 Belgians living in the Belgian Congo had left; most others followed soon after. During good years Spain attracted immigrants from Argentina and other Spanish-speaking countries in the Americas, and significant numbers of Moroccan immigrants.

Such migration had analogs elsewhere. Britain's population changed significantly from the 1950s as a result of immigration from the British West Indies, south Asia (Pakistan and India), north Africa, the Middle East, Africa, Canada, and Australia and New Zealand. The British politician Enoch Powell's "Rivers of Blood" speech in Birmingham in 1968 cast immigration in apocalyptic terms, and restrictions on immigration followed in the 1970s. As noted, hundreds of thousands of *pieds noirs* left Algeria at the end of the war there, as did thousands of *harkis*, Algerians who had fought alongside the French. France drew on its connections to Morocco, Algeria, and Tunisia in subsequent years to attract cheap labor during the boom years from 1945 to 1975. There were large numbers of French people of Algerian descent who had been born in France, such as Azouz Begag, as well as former *pieds noirs* who had been born in Algeria but had relocated to France, like one of Begag's schoolteachers (discussed earlier).

Significant numbers of white colonials migrated within the European empires as the terrain shifted. Some Anglo-Indians ended up in British African colonies. Former British colonials sometimes bought retirement homes in Portugal under the Salazar regime, perhaps because they were comfortable with the government's authoritarianism or its outlook on Africa. When independence arrived, these white European colonials sometimes would leave a recently or soon to be "lost" area to relocate to a place where colonial rule endured, for as long as it lasted anyway, for example they might move from Katanga to Rhodesia, then from Rhodesia to South Africa.

Postcolonial immigration was not always to the former colonial master's territory. Large numbers of so-called *Gastarbeiter*, or "guest workers," in Germany were Spaniards, Portuguese, Turks, or Kurds. Only a tiny percentage of the large numbers of immigrants to Belgium were Congolese, most of them being Italian, Portuguese, or Maghrebi. More Congolese left central Africa for France than for Belgium, and by 1992, 52 percent of all the Congolese in Europe resided in the France and only 29 percent in Belgium. North Vietnam's victory over South Vietnam in 1975 was accompanied by the flight of thousands of Vietnamese, many of them anticommunists from the South who had aided the French or the Americans, or both. Further warfare in mainland southeast Asia in the late 1970s led to even greater numbers fleeing, many by boat. These Vietnamese "boat people" ended up in France; in nearby countries like Indonesia, Malaysia, or the Philippines; or even in Canada or the United States.

Forms of Decolonization

Equally important as colonial rule and resistance were the specific forms that decolonization took as many dozens of countries came into being as independent states in the twentieth century, while others lost empires. France and Zimbabwe are illustrative examples.

Changing ideas of citizenship in France resulted from the 1954–1962 conflict in Algeria and decolonization. French officials shifted from a legalistic view of Algeria and Algerians, and by extension France and the French, to a view centered on "origins." No longer would citizenship be blind to race or ethnicity: nationals had to be "Europeans"; Algerians were "Muslims" and "white" French men and women were not. The French considered European repatriates from Algeria as "French" and Muslims as "refugees." The use of familial language linked the *pieds noirs* to the French "family" but not Muslims or the radical OAS. An ethnic definition of citizenship is important because not all French were "white," and as immigration from non-European countries proceeded apace, in particular from the Maghreb, this tested the nature of the French Republic.

Southern Rhodesia was another case entirely. The white settlers who formed the base of Prime Minister Ian Smith's supporters wanted to keep their privileges and control over the country. There were profound suspicions that the British government was going to transition toward independence with a more representative government. As noted, Prime Minister Macmillan made his "Winds of Change" speech in 1960. Apartheid South Africa declared itself a republic in 1961. By 1964 Britain had already conceded to majority rule in many places, even in settler colonies, for example Kenya. White settlers in

Rhodesia, being in the minority, felt the need to seize control. Smith's government made a Unilateral Declaration of Independence in 1965, taking Rhodesia out of the British Commonwealth and setting off on its own.

Rhodesia's Unilateral Declaration of Independence led to a long-drawn-out war. Different groups fought against the government, donning the mantle of nationalism and anticolonialism. Unwilling to cede to reality, Smith's government characterized Africans fighting for their freedom as terrorists or "terrs." Embattled white settlers discovered that they could not control the vast hinterlands of the country. On a map of Africa, Southern Rhodesia (present-day Zimbabwe) might look small, especially in comparison to nearby Angola, Mozambique, or South Africa, but it is about the size of the US state of Montana. The regime poured money into defense, but sanctions and isolation by Britain and countries worldwide – not even South Africa recognized Rhodesia's white-ruled government – sapped its ability to prosecute the war. As the last quarter of the twentieth century dawned, it was anything but clear what would happen next.

Conclusion

Decolonization's second wave witnessed both peaceful handovers of power and violent anticolonial wars of independence, with the presence or absence of significant European settler populations playing a fundamental role. As formal empire broke down again and again, people struggled over what form decolonization and independence would take, and this was contingent on innumerable factors. Decolonization reshaped both European nation-states and former colonies, although it was newly independent states that suffered most acutely from political, ethnic, religious, gender, linguistic, and regional divisions as well as, oftentimes, the aftereffects of violent anticolonial wars of freedom. Nonetheless, this was a time of great optimism as many countries celebrated successful struggles to throw off foreign rule. That said, in many cases Europeans ceded ostensible political control while continuing to wield real power in myriad ways, and the extent to which the end of empire really meant an end to European overseas imperialism in all its aspects remained to be seen.

Citations

Page   Source
185   "The All-African People's Conference…" "Resolution of the All-African People's Conference at Accra, Ghana, on Imperialism and Colonialism, 1958," in *The Imperialism Reader: Documents and Readings on Modern Expansionism*, edited by Louis L. Snyder (Princeton: D. Van Nostrand, 1962), 174.

187 "Va-t-elle se portugaliser?" Quoted in Elizabeth Buettner, *Europe after Empire: Decolonization, Society, and Culture* (Cambridge: Cambridge University Press, 2016), 160.
188 "never accept any control..." Kautsky to State Department, despatch 764, January 22, 1954, document 755a.00/1-2254, National Archives and Records Administration, College Park, MD, USA.
189 "in the Americas." *The Sacred Mission of Civilization: To Which Peoples Should the Benefits Be Extended? The Belgian Thesis* (New York: Belgian Government Information Center, 1953).
191–2 "historically unthinkable..." Quoted in Frederick Cooper, *Colonialism in Question: Theory, Knowledge, History* (Berkeley: University of California Press, 2005), 228
192 "not a single indigenous organization..." David Van Reybrouck, *Congo: Une Histoire* [Congo: A History], translated by Isabelle Rosselin (Arles, France: Actes Sud, 2012), 249 (my translation).
192–3 "The independence of the Congo..." "Marred," *Guardian*, July 1, 1960, at https://www.theguardian.com/world/1960/jul/01/congo, accessed October 3, 2017.
193 "Men and women..." Quoted in Suzanne McIntire, with William E. Burns, *Speeches in World History* (New York: Facts on File, 2009), 438.
195 "During my lifetime..." Nelson Mandela, *No Easy Walk to Freedom* (Oxford: Heinemann, 1965), 189.

Bibliography

Betts, Raymond F. *France and Decolonisation 1900–1960*. New York: St. Martin's Press, 1991.
Buettner, Elizabeth. *Europe after Empire: Decolonization, Society, and Culture*. Cambridge: Cambridge University Press, 2016.
Elliott, Duong Van Mai. *The Sacred Willow: Four Generations in the Life of a Vietnamese Family*. Oxford: Oxford University Press, 1999.
Gerard, Emmanuel, and Bruce Kuklick. *Death in the Congo: Murdering Patrice Lumumba*. Cambridge, MA: Harvard University Press, 2015.
Horne, Alistair. *A Savage War of Peace: Algeria 1954–1962* (1977). New York: New York Review of Books, 2006.
Mandela, Nelson. *No Easy Walk to Freedom*. Oxford: Heinemann, 1965.
Namikas, Lise. *Battleground Africa: Cold War in the Congo, 1960–1965*. Washington, DC: Woodrow Wilson Center Press, 2013.
Olson, James Stuart, and Randy W. Robert. *Where the Domino Fell: America and Vietnam 1945–2010*. 6th ed. Malden, MA: Wiley Blackwell, 2014.
Shepard, Todd. *The Invention of Decolonization: The Algerian War and the Remaking of France*. Ithaca, NY: Cornell University Press, 2008.
Thompson, Leonard. *A History of South Africa*. 3rd ed. New Haven: Yale University Press, 2000.

9

Empire After Imperialism
1975–1999 and Beyond

> *Berlin of 1884 was effected through the sword and the bullet. But the night of the sword and the bullet was followed by the morning of the chalk and the blackboard. The physical violence of the battlefield was followed by the psychological violence of the classroom.*
>
> Ngũgĩ wa Thiong'o, *Decolonising the Mind* (1986)

In May 2012 a settlement was reached allowing male Sikh New York City transit workers to wear the distinctive Sikh turban without an identifying Metropolitan Transportation Authority (MTA) logo on the front. This reversed a policy imposed after the September 11, 2001, attacks on New York and Washington, DC, which identified – branded, some said – Sikhs as MTA workers. The settlement echoed a decades-old ruling in English courts. In Wolverhampton, England, in 1959 G. S. Sagar, a Sikh, was turned down for a bus driver position because he insisted on wearing his turban rather than the uniform cap required of all city bus drivers. The Sikh leader Sohan Singh Jolly threatened to commit suicide by self-immolation if the rule banning turbans (and beards) was not lifted. A group of Sikh men argued that the turban was essential to the Sikh religion. The dispute lasted years before being resolved in favor of the Sikhs.

Such legal cases can be ranked as victories for religious tolerance and civil rights, and against workplace discrimination. They also reveal profound and unanticipated cultural effects of European imperialism. Today's distinctive Sikh turban is not mentioned in early accounts of Sikhism, which emerged as a religion in sixteenth-century India as a syncretic faith combining aspects of Islam and Hinduism. Sikhism developed a number of rules, including the requirement

---

European Overseas Empire, 1879–1999: A Short History, First Edition. Matthew G. Stanard.
© 2018 John Wiley & Sons, Inc. Published 2018 by John Wiley & Sons, Inc.

that males' hair remain unshorn; that alcohol, tobacco, or meat butchered in the Muslim fashion be prohibited; and that Sikhs take the surname Singh. Although the early Sikh community was generally pacifist, persecution at the hands of Muslim Mughals led to their become more militant. Despite their having been defeated by the EIC in 1849, the British believed Sikhs to be good warriors and recruited them as soldiers. During the 1857 mutiny, Sikh troops proved themselves willing and effective soldiers against rebellious Muslim and Hindu sepoys.

Sikhs did have long hair, and their turbans distinguished them from Muslim and Hindu soldiers in the British Raj. Because they were neither Hindu nor Muslim, the British felt more confident using them in cases where sectarianism might undermine the steadfastness of colonial troops. The turban became part of Sikh regiments' uniforms, and the British reliance on Sikhs grew, so that, while they made up only 1 percent of India's population, Sikhs eventually constituted some 20 percent of the colony's soldiers. By the time British rule ended in 1947, the turban had become synonymous with Sikhism.

Such examples of the cultural impact of the colonial situation can be multiplied, from the global reach of football (soccer) to the many millions of people outside Portugal who speak Portuguese, to the Basilica of Our Lady of Peace in Yamoussoukro, Côte d'Ivoire, which by many measures is the world's largest church building. Although by the late 1970s the world seemed to have become "postcolonial" – for most formerly colonized territories had achieved independence – it became clear that political independence was only one facet of freedom from the colonial yoke. Although the transfer of power from foreign to native rule entailed political independence, forms of colonialism endured, for instance in the configurations of preferential trade agreements, financial dependency, cultural influence, military agreements, even humanitarian interventions. Cold War interference by the United States, the Soviet Union, and their allies and proxies circumscribed the freedom of newly self-governing states and their peoples. The cultural and social effects of imperialism also endured, many of which have lasted longer than the period of formal colonial rule. Greater distance from the past shows that, while colonialism's nonpolitical effects were great, as seen, for example, in the identification of Sikhs with turbans, in important ways the colonial era represented just one stage, albeit an important one, in the longer histories of Africans, Indians, and others of the formerly colonized world. The book closes with this chapter, but it is a conclusion that does not conclude as people worldwide continue to grapple with imperialism's legacies.

The "Confetti" of Empire

With Portugal's colonies achieving independence in 1975, Papua New Guinea breaking free from Australia, and most of the Comoros from France, the number of non-self-determining colonized territories across the globe had shrunk to a very small number. Many of these were islands, the so-called confetti of empire. Their number continued to shrink as territories negotiated independence, which took many years in some cases, facilitated by the United Nations' Special Committee on Non-Self-Governing Territories. Djibouti on the Horn of Africa separated from France in 1977, and Belize and Brunei from Britain in 1981 and 1984, respectively. Timor-Leste (East Timor), which broke from Portugal in 1975, was invaded almost immediately by its larger neighbor Indonesia, leading to over two decades of occupation. UN involvement led to Timor-Leste's liberation by 2002 and an ongoing United Nations presence in what is one of the world's youngest countries.

In some cases territories opted for continued or even closer or renewed association with the metropole. When Comoros declared independence from France in 1975, the island of Mayotte went its own way, eventually becoming a French overseas department. Britain still holds islands in the Indian Ocean, in the Caribbean (for instance, Monserrat), and in the Atlantic, including Bermuda; Saint Helena, Ascension, and Tristan da Cunha; South Georgia and the South Sandwich Islands; and the Falkland Islands. Such territories in the Pacific include French Polynesia and New Caledonia (French), the Pitcairn Islands (British), American Samoa and Guam (US), and Tokelau (New Zealand). These are remote, sparsely populated places. The Pitcairn Islands, for example, are populated by only about 50 people, most of whom are descendants of those involved in the mutiny on the *Bounty*.

At century's end, the last European colonial holdings in east Asia disappeared. The United Kingdom turned over Hong Kong in 1997, and the Portuguese gave up Macau in 1999 after nearly four and a half centuries of rule there. Both became Special Administrative Regions of the People's Republic of China. Today the only European landholdings on mainland Asia, Africa, or North and South America are French Guiana (part of France since 1946) and Spanish Ceuta and Melilla in north Africa.

White Rule in Southern Africa

The arrival of self-determination in southern Africa was complex and difficult. By 1975 the Portuguese had gone (as they had from Guinea-Bissau and the Cape Verde Islands in west Africa), and the only parts of sub-Saharan Africa where white minority rule persisted were Rhodesia, South Africa, and South West Africa. Rhodesia's white minority government under Ian Smith had issued a Unilateral Declaration of Independence in 1965 to retain white minority rule, and war followed, which lasted from 1965 to 1979. Rhodesia's isolation heightened after neighboring Mozambique and nearby Angola achieved independence, after which Smith's government prosecuted the war not to win but to secure a position of strength for negotiations. Those negotiations led to the emergence of independent Zimbabwe, and Robert Mugabe, a freedom fighter and leader of the Zimbabwe African National Union, was elected in 1980.

Rather than attaining freedom, however, Zimbabweans exchanged one form of minority rule and oppression for another. Multiple groups had fought for independence, but the leading postindependence political parties did not represent all people in the country, not least of all women, since anticolonialist and nationalist groups were overwhelmingly male dominated. The dictatorship that developed saw white minority rule replaced by minority rule under Mugabe, who ruled Zimbabwe as a dictator until 2017.

Despite events in Rhodesia, white minority rule endured in South Africa, the continent's largest economy, where apartheid survived. A towering figure of the anti-apartheid movement was Nelson Mandela but, considering that he was imprisoned for decades from 1964, other factors precipitating apartheid's demise must be taken into account. By the late 1960s, it appeared that the South African government had the situation well in hand and that Afrikaner and white domination would persist indefinitely. Mandela and other key ANC leaders were in prison. In 1970 the government passed the Bantu Homelands Citizenship Act, denying black South Africans citizenship (although no other nations recognized this). In 1978 B. J. Vorster became prime minister, a man who had been interned during World War II for his overt Nazi sympathies. South Africa controlled South West Africa as a mandate but ran it as a colony; it attempted to annex it and relented only in the face of international pressure. South Africa enjoyed one of the world's highest standards of living – but only if you were white. The ruling party cracked down on dissent and imposed terrible burdens on the country's black population. In her memoir *Strikes Have Followed Me All My Life* (1989), the South African labor leader Emma Mashinini recalled the harsh prison conditions and the psychological torture she suffered at the hands of her warders. Subjected to prolonged solitary confinement, she forgot her own daughter's name at one point, which traumatized her: "I struggled and struggled. I would fall down and actually weep with the effort of remembering the name of my daughter."

Several factors, including labor union activity by Mashinini and others, put the apartheid regime under pressure. South Africa suffered the world economic downturn of the late 1970s. In 1980 Rhodesia became Zimbabwe. By the 1980s hundreds of thousands of black South African men and women were trapped in low-paying work and deplorable living conditions from which they were unable to escape, trapped by their circumstances and by whites' monopoly of power. Growing pressure on land resources, deleterious legislation, stricter police controls, and low mine wages led to the proletarianization and concentration of blacks in densely populated and undesirable areas such as the Rand mine compounds and Cape Town hostels. Government crackdowns on township protests in the mid-1980s led foreign nations to impose sanctions. Over time, demographic and other pressures became evident. Because the country's black population grew faster than its white population, if its economy was to survive, black Africans had to be empowered as consumers and producers. All the while, anti-apartheid leaders continued the pressure, under Mandela's leadership, albeit from a remove. In 1989, the year the Cold War ended in Europe, the conservative Nationalist Party leader F. W. de Klerk became prime minister. Nationalist Party principals believed that any communist support for the ANC would melt away, and that they might lose support in the West. They decided to act while still in a strong position.

Thus a confluence of factors drove Nationalist Party leaders to open negotiations before events got ahead of them. In 1990 South Africa – under great international pressure – left South West Africa, which became independent Namibia. De Klerk's government released Mandela provisionally, then completely, legalized the ANC and the PAC, and acceded to negotiations that led to the country's first democratic elections in 1994. Amazingly, South Africa did not erupt into civil conflict. A Truth and Reconciliation Commission and a large Reconstruction and Development Programme aided in the transition. South Africa emerged as a democracy and remains Africa's largest economic power, even while it is plagued by persistent problems including racism, crime, low levels of education, an HIV/AIDS epidemic, slowing economic growth, and the emergence of a one-party state under the ANC.

Another major development of 1994 was a genocide in Rwanda. The populations of neighboring Rwanda and Burundi, both former Belgian mandates, were approximately 84 percent "Hutu," 15 percent "Tutsi," and 1 percent "Twa." Hutu and Tutsi designations were changeable, but the German and then the Belgian authorities had reinforced distinctions between them over the decades by labeling people as one or the other, by conducting censuses using the designations, and by requiring identity cards indicating ethnicity, all of which had the effect of "fixing" ethnic identity. The Belgians also elevated Tutsis to positions of authority, which stoked resentment among the Hutus.

In Rwanda, Hutus had rebelled against Tutsis since 1959. Tutsis remained in power in Burundi – often through severe repression – from the 1960s to 1993, when elections brought the Hutus to power. Two major results of Hutu–Tutsi competition over the years were tens of thousands of victims of ethnic killings as Hutus and Tutsis vied for power in both countries, and large numbers of refugees, both internally displaced persons and others living in neighboring Congo and Uganda. Some included armed refugee militias such as the Tutsi Rwandan Patriotic Front (RPF) in Uganda. Adding to tensions was competition over resources, especially land, since Rwanda and Burundi were two of the most densely populated countries of the world. There were also growing calls for democratization.

In April 1994 the Rwandan president (and Hutu) Juvenal Habyarimana's plane was shot down as he returned from a regional security and peace conference in Uganda, also killing Burundi's president, Cyprien Ntaryamira (a Hutu), who was on board. This sparked a genocide in Rwanda. Hutu extremists in Rwanda who were intent on eliminating the Tutsi presence in the country organized and instigated the killing of Tutsis and of moderate Hutus. Hutu paramilitary groups like the Interahamwe played a leading role in the genocide. The RPF, led by Paul Kagame, fought toward the capital, Kigali, which led to more violence and pressure on Hutus there and elsewhere and accelerated the killing. In response to US State Department official Prudence Bushnell's plea that the RPF halt its advance, Kagame replied, "Madame, they're killing my people." After 100 days, the RPF took Rwanda in July 1994, ending the genocide. By that time, Hutus had murdered some 800,000 people.

What Did Decolonization Really Mean?

Nkrumah, Nasser, Gandhi, Lumumba, Mandela, and other such leaders instilled fear in the hearts of Western conservatives but inspired hope among so many more. Steve Thomas, an American soldier fighting in South Vietnam against the Viet Minh in the late 1960s, questioned the entire enterprise when Ho Chi Minh's death was announced in 1969. He thought that the South Vietnamese would greet the communist dictator's demise with celebration. Instead, he found villagers mourning Ho's passing.

The array of new countries emerging from oppressive colonial rule raised expectations about the future. Some called the 1960s "the decade of Africa." New history writing reinforced hope, helping to set up unrealistic expectations through skewed depictions of the past. During the colonial era, many Western scholars and writers had denigrated non-Western societies and cultures and their histories. Now the pendulum swung back as writers of fiction, historians, and other scholars idealized precolonial history when writing about Asian, African, and American pasts. As the 1970s unfolded into the 1980s, historians and others discovered that the picture of colonialism, late colonialism, decolonization, and their aftermath were more complex than previously thought.

Decolonization's second wave from the 1960s to the mid-1970s was a period of great achievement and liberation. Yet, from the mid-1970s, hopes began to dim. The exodus of Vietnamese boat people that started in 1978–1979 and continued for years kept the traumatic legacies of empire in Asia in the headlines. Many had called the 1960s the decade of Africa, yet by 1970 about half of Africa's independent states had already fallen under some kind of military rule. Ethiopia's famine in 1983–1985 brought mismanagement and human rights abuses by African governments to global attention. There were several reasons for Africa's problems from the 1970s. First, parliamentary and administrative institutions had failed to overcome destructive regionalism or a threat of separatism – for example, the case of Nigeria and the Biafran War of 1967–1970 – or state parliamentary and administrative institutions had been unable to prevent a collapse of political power into intrigue and corruption. Second, popular discontent, largely economic in origin, had reached a breaking point that undermined law and order. Third, in weak countries, foreign interests or foreign governments sometimes provoked a change of government in their favor. Fourth, personal ambition for power and privilege, backed by various support – from clans, particular elites, tribal groupings – undermined good governance. All this did not make African states uniquely unstable, especially in light of some of European history in the twentieth century. The German military and government collapsed in 1918 at the end of World War I, and within a matter of years Germany had fallen under a totalitarian dictatorship. Russia entered into a brutal revolution and then civil war, beginning in 1917, that led to the imposition of a violent, one-party rule for most of the twentieth century. During the interwar years, Austria, Poland, Hungary, Romania, and other eastern European states all slid into dictatorships of one form or another. Both Spain and Portugal were ruled by repressive dictatorships from the 1930s to the mid-1970s.

As the years unfolded and more countries achieved independence only to suffer ongoing problems – many seemingly rooted in colonial-era relations – more and more people asked themselves what exactly decolonization was and whether it had really happened. "Decolonization" initially referred to the political independence of colonies from a controlling imperial metropole. As discussed, this traditional interpretation was captured in the British expression "transfer of power," referring to the idea of the colonial authorities bestowing power on recognized indigenous political leaders in a handover. This was manifested in events held to mark the transfer of power, at which the flag of the imperial power was lowered, followed by a flag raising for the newly independent nation-state. Most decolonization, in the strict political sense of the term, occurred from around the time of India's and Pakistan's independence in 1947 to the end of the Portuguese empire around 1975. Thus "postcolonial" refers, again strictly speaking, to the period after around 1975, with, as we saw, the few exceptions of the confetti of empire. But "postcolonial" also refers to something else culturally. Decolonization occurred in different ways when it came to economics, culture, language, and society.

As the years passed, it became evident that, in many ways, former colonies – their economies, societies, cultures, and even people's minds – remained "colonized." Newly independent states were products of the colonial era, from their borders to their forms of government, to their historical narratives of national independence. Countries came to define themselves against the colonial experience, and leaders used colonialism to mobilize their populations. In Mozambique, for example, after 1975 FRELIMO created myths to bolster the nation and its own legitimacy. This encouraged the creation of "useful" histories that cast anyone who had been on the fence during the country's anticolonial conflicts as a potential collaborator. "The myth of the guerrilla nationalist was created as an attempt to generate new political identities during the first years of independence," as the war against Portugal became the nation's defining moment. This ignored distinct ethnicities, different experiences, and varied reactions to the Portuguese colonial regime. Another example of such mobilization around anticolonialism took place in Algeria, where the anticolonial struggle against France essentially became the basis for national identity. This was most egregious in Zimbabwe, where the corrupt dictator Robert Mugabe held power for years, in part by using anticolonialism as a rallying cry while attacking his own country's people, both blacks and the few remaining whites, for example through land seizures. Frantz Fanon had predicted as much. In *The Wretched of the Earth* (1961), he had warned against the national middle class of the emerging independent countries, saying that it would simply replace the colonial class it had displaced. The national middle class would not act as a transformative force, rather would perpetuate aspects of the colonial situation that benefited itself. Thus the new independent bourgeoisie would be incapable of leading a thorough revolution that resulted in real independence and transformation.

Legacies of colonial rule

It also became evident by the late twentieth century that imperialism had profoundly remade the world's populations. Of course the populations of European descent in Canada, Australia, and New Zealand had grown tremendously by the second half of the twentieth century, through both natural growth and immigration. Although there was an outflow of European settlers in many parts of south Asia and Africa, there remained a presence, in particular missionaries and the white populations in Zimbabwe and South Africa. In the latter, people of Indian descent made up a major part of the country's population, as they did in Uganda, as the world was brutally reminded when the Ugandan military ruler Idi Amin expelled the country's entire Indian population in 1972. Or consider Guyana, formerly British Guiana, where, on terminating the system of indenture in 1919, the British promised all so-called coolies passage back "home." Many boats transported laborers back to India, the last of which, the MV *Resurgent*, left in 1955. Still, "only about one quarter of indentured servants taken to the West Indies ever returned to India."

Another result of the late colonial state and decolonization was a legacy of violence. Long histories of conflict and destruction burdened many newly emergent states. As we have seen, India's botched partition killed hundreds of thousands. Algeria's 1954–1962 war against France killed more than one million Algerians. Ethiopia, conquered in a horrific Italian invasion in 1935–1936 and liberated during another war in 1941, suffered hundreds of thousands of deaths. Vietnam endured war from 1945 to 1979. Portuguese Guinea, Angola, and

Mozambique were at war with Portugal from 1961 to 1974, and the civil wars in Angola and Mozambique that followed continued for years. Zimbabwe's war of independence lasted from 1965 to 1980. South West Africa suffered numerous interventions before 1990. The list goes on.

Of course there were at least quasi-positive legacies, for instance built infrastructure: railway lines, ports, hospitals, schools, buildings, and roads. Another was the development and diffusion of health and medical knowledge, much of which had emerged along with and as a product of colonialism: a better understanding of germs, psychiatric illnesses, and endemic diseases like malaria and trypanosomiasis; better vaccines and other prophylactics; knowledge about sterility, pre- and postnatal care; and so forth. In some places this led to a population explosion. Whether or not Western development actually led to the so-called Green Revolution, Africa and Asia in the twentieth century escaped the Malthusian trap just as Europe had done so in the late eighteenth century. By 2017 India's population surpassed 1.3 billion, while in Nigeria the population increased from 17 million in the 1890s to 39 million at independence, to 182 million in 2017.

International borders were another enduring colonial legacy. It is often said that the world's nation-state system resulted from the Peace of Westphalia which ended the Thirty Years' War (1618–1648). As important, if not more, are the expectations and norms that resulted from European imperialism and the end of empire in the twentieth century. Most present-day international frontiers date back to borders either drawn up by European powers following their conquest of different areas of Asia and Africa or negotiated at the time of decolonization, and numerous border conflicts have roots in this more recent era. The decades-old Arab–Israeli conflict originated in the Ottoman empire's collapse, modern Jewish nationalism, the Sykes–Picot Agreement, British promises to Zionists, and the Palestinian Mandate. The entire modern map of the Middle East dates back to World War I. Large African states in which people of multiple ethnicities or religions were lumped together by colonial-era borders have threatened to break up, as in Nigeria during the 1967–1970 Biafran War. Sudan, which divided into Sudan and South Sudan in 2011, has in many ways ceased to exist as a state, as have Libya and Somalia. The Democratic Republic of the Congo, which suffered devastating civil wars in the 1990s and early 2000s, also no longer exists as a viable state.

All this said, the problem of (colonial) borders lumping together disparate ethnicities, religions, language groups, and even nations is not unique to former colonies, as some would have it. This line of thinking implies that other national frontiers, say of the United States or in Europe, are "natural" or at least historically less problematic. The opposite is true. Spain's and Portugal's shared border has remained unchanged for about 500 years, longer than any other national frontier in Europe. It is a rare exception. Most European borders have been subject to innumerable, more often than not bloody, changes over time. Britain's borders, for example, have changed numerous times in the twentieth century alone, and, given the possibility of Scottish independence, may yet change again. As noted, Spain today still includes populations – some say "nations" – who speak different languages. There was no "natural" form for a united Germany when it emerged in 1871, and Germans had debated a *Kleindeutsch* versus a *Grossdeutsch* solution to German unification for years. Moreover, Germany's borders have changed drastically between 1871 and today. Although many characterize civil conflicts in south Asia, the Middle East, and Africa as eternal communal conflicts among backward peoples – as opposed to peace in the more enlightened West – until very recently, armed conflict was perennial in Western countries, from endemic warfare in Europe to the centuries-long murder and expulsion of native peoples across the Americas. A major reason why Europe has remained peaceful in the latter half of the twentieth century – with the exception of Yugoslavia in the 1990s and, more recently, the conflict between Ukraine and Russia – is exactly because of war and ethnic cleansing, from the Spanish monarchy's expulsion of Jews and Muslims in 1492 to postwar population exchanges after 1918, to the massive forced migrations and genocidal killings of World War II.

Neo-imperialism's many guises

The continuation of colonialism after formal political independence is achieved is often termed neocolonialism or neo-imperialism. Politically, the reason so many governments of former colonies resemble those of their former metropoles – parliamentary democracies, at least on paper – is because of British, French, Belgian, and Portuguese rule and decolonization. That so many former colonies maintained close relations with the former metropole is indicated by the fact that France even had a name for its relations with former African colonies, *Françafrique*. France's relations were at times blatantly neocolonialist, as the goal of successive governments was to maintain influence in Africa to sustain France's global position despite not having a formal empire. The postcolonial era witnessed innumerable military interventions by erstwhile colonial powers during the Cold War. The United States cultivated relations with Pakistan, Iran, and the Congo under Mobutu Sese Seko. The Soviet Union sponsored or supported Egypt, communist Vietnam, and Haile Mariam Mengistu's regime in Ethiopia from 1976 to 1991. Cold War rivalry led to interventions, from the Cubans in Angola to China's invasion of Vietnam in 1979, undermining development efforts.

Neocolonialism has also been economic. Some former colonies remained economically dependent upon their former colonial power. European states, recognizing the fragile nature of many now independent former colonies, negotiated support for them. The 1962 Yaoundé Conference of former colonial powers and African nations, for instance, arranged "reverse preferences" whereby European countries agreed to buy primary products at certain prices. European nations also promised money for newly independent countries. The 1975 Lomé Convention included an expanded number of former European powers (nine) and 46 former colonies, coming together to agree on trade arrangements and financial support.

That the economies of former colonies remained dependent on their former metropoles into the postcolonial era is unsurprising because their development over decades had been oriented toward the latter's economies. Continued investment in economies in Asia and Africa largely went to agriculture and primary materials extraction in what some have called "underdevelopment." This also played to some strengths, because the colonial powers bequeathed infrastructure to extract raw materials – as opposed to infrastructure that might facilitate the movement of people, encourage industrialism, or foster intellectual capital development. Partly as a result, Africa remains today what it was 200 years ago: a continent of mainly agriculturalists and pastoralists. In western Europe, by contrast, the percentage of the working population engaged in agriculture, forestry, and fishing declined between 1954 and 1992 from 28.2 percent to 5.2 percent; those in industry declined from 37.1 to 28.9 percent; while the service sector ballooned from 34.7 percent in 1954 to 65.9 percent in 1992. In contrast, in 2006 most African workers were still agriculturalists: Côte d'Ivoire (68 percent); Ethiopia (80 percent); Rwanda (90 percent); Burundi (90 percent); Tanzania (80 percent); Ghana (60 percent).

During the 1970s the world was caught in a serious economic downturn, and many former colonies' economies were still dominated by export-oriented industries that suffered greatly any time there were significant price drops for raw goods. Some former colonies did excel, as in South Korea, while others took collective measures to address economic challenges, including the risk associated with dependence on exports and commodities. In 1975, for example, 16 West African states picked up on the theme of the European Economic Community and came together to form the Economic Community of West African States (ECOWAS). The problem was that, unlike in Europe, member states traded little with each other. The drop in global commodity prices coupled with the oil shock created a double whammy.

Colonial states that Europeans had created in Africa were not good at much besides gatekeeping. Europeans had had limited goals for their colonial states – conquest, administration, and the extraction of natural resources for profit – and so they carried out limited functions. A colony was a strong state in the sense that it had a military that could defeat organized resistance, backed up by a military power in Europe. Beyond this, the colonial state controlled flows of investment from the metropole to the colony, the purchase of raw materials, and outflows from the colony, as well as people traveling in and out of the colony. In other words, colonial states did not reach very deep into African societies and were not firmly rooted in them. But, whereas in earlier times it was clearly the European power that was in charge of the gatekeeper state, now who was in control could not be taken for granted. The goal was to be in control in order to determine where assets went, which set the stage for corruption, clientelism, and civil conflicts over control of the levers of power.

Culturally, the former colonial powers continued to exercise influence over south Asia and Africa, sometimes deliberately, such as in the French promotion of *Francophonie* or the lusophone Comunidade dos Países de Língua Portuguesa. The British maintained political ties not only through the queen remaining head of state in many instances, but also by transforming the former empire into the Commonwealth. But the Commonwealth was not only a political entity – it also fostered intercultural cooperation, and it perpetuated Britain's influence by acting as a continuation of the British empire. The Commonwealth Games, for example, rival the Olympics for their global reach. Whereas this effort was particularly forthcoming from the British, the French, and the Portuguese, it was less so with the former colonial powers Germany, Italy, Belgium, and the Netherlands. These countries tended to promote cultural cooperation more generally, for instance Germany's Goethe Institute.

At a cultural level neocolonialism was often indirect, for example the image of the Sikh turban (discussed earlier). There is the global importance of football and cricket, the popularity of foods with European connections such as bánh mì (*baguette*), which is popular in Vietnam. Language is one of the most evident signs of long-lasting cultural effects. European tongues, primarily French, British, and Portuguese, became lingua franca, as many newly independent countries were divided by dozens of languages, as in India, or even by hundreds, as in Nigeria or the Congo. As Ngũgĩ wa Thiong'o observed, "The choice of language and the use to which language is put is central to a people's definition of themselves in relation to their natural and social environment, indeed in relation to the entire universe." The percentage of people who could speak French in francophone sub-Saharan Africa increased after 1960, the year in which most French colonies and the Belgian Congo received their independence. When colonial restrictions on education were lifted around 1960, more people could go to school and for longer, and many people sought to learn French, English, or Portuguese to better themselves.

The spread of Christianity had long-lasting consequences. This was more marked in those parts of the world where there were fewer large-scale organized religions before the advent of European colonial rule, as in Muslim-majority north Africa, where Christianity made little headway. The same was true in India where, as in north Africa and the Middle East, the colonial power decided not to try and impose its religions and threaten colonial stability. But in other places Christianity advanced substantially. In Vietnam, a sizable Catholic minority continues to exist. In British white settler colonies, Christianity became the dominant religion and culture. In much of sub-Saharan Africa, Christianity found millions of converts as well, both Protestant and Catholic. Some say that, while the nineteenth century witnessed Europe's evangelization of Africa, the twenty-first century will witness Africa's evangelization of Europe, considering the strength of Christian churches in Africa and the secularization of European society.

That the transfer of power often led to ostensible rather than real independence should not obscure unexpected yet important ways in which real decolonization proceeded apace. Many dominions of the British empire gained self-rule earlier in the twentieth century, but it was only in the 1960s that they achieved real independence, and only in the 1970s and 1980s that they moved away from Britain. It was then that places like Australia and Canada saw a decline in the popularity of Britain, a decline in British immigration, and controversy over loyalty to the British monarchy, for instance at the time of royal visits. There was also a resurgence of attention to indigenous peoples in former dominions. The accelerated flow of ideas and communications, especially after 1989, facilitated change. Trade connections with Britain weakened. In 1961 Britain applied to join the European Economic Community, marking a turn, of sorts, to Europe and away from empire. And new nations did develop growing degrees of real political independence, which could be seen at the United Nations, which increased in membership from some 50 members to nearly 200, making it much less of a Western club.

Colonialism and Knowledge

With time and reflection it became clear that modern imperialism affected what we know and even how we know it. The entire imperial project was premised on the superiority of Western culture, knowledge, and learning, and this permeated education and thought to the detriment of non-European cultures. As Ngũgĩ wa Thiong'o puts it in this chapter's epigraph, violence allowed for physical conquest, but it was what followed – Eurocentric education, proselytization, cultural denigration – that caused the greatest harm. Or, as the first president of Guinea, Ahmed Sékou Touré, put it:

> While we were learning to appreciate [French] culture and to know the names of its most eminent interpreters, we were gradually losing the traditional notions of our own culture and the memory of those who had thrown lustre upon it. How

many of our young schoolchildren who can quote Bossuet, are ignorant of the life of El Hadj Omar? How many African intellectuals have unconsciously deprived themselves of the wealth of our culture so as to assimilate the philosophic concepts of a Descartes or a Bergson?

The structures of Western colonialism included knowledge formation, and this had injected a long-lasting Eurocentrism into the production of knowledge.

History writing empowered certain forms of knowledge and knowledge production and discounted or even excluded others. Following Western traditions, history writing has long depended on official accounts and archives as its main sources, with memoirs, unofficial reports, newspapers, and other such documents providing additional sources. This ingrained official, colonialist views into our knowledge of the past, and ignored the views of people who were illiterate or powerless, and often of women. An example is the exclusion of female voices in the history of *sati* in the British Raj: we know about the practice (and British attempts to abolish it) not through the voices of Indian women who had engaged in or witnessed it, but through official reports. In the postcolonial era the school of subaltern studies revealed and emphasized that the discourse of history derived from written archives, that is, the discourses of a literate, often official elite, and hence marginalized the illiterate, the masses: "It is important to recognize that the critique of the West is not confined to the colonial record of exploitation and profiteering but extends to the disciplinary knowledge and procedures it authorized – above all, the discipline of history." Because history traditionally empowers certain kinds of knowledge and not others, it must be subjected to postcolonial criticism as well.

The nationalist agendas of liberation movements and the governments that followed them depended in part on nationalist historiographies affirming not only the existence of the nation but also its deep historical roots. History writing became enmeshed with nationalist discourses, for instance in India, where history entrenched and legitimized the "Indian nation" – and thereby its elites – even though the Indian nation-state is a very recent phenomenon. Thus the 1857 Sepoy Rebellion became India's First War of Independence even though it was in reality an anticolonial revolt. The same is true in the case of African history, a field that hardly even existed during the colonial era because most academics who studied Africa (mainly Europeans) believed that the continent and its peoples had no "history." After independence and as history writing developed, and as more Africans gained doctorates in the field, more nationalist histories emerged to validate the nations. That this occurred is hardly surprising: the origin of national history writing in Europe saw scholars valorizing the nation through scholarship, for instance Jules Michelet's monumental *Histoire de France* (1833–1867). It has been a challenge to disengage from these tendencies and to recognize that not everything in the precolonial past was admirable, that some "nations" had not existed then, and that the colonial era was indeed an important episode for non-Europeans, albeit only one in what were much longer histories.

Even well-intentioned, dedicated scholars from former colonies revealed "colonized" mindsets when it came to writing. During the colonial era and into the decolonization period, many had seen socialism generally, and Marxist socialism specifically, as a liberationist ideology. Yet Marxist and Western historiography interpreted history from a framework that took Western history as the norm. Marx himself developed his supposedly all-encompassing theories based on a partial reading of history that focused overwhelmingly on the West. As Dipesh Chakrabarty puts it, "There is a peculiar way in which all these other histories [of other world areas] tend to become variations on a master narrative that could be called 'the history of Europe.'" In the case of India, Marxist history always cast India as backward and its history as one of "lacks": it had never experienced a bourgeois revolution, for example, a step that was regarded as essential in the Marxist view of history. Key terms that historians use reflexively and with little thought, such as "bourgeoisie," "revolution," and "modern," are all Western constructions, and as such need to be taken apart and reconsidered when writing the history of peoples across the world on their own terms. In this sense Marxist interpretations have not been liberating.

European cultures and empire

It has long been understood that colonialism reshaped non-European cultures, but only more recently has it been recognized that it remade Europe as well. Both can be seen in how imperialism figures as a prominent theme in the literature of both colonizer and colonized. In this book, we have had glimpses of *Palace Walk* by the Nobel Prize winner Naguib Mahfouz, of *Things Fall Apart* by Chinua Achebe (who was awarded the Man Booker International Prize in 2007), and of *A Bend in the River* by V. S. Naipaul, another Nobel Prize winner (in 2001). In 1983 Léopold Sédar Senghor, poet, author of "Poème à mon frère blanc" (Poem to My White Brother), and first president of independent Senegal, was elected to the Académie Française, the most prestigious body in France on matters of the French language. In this short book we also have read passages from *The Heart of the Matter* by Graham Greene (who was shortlisted for the Nobel Prize in 1967), from *Kim* and "The White Man's Burden" by Rudyard Kipling (1907 Nobel Prize winner), *A Passage to India* by E. M. Forster (nominated for the Nobel Prize multiple times), as well as from works by two of the greatest English-language writers of all time, Joseph Conrad and George Orwell. These literatures intertwine. The recent well-received novel *The Meursault Investigation* (2013) by Kamel Daoud sheds new light on Albert Camus's classic

The Stranger, but at the same time it can be understood only in relation to Camus's novel. Such works reveal not merely that imperialism left its mark on the literatures of Europe and its (former) colonies, but rather that modern European, African, Caribbean, and Asian literatures emerged from the colonial experience in tandem, as interchanges between peoples who were often inextricably intertwined remade their cultures.

That the view that empire mainly affected the non-European world and not the other way around persisted for so long was itself a symptom of imperialism. Europeans had such faith in their own superiority that they believed that other cultures could only have limited influences on their own. We now know differently. A milestone publication was Edward Said's *Orientalism* (1979), which showed how Europe defined itself against the non-Western (colonial) world. We have since learned the myriad ways in which the imperial experience affected, shaped, and reshaped Europe, which demonstrates again how imperialism was about exchange rather than about a one-way outward projection of Europe. There is the influence of the non-European world on European languages, introducing into the English language words like "punch" and "thug," as we have seen.

European and American screenwriters and directors have turned repeatedly over the years to colonial themes in films like *Lawrence of Arabia* (1962), *The Man Who Would Be King* (1975), *Noirs et Blancs en Couleur* (Black and White in Color, 1976), *Breaker Morant* (1980), *Gandhi* (1982), *A Passage to India* (1984), *Out of Africa* (1985), *Indochine* (1992), *Nirgendwo in Afrika* (Nowhere in Africa, 2001), *Caché* (Hidden, 2005), *Indigènes* (Days of Glory, 2006), and *Loin des Hommes* (Far from Men, 2014), to name just a few. Imperialism found its way into street names in Europe, one study of Paris suggesting that some 275 streets in the city's 20 arrondissements bear names of people or places linked directly to colonies. Brussels, likewise, has numerous streets named after Belgian former colonial officials and colonial heroes. The imperial experience changed food: people go out for a curry in Britain, and tikka masala has just about displaced fish and chips as the national dish. Merguez and couscous are now staples in France, and there are now halal butcher shops in many cities because of the increase in the number of Muslims living in Europe, many of whom trace their origins back to colonial networks of migration.

Indeed, colonialism and its aftermath have transformed populations in Europe. As we have seen, migration to France in the second half of the twentieth century included hundreds of thousands of *pieds noirs* and *harkis* from Algeria from the time of that country's independence in 1962, as well as influxes of Vietnamese, Cambodians, Cameroonians, Moroccans, Tunisians, and other Algerians, among others. "Colonial" immigrants from south Asia, Jamaica, South Africa, Uganda, and many other former colonies have also changed Britain. A significant percentage of Belgium's entire population is now of non-European origin – Turkish, Moroccan, Algerian, or Congolese. Around the time of Suriname's independence in 1975, many Indo-Surinamese migrated to the Netherlands, and there are today nearly as many people of Surinamese origin in the former metropole as there are in Suriname itself. As discussed, the arrival "back home" of nearly 500,000 *retornados* from Africa to Portugal in 1974–1975 increased that country's population by 5 percent.

Many Europeans who had formerly lived and worked in the colonies looked back on the late colonial era as "golden years" before the end of the good times, which highlights how memories of the colonial era reshaped European culture. Once they returned home, many Italian and Belgian former colonial officials believed themselves to be victims – of changed circumstances that came with the end of empire, of history perhaps, or of decolonization – and many felt unwelcome. Some opted for destinations where authoritarianism survived, for example Britons who moved to Portugal during the waning years of the Salazar regime, where they may have felt more comfortable because Portugal continued to hold onto its African colonies. Events at the end of empire often only confirmed former colonials in their convictions, even when it was the colonial situation itself, or poor planning by European administrators, or both, that provoked violent episodes or breakdowns in order. Killings at the time of India and Pakistan's partition and independence in 1947 reinforced the impression among staunch pro-empire supporters that British colonial rule had been a good and a necessary thing. Belgians who had lived and worked in the Belgian Congo and who repatriated to the metropole had little to say at first, perhaps because the prolonged, violent, and embarrassing Congo Crisis was such a clear manifestation of poor planning on the part of the former colonial master. But they, like their British counterparts, ended up looking back on the last years of colonial rule, in their case the whole of the 1950s, through rose-tinted glasses. After 1962 many French former colonials likewise looked back on the 1950s as a golden age.

Although imperialism is now thoroughly discredited, how the colonial era should be taught, remembered, and commemorated is anything but straightforward. A famous French law of 2005, which was later rescinded, required the teaching of positive aspects of France's colonial history in school classrooms. Some Belgians continue to honor Belgium's King Leopold II, but other Belgians have attacked his statues (Figure 9.1). In December 2015 a ceremony that was meant to take place at the foot of a monument to Leopold II in Brussels, to celebrate the one hundred and fiftieth anniversary of his ascent to the throne, was cancelled. The Belgians had erected an identical statue in the Congo's capital in the late 1920s, which Mobutu's government removed in the late 1960s as part of his *recours à l'authenticité*, a movement to emphasize "authentic" African culture and to solidify his hold on power. Congo's government re-erected the statue in 2005, although it came down again after just one day. By contrast, the Republic of Congo – the former French Congo – put up a monument to the explorer Pierre Savorgnan de Brazza in 2006, which remains. Despite Gandhi having

Figure 9.1 Statue of Leopold II in Brussels, Belgium, with wreaths, December 2009. *Source*: Photograph by the author.

been a champion of local self-rule during the colonial era, activists in Ghana recently removed a statue of Gandhi in Accra, decrying his racist attitudes toward black Africans early in his public career. Aside from a few notable exceptions, such as the controversy over a statue to Cecil Rhodes at the University of Oxford, in most of Europe colonial monuments and memorials have been allowed to stand, and streets and squares named after colonial officials remain. Does this signal tacit support in Europe for the ideals and practices of the colonial past?

Such debates about the colonial past vary across Europe. In Italy and Germany there has been little coming to terms with the colonial past. In Italy the evils of colonialism were associated almost exclusively with the country's fascist regime, despite the fact that overseas expansion was part of liberal Italy's drive for legitimation following unification in 1870, and that the period from Italy's takeover of Eritrean territories on the Red Sea to the advent of the fascist regime (some

Empire After Imperialism: 1975–1999 and Beyond

36 years) was much longer than the fascist era (1922–1943) itself. Italians could still see themselves as victims of fascism, *brava gente*, not imperialists. There were few like the scholar Angelo Del Boca who confronted Italy's history of overseas colonialism head-on. In Germany, its Nazi past overshadowed the history of overseas colonies, and it was not until 2004 that Germany apologized for the 1904 genocide in South West Africa. Why was there this longstanding ignorance of the colonial past? One factor is that, after World War II, the Germans and the Italians, like other Europeans, downplayed the colonial past so as to move forward and reconstruct. Although there were many fascist parties elsewhere, it was only in Italy and Germany that fascists came to power, and that story and World War II loomed large. It is also important that both countries lost their colonies at the hands of other European powers – the Treaty of Versailles for Germany and defeat in World War II for Italy – and not as a result of nationalist movements or violent anticolonial wars of liberation, which might have precipitated greater soul searching.

Empire continued to exercise a profound influence on European mentalities well into the postcolonial era, as witnessed by events surrounding the Falkland War. By the late 1970s the United Kingdom had been shedding overseas colonies for three decades. The 1982 Falkland War gave the British something they had not had since 1945: a clear victory. Prime Minister Margaret Thatcher had come to power intent not on achieving parliamentary compromise and building consensus but rather on overcoming economic recession and inflation in Britain, which was a result of the global downturn of the 1970s. Thatcher attempted to do this through a deflationary monetary policy and through budget cuts in education, health, public housing, and other areas of government expenditure, and by lowering taxes to stimulate private economic initiative. Her policies were effective at bringing down inflation and at making Britain much more competitive on the world market, but led to high unemployment. When Labour left power in 1979, unemployment stood at 5.6 percent, but by 1982 it had risen to 12.2 percent and kept increasing to the extent that more than three million workers were out of work. However, the general election of 1983 swept Thatcher back into office. Why? In 1982 the Argentine military had invaded the Falkland Islands, an outpost of the now much reduced British empire in the southernmost reaches of the South Atlantic. Led by Thatcher, the British took back the islands in less than two months in a resounding defeat of Argentina.

We are only beginning to understand how the colonial era and decolonization reshaped European politics and governments. Between 1958 and 1975, colonial conflict led to the overthrow of multiple governments, and not for the first time, as Spain's poor showing in the Rif War had precipitated Primo de Rivera's coup in 1923. In 1958 war in Algeria led to a coup in France that ended the Fourth Republic and returned de Gaulle to power. Belgium's sudden loss of the Congo in 1960 coincided with the beginning of the end of the Belgian unitary state. Portugal's long-lasting colonial wars precipitated the Carnation Revolution of 1974 which overthrew the Estado Novo.

Conclusion

Much work remains to be done to explain the many afterlives of empire. In that sense, this is a conclusion that does not conclude. Whereas we used to refer to decolonization in the past tense, more recent studies show that it has been more complex than we first thought, and that it is ongoing. By 1999 virtually every corner of the formerly colonized world had achieved political independence. Yet, as we have seen, forms of colonialism endured in myriad ways, from changed demographics and cuisine to intractable and fundamental remainders in important realms such as knowledge formation, international relations, and economics. Among the many forces influencing the trajectory of world history over the past century and a half, European overseas colonialism is one of the most significant. In many ways, we continue to live in a world shaped by empire.

Citations

Page	Source
204	"I struggled..." Emma Mashinini, *Strikes Have Followed Me All My Life* (New York: Routledge, 1991), 86.
206	"Madame, they're killing my people." Quoted in "Ghosts of Rwanda [transcript]," at http://www.pbs.org/wgbh/pages/frontline/shows/ghosts/etc/script.html, accessed October 5, 2017.
206	"Steve Thomas." James S. Olson and Randy Roberts, *Where the Domino Fell: America and Vietnam 1945–2010*, 6th ed. (Malden, MA: Wiley Blackwell, 2014), 190–191.
208	"The myth of the guerrilla..." Maria Paula Meneses, "Images Outside the Mirror? Mozambique and Portugal in World History," *Human Architecture: Journal of the Sociology of Self-Knowledge* 10, no. 1 (2012), 121–136 (quotation at 129).
208	"only about one quarter..." Gaiutra Bahadur, *Coolie Woman: The Odyssey of Indenture* (Chicago: University of Chicago Press, 2014), 166; quotation at 172.
212	"The choice of language..." Ngũgĩ wa Thiong'o, *Decolonising the Mind: The Politics of Language in African Literature* (London: James Currey, 1986), 4.
213–4	"While we were learning..." Sékou Touré, "The Political Leader Considered as the Representative of a Culture," in J. Ayo Langley, *Ideologies of Liberation in Black Africa, 1856–1970* (London: Rex Collins, 1979), 607.
214	"It is important to recognize..." Gyan Prakash, "Subaltern Studies as Postcolonial Criticism," *American Historical Review* 99, no. 5 (1994), 1483 and passim.
215	"There is a peculiar way..." Dipesh Chakrabarty, "Provincializing Europe: Postcoloniality and the Critique of History," *Cultural Studies* 6 (1992), 337.

217 "golden age." Elizabeth Buettner, *Europe after Empire: Decolonization, Society, and Culture* (Cambridge: Cambridge University Press, 2016), 39, 456.

Bibliography

Andall, Jacqueline, and Derek Duncan. *Italian Colonialism: Legacy and Memory*. Oxford: Peter Lang, 2005.

Begag, Azouz. *Shantytown Kid*. Translated by Naïma Wolf and Alec G. Hargreaves. Lincoln: University of Nebraska Press, 2007.

Buruma, Ian. *Murder in Amsterdam: Liberal Europe, Islam, and the Limits of Tolerance*. New York: Penguin, 2007.

Chakrabarty, Dipesh. *Provincializing Europe: Postcolonial Thought and Historical Difference*. Princeton: Princeton University Press, 2007.

Davidson, Basil. *The Black Man's Burden: Africa and the Curse of the Nation-State*. New York: Times Books, 1992.

Godwin, Peter. *Mukiwa*. New York: Harper Perennial, 1996.

Ngũgĩ wa Thiong'o. *Decolonising the Mind: The Politics of Language in African Literature*. London: James Currey, 1986.

Nicolaïdis, Kalypso, Berny Sèbe, and Gabrielle Maas, eds. *Echoes of Empire: Memory, Identity and Colonial Legacies*. London: I. B. Tauris, 2015.

Said, Edward. *Orientalism*. New York: Vintage, 1979.

Westad, Odd Arne. *The Global Cold War: Third World Interventions and the Making of Our Times*. New York: Cambridge University Press, 2007.

Index

References to illustrations are in italics, e.g. *16*.

Aba Women's Riots, 121, 125
Abbas, Ferhat, 127
Abbasid caliphate, 7, 8
Abdelaziz, 91
Abdelhafid, 68, 91
Abd el–Kader, 29
Abd el–Krim, 116
Abdul Hamid II, 20, 70, 89
Abdul Mejid, 20
abolitionism, 13, 14, 27–28
Abrahams, Peter, 170
Aceh sultanate, 36, 69
Achebe, Chinua, 78, 215
African National Congress (ANC), 115, 125, 170, 194–195, 204–205
African Party for the Independence of Guinea and Cape Verde, 196
Afrikaners, 114, 169 *see also* Boers; South Africa
Afrique Équatoriale Française (AEF), 62, 74, 118, 119, 126, 145, 147, 165–166, 190
Afrique Occidentale Française (AOF), 59, 62, 74, 98, 118, 121–122, 165–166, 190

Ahmad, Muhammad, 41
Ahmad Shah Qājār, 68
Ahmadu Seku, 38
Alaska, 20, 63
Alexander the Great, 6–7
Alexander II, 21
Algeria, 5, 20, 27, 28–29, *29*, 35, 42, 52, 56, 57, 59, 61, 62, 78, 94–95, 113–114, 120, 127, 139, 145, 154, 160, 165, 167, 168, 184, 185–188, 190–191, 193, 197, 208, 216
    war with France (*see* French–Algerian War)
Al hajj Umar *see* Umar Tal
All-African People's Conference, 168, 184–185
Alleg, Henri, 176, 186
All India Home Rule League, 125, 127
All-India Muslim League *see* Muslim League
Alsace–Lorraine, 18, 59, 119
Ambiguous Adventure (1963), 122
Amery, Leo, 147
Amin, Idi, 208
Amritsar massacre, 110–111, 115, 125

European Overseas Empire, 1879–1999: A Short History, First Edition. Matthew G. Stanard.
© 2018 John Wiley & Sons, Inc. Published 2018 by John Wiley & Sons, Inc.

Index

Anglo–Belgian India Rubber Company, 81
Anglo–German Treaty (1890), 39, 90
Anglo–Indians, 22–23, 138, 156, 197
Anglo–Japanese Treaty (1902), 48
Angola, 1, 24, 39, 42, 63, 73, 164, 185, 196, 203, 208–209, 210
Annam *see* Indochina
anticolonialism *see* resistance
apartheid, 155, 168–170, 177, 194–196, 204–205
Arab–Israeli conflict, 209
Arab–Swahili, 24–25, 37, 40, 54
Argentina, 18, 197, 219
askaris, 93, 101, 104
Atatürk *see* Kemal, Mustafa
Atlee, Clement, 156
Australia, 4, 14, 18, 19, 27, 36, 41, 42, 49, 53, 62, 85, 94, 102, 146, 185, 189, 202, 213
Australia and New Zealand Auxiliary Corps (ANZAC), 94, 99, 104
Austria, 101, 144, 207 *see also* Habsburg empire
Austria–Hungary *see* Habsburg empire
Auteuil, Daniel, 173
Azikiwe, Nnamdi, 127, 162
Azores, 39
Aztec Empire, 26

Babur, 8
Badis, Ben, 127
Bailundo revolt, 73
Baker, Samuel, 24
Bakouba (1952), 153–154
Balfour, Arthur, 96
Balfour Declaration (of 1917), 96, 131, 171
Balfour Declaration (of 1926), 120
Bandung Conference, 159
Bangladesh, 157, 194
Banks, Joseph, 52
Bardo Treaty *see* Treaty of Bardo (1881)
Baring, Evelyn (Lord Cromer), 35, 60
Batavia, 13, 58

Battle of Adowa, 40, 142
Battle of Algiers, 176, 185–186
Battle of Dien Bien Phu, 160–161, 168, 176
Battle of Isandhlwana, 35
Battle of Lepanto, 19, 26
Battle of Majuba Hill, 35
Battle of Omdurman, 41, 48, 148
Battle of Pavia, 26
Battle of the Somme, 100
Battle of Verdun, 98, 100
Baudouin (Belgian king), 164, 192–193
Bechuanaland, 28 *see also* Botswana
Becker, Jérôme, 55–56
Begag, Azouz, 181, 183–184, 197
Belgian Congo, 5, 72, 74, 76, 80, 93, 113, 120–121, 122, 126, 133, 147, 148, 167, 181–182, 184, 185, 192–193, 197, 212, 217
Belgium, 5, 19, 50, 52, 70, 83, 89–90, 93, 96, 101, 102, 125, 144, 164, 181–182, 188–189, 198, 216, 219–220
Belize, 203 *see also* British Honduras
Belloc, Hilaire, 44
A Bend in the River (1979), 135, 215
Benga, Ota, 58
Bengal famine, 147
Berlin Conference, 36–37, 43, 90, 103
Berry, Martha, 34, 51
Besant, Annie, 127
Blixen, Karen, 80
Boali, 81
Bodson, Omer, 46–47
Boers, 11, 27–28, 42, 59, 93, 104, 114 *see also* Afrikaners
Boer War (1899–1902), 48–49, 56, 74, 91, 93, 114
Boisson, Pierre, 145
Bolsheviks, 9, 101, 124, 143–144
Bond, Horace Mann, 162
Bose, S. C., 146
Bosnia–Herzegovina, 35, 88, 89
Botha, Louis, 114
Botswana, 185
Bourguiba, Habib, 185

Index

Boxer Rebellion, 47–48, 70
Brazil, 13, 24, 27
Brazzaville Declaration, 145–146
Britain, 1, 4, 6, 9, 13, 15, 17, 18, 19, 21–23, 25, 27, 30, 35, 36, 37, 40, 41, 48, 50, 52, 60, 61, 70, 74, 77, 78, 83, 89–90, 91, 94, 100, 101, 102, 103, 105, 110, 114, 115–117, 124, 128, 131, 132, 135, 146–147, 156, 163, 166, 169, 170–172, 176–177, 185, 188, 189, 197, 199, 203, 209, 212, 213, 219
British Commonwealth, 166, 168, 189, 199, 212
British East India Company (EIC), 18, 21–23, 27, 59, 109, 202
British Empire League, 60
British Guiana, 27, 69, 84, 111
British Honduras, 27, 69 see also Belize
British India, 22, 33, 62, 74–75, 76, 77, 78, 79, 80, 94, 109–112, 121, 126, 139, 146, 156–158, 202, 214 see also India
British Raj see British India
British South Africa Company (BSAC), 39
Brunei, 203
Buchan, John, 60
Buganda, 24–25, 37, 84 see also Uganda
Bulgaria, 20, 35, 90, 94, 101
Burke, Robert O'Hara, 54
Burma, 36, 62, 135–136, 147, 157
Burmese Days (1934), 135–136
Burton, Richard, 52, 53, 54
Burundi, 205–206, 211 see also Ruanda–Urundi

Cabral, Amílcar, 196
Caetano, Marcello, 196
Caillé, René, 52
California, 19, 49
Camara Laye, 122
Cambodia, 36, 54, 159, 160, 189, 190 see also Indochina
Cameron, Verney Lovett, 54
Cameroon, 39, 76, 93, 102, 119
Camus, Albert, 173, 174, 215–216
Canada, 18, 41, 62, 69, 146, 213

Canisius, Edgar, 39–40
Can Vuong movement, 43
Cape Colony, 27–28, 35, 36, 59, 79, 158 see also South Africa
Cape Verde, 164, 196
capitalism, 2, 49–50, 149
Casement, Roger, 60, 72, 73, 81, 101
caste system, 23
Catherine the Great, 20
Catholicism see Christianity
Cawnpore, 21, 22
Central African Federation (CAF), 166, 167
Césaire, Aimé, 141
Cetshwayo, 35
Ceuta, 116, 183, 203
Ceylon see Sri Lanka
Chad, 119, 145
Chamberlain, Joseph, 84
Chamoun, Camille, 173
Chandernagore, 158
Charles V (Holy Roman Emperor), 26
Charles X (French king), 28
Charmes, Gabriel, 60
"The Chess Players," 109–110, 111
Chiang Kai-shek, 142, 158, 159
China, 1, 2, 13, 14, 15–16, 17, 18, 19, 36, 40, 43, 47–48, 69–70, 77, 83, 84, 92, 99, 101, 102, 106, 120, 138, 142, 147, 181, 190, 203
 1949 communist victory, 159, 182
 Ming dynasty, 7, 8, 99
 Qin dynasty, 7
 Qing dynasty, 3, 8, 15–16, 17, 43, 47–48, 62, 99
 revolution of 1911–12, 120
 Tang dynasty, 7
 Xuantong emperor, 68, 142
 Yuan dynasty, 7
Christianity, 11, 23, 34, 36, 51, 73, 78, 212–213
Churchill, Winston, 60, 109, 111, 118, 127, 146, 149, 156, 157
Church Missionary Society, 37, 51
civilizing mission, 33–34, 51, 68, 117–119, 127–128, 138
Clauzel, Bertrand, 61

Index

Clemenceau, Georges, 101
Climbié (1956), 122, 123, 136
Cochinchina, 27, 36, 59 *see also* Vietnam
code de l'indigénat, 113, 125, 173
Cold War, 124–125, 150, 158, 159, 163, 182, 183, 189–190, 210
Colijn, Hendrikus, 69
colonial administration, 22–23, 67–68, 74–78, 79, 120–121, 133, 163–168, 174
colonial development *see* colonial investment
Colonial Development Act of 1929, 119
Colonial Development and Welfare Act of 1940, 164
Colonial Development and Welfare Act of 1945, 164
colonial education, 75, 121–123
colonial expositions, 140–141, 184
colonial investment, 22, 49–50, 68, 71, 77, 119–120, 124, 133, 163–164
colonialism, definition of, 3–5
colonial knowledge, 22–23, 44, 53, 56, 154, 213–215, 220
colonial taxation, 22, 23, 73, 75, 77, 99, 111, 113, 120, 121, 127, 133, 167
colonial trade, 50, 83–85, 163
Columbus, Christopher, 5, 8, 26, 83
Comité de l'Afrique Française, 60
Comité de l'Asie Française, 60
Comité de Madagascar, 60
Comité du Maroc, 60
communism, 2, 124–125, 150, 156, 158, 170
Comoros, 202–203
Compagnie du Katanga, 44
Comte, Auguste, 51
concessionary companies, 39
Congo *see* Belgian Congo; Congo Free State; Democratic Republic of the Congo; French Congo; Republic of Congo
Congo Free State (CFS), 39–40, 42, 44–47, 55, 63, 71–72, 75–76, 79, 82, 84
Conrad, Joseph, 11, 27, 67, 71, 79, 215

Convention People's Party, 176–177
Cortés, Hernán, 25, 26
Côte d'Ivoire, 25, 122, 136, 165–166, 191, 202, 211
Coty, René, 186
Crémieux Decree, 57, 114
Crimean War (1853–56), 13, 20–21, 56
Cromer, Lord *see* Baring, Evelyn
Cuba, 13, 26, 27, 47, 69
culture and empire, 22–23, 137–141, 154, 201–202, 212, 215–220
Curaçao, 69, 183
Curzon, George, 62, 75
Cyrus (Persian king), 6
Czechoslovakia, 144

Dadié, Bernard, 122, 123, 136
Daman, 158, 164, 196
Damas, Léon, 141
Daoud, Kamel, 215–216
Darius (Persian king), 6
The Dark Child (1953), 122
Darwin, Charles, 51, 57–58
d'Azeglio, Massimo, 27, 123
De Boe, Gérard, 153
de Brazza, Pierre Savorgnan, 52, 217
decolonization, 5, 182–184, 207, 220
Decoux, Jean, 146
Defferre, Gaston, 165
de Gaulle, Charles, 144–145, 183, 186–187, 190–192, 219
de Gobineau, Arthur, 57
Dekker, Eduard Douwes, 73
de Klerk, F.W., 205
Delacroix, Eugène, 138
Delavignette, Robert, 117
Del Boca, Angelo, 219
Democratic Republic of the Congo, 181, 193, 205, 209, 210, 212 *see also* Belgian Congo; Congo Free State
Denmark, 144
Dequae, André, 188
de Rivera, Primo, 219
Dernburg, Bernhard, 74
Déroulède, Paul, 59
The Descent of Man (1871), 52, 58
Diagne, Blaise, 99

diamonds, 28, 35, 42, 49, 61, 84, 120, 133, 169
di Lampedusa, Giuseppe, 153, 154
Dingane, 12
Dingiswayo, 12
disease, 25, 48, 55–56, 75–76, 79, 104, 105, 209
Diu, 158, 164, 196
Djibouti, 40, 203
Dodecanese islands, 89, 102, 147
Domont, J.-M., 136–137
Doudart de Lagrée, Ernest, 54
Doumer, Paul, 36, 68
du Chaillu, Paul, 53
Dulles, John Foster, 162
Dutch East India Company *see* Vereenigde Oostindische Compagnie (VOC)
Dutch East Indies, 13, 27, 36, 58, 63, 73, 74, 75, 81–82, 94, 119, 124, 146, 147, 150, 158–159, 197 *see also* Indonesia
Dutch Guiana, 27, 63, 69, 117, 183 *see also* Suriname
Dyer, Reginald, 110

"Eastern Question," 69–70, 89, 96
Éboué, Félix, 145
École Normale William Ponty, 122
Economic Community of West African States (ECOWAS), 211
Edward VII, 62
Egypt, 19, 23–24, 35, 37, 41, 52, 61, 91, 102, 115–116, 120, 140, 171–172, 210
Eisenhower, Dwight, 172–173
   presidential administration, 160–161, 163
El Hadj Omar *see* Umar Tal
El Mogdad Seck, Bou, 43
El-Mokrani, Mohamed, 29, 42, 114
Emmanuel III, Victor, 147
empire, definition of, 3–4
England *see* Britain
Enlightenment, 13, 57
entente cordiale, 41, 78, 90–91, 144
Equatorial Guinea, 116
Eritrea, 40, 59, 79, 143, 147
État Indépendant du Congo *see* Congo Free State (CFS)

Ethiopia, 40, 43, 54, 69, 142–143, 147, 208, 210, 211
   famine in, 206
European Economic Community, 187, 211, 213
exploration, 52–55
Eyre, Edward John, 54

Faidherbe, Louis, 27, 43
Falkenhayn, Erich, 100
Falkland Islands, 69, 183, 203, 219
Fanon, Frantz, 175, 208
Fashoda crisis, 40–41, 78, 91
Feraoun, Mouloud, 174–175, 187
Ferdinand (Aragonese king), 25, 26
Ferdinand, Franz, 88, 90, 106
Ferry, Jules, 60
films, 54, 80, 153–154, 216
First Indian War of Independence *see* Sepoy Uprising
First World War *see* World War I
Foccart, Jacques, 183
Fonds d'Investissement pour le Développement Économique et Social, 164
forced labor, 39–40, 71–72, 82, 99–100, 167 *see also* slavery
Force Publique, 39–40, 93
Forster, E. M., 118, 131, 134, 215
Fourah Bay College, 51, 122
Françafrique, 183, 210
France, 3, 4, 13, 15, 17, 20, 21, 27, 28–29, 35, 37, 40–41, 49, 50, 52, 56, 57, 58, 59, 60, 61, 83–84, 87, 89–90, 91, 95, 96–98, 100, 101, 102, 104, 116, 120, 121, 124, 132, 144, 147, 159–161, 163, 164–165, 168, 170–172, 177, 184, 188, 197, 198, 202, 210, 216
Fifth Republic, 186
Fourth Republic, 154, 159, 186, 219
Free French, 144–146, 150, 186
French Second Empire, 57, 61 (*see also* Napoleon III)
French Second Republic, 57
   revolution of 1789, 14, 51, 61
   revolution of 1830, 28

France (cont'd)
  Third Republic, 18, 51, 57, 77, 96, 145
  Vichy regime, 145–146, 150
  war with Algeria (see French–Algerian War)
Francophonie, 212
Franco–Prussian War (1870–71), 59, 90
French–Algerian War (1954–62), 173–176, 177, 183, 185–188, 190, 208
French Community, 190
French Congo, 79, 148, 217 see also Republic of Congo
French Guiana, 27, 42, 63, 69, 183, 203
French Guinea, 122, 163, 191 see also Guinea
French Polynesia, 183, 203
French Somaliland, 41
French Union, 164–165, 167, 190
Frente de Libertação de Moçambique (FRELIMO), 196, 207
Front de Libération Nationale (FLN), 174–176, 185–188, 193
Fuad (Egyptian king), 115

Gabon, 47, 75, 118
Gaffarel, Paul, 60
Galton, Francis, 57
the Gambia, 62, 74
Gandhi, Mohandas, 80, 109, 110, 111–112, *112*, 126–127, 156–157, 206, 217–218
Garanganja Kingdom, 44–45
Garner, Richard Lynch, 75
Garnier, Francis, 54
Gauguin, Paul, 75, 117
Geeraerts, Jef, 137
gender *see* sex
Generación del '98, 116, 138
Genghis Khan, 7
Geoffroy Saint-Hilaire, Albert, 58
geographical societies, 51–53
George V, 68, 75
Georgia (U.S. state), 34
German East Africa, 73, 84, 93, 102
German East Africa Company, 37, 38, 84
German New Guinea, 94, 102
German Samoa, 94, 102

German South West Africa, 72–73, 84, 93, 103, 219 see also Namibia; South West Africa
and the Holocaust, 148
Germany, 9, 13, 18, 23, 27, 36–37, 49, 50, 57, 58, 59, 60, 63, 69, 70, 78, 88–90, 91, 93–95, 96, 100, 101, 104, 114, 118, 119, 126, 128, 132, 144–145, 147, 186, 189, 198, 207, 218–219
  Nazi regime, 124, 142, 144, 148, 155, 169
  unification of, 13, 18, 27, 210
Gesellschaft für Deutsche Kolonisation *see* Society for German Colonization
Ghana, 154, 162, 168, 176–177, 184, 190, 192, 211 see also Gold Coast
Giles, Ernest, 53
globalization, 1, 2, 83–85
Goa, 158, 164, 168, 196
gold, 8, 19, 26, 39, 42, 48, 49, 84, 120, 169–170
Gold Coast, 25, 38, 62, 74, 120, 133, 176–177 see also Ghana
Golden Stool, 38
Gordon, Charles, 24
Government of India Act (1935), 120, 126
Graves, Robert, 117
Graziani, Rodolfo, 125
Great Britain *see* Britain
Great Depression, 124, 125, 132–134, 142, 151
Greater East Asia Co-Prosperity Sphere, 142, 147
Great Trek, 28, 169
Greco–Turkish War (1919–22), 101–102, 105
Greece, 20, 70, 89–90, 95, 101–102, 103, 147
Greene, Graham, 137, 215
Grierson, George, 80
Guadeloupe, 61, 69, 165
Guam, 183, 203
Guèye, Lamine, 165
Guinea, 184, 191, 213 see also French Guinea
Guinea-Bissau, 196 see also Portuguese Guinea
Guyana, 208 see also British Guiana

Habsburg empire, 9, 18, 35, 49, 68–70, 88–90, 91, 94, 100
Habyarimana, Juvenal, 205
Hagenbeck, Carl, 58
Haggard, H. Rider, 80–81
Haiti, 13, 61
Hammurabi, 6
Hanoi, 67, 69, 77
harkis, 168, 187–188, 197, 216
Harris, Alice Seeley, 72
Hatta, Mohammad, 150
Hawai'i, 47, 63, 147
The Heart of Africa, (1874), 25
Heart of Darkness (1902), 11, 67, 71
The Heart of the Matter (1948), 137, 215
Hergé, 122
Hertzog, J. B. M., 114
Herzl, Theodor, 96
Hinden, Rita, 119
Hind Swaraj (1909), 111
Hinduism, 23
historiography of imperialism, 2, 5, 206, 207–208, 214–216, 219 *see also* colonial knowledge
Hitler, Adolf, 124, 126–127, 144
Hoang Cao Khai, 43
Hobson, J. A., 49, 60, 92
Ho Chi Minh, 102, 115, 125, 160, 189, 206
Hodgson, Frederick, 38
Holocaust, 148, 171
"home rule," 43, 89, 101, 146
Hong Kong, 70, 203
Hong Xiuquan, 15, 17
Hornemann, Friedrich, 52
Houphouët-Boigny, Félix, 165–166, 191, 193
human zoos, 58, 184
Hungary, 7, 101, 172, 207
"Hun speech," 47
hunting, 71, 72, 75, 118, 137
Hussein (sharif of Mecca), 95
Huxley, Elspeth, 80, 119

Idris (Libyan king), 171
Ifni, 164
Imperial British East Africa Company (IBEAC), 37, 84
Imperial Federation League, 60
imperialism
  causes, 49–61
  definition of, 4
Imperial South Africa Association, 60
indentured labor, 42, 80, 82, 208
India, 1, 6, 21–23, 27, 35, 36, 37, 43, 53, 56, 59, 62, 68, 73, 82, 84, 109–112, 133, 135, 138, 182, 194, 196, 209, 212, 214–215 *see also* British India
  partition, 156–157, 162, 177, 194, 208, 217
Indian Army, 23, 99, 146, 156, 168 *see also* sepoys
Indian National Congress, 43, 73, 110–111, 125, 146
Indian Rebellion of 1857 *see* Sepoy Uprising
Indochina, 36, 50, 56, 59, 61, 63, 67–68, 69, 119, 146, 150, 155, 159–162, 176, 185, 186
Indochinese Communist Party, 160
Indonesia, 158–159, 168, 182, 183, 189, 197, 203 *see also* Dutch East Indies
Indo–Pakistani War of 1971, 157
industrialization, 16–17, 19, 21, 30, 40, 44, 49, 106
The Influence of Sea Power on History, 37
Iran, 68, 171, 172, 190, 210
Iraq, 6, 7, 95, 116, 120, 172
Ireland, 9, 43, 50, 89, 101, 104–105
Irish War of Independence (1919–21), 101
Isabella (Castilian queen), 25, 26
Islam, 23, 38, 94–95, 190
Ismail Pasha, 24
Israel, 171, 172, 190 *see also* Palestine
Istiqlal party, 171
Istituto Coloniale Italiano, 60
Italian Somaliland, 4, 59, 79, 147
Italo–Turkish War (1911–12), 89, 90, 102
Italy, 35, 40, 49, 56, 58, 59, 60, 63, 76, 88, 89, 91, 93, 95, 96, 99, 101, 102, 115, 116, 123, 126, 144, 147, 185, 218
  fascist regime, 124, 128, 142–143, 218–219
  unification of, 13, 18, 27, 218
  war against Ethiopia (1935–1936), 142–143, 208

Index

Itzcóatl, 8
Ivory Coast *see* Côte d'Ivoire

Jacques, Jules, 42
Jallianwala Bagh *see* Amritsar massacre
Jameson, L. S., 48
Jameson raid, 48
Japan, 1, 7, 16–17, 30, 35, 40, 48, 68,
    70–71, 78, 83, 89–90, 93–94, 101,
    102, 105, 141–142, 144, 146–147,
    149–150, 189
  Meiji Restoration, 16, 19, 142
  Tokugawa shogunate, 16
jihad, 94–95
Jinnah, Muhammad Ali, 111–112, 127,
    156–157
Jolly, Sohan Singh, 201
Jünger, Ernst, 87–88, 99

Kagame, Paul, 206
Kane, Cheikh Hamidou, 122
Karikal, 158
Kemal, Mustafa, 102, 103
Kennan, George, 147
Kenya, 74, 80, 93, 113, 117, 155, 168,
    177, 194
Khama, Seretse, 185
Khrushchev, Nikita, 181
Kim (1901), 43, 78, 122, 215
Kimberly, 28, 35, 49, 61
King Solomon's Mines (1885),
    80–81
Kipling, Rudyard, 33–34, 43–51, 55, 75,
    78, 110, 122, 215
Kitchener, Horatio, 40–41, 48
Knox, Robert, 57
Korea, 5, 15, 40, 68–69, 70–71, 159
  North Korea, 160, 189
  South Korea, 211
Korean War (1950–53), 159
Kublai Khan, 7
Kuwait, 95

La Force noire (1910), 98
Laing, Alexander Gordon, 52
La mise en valeur des colonies francaises
    (1923), 119

language, 26–27, 34, 43, 54, 75, 83, 91,
    114, 123, 138–141, 190, 194, 202,
    209, 212, 215–216
Laos, 36, 159, 160, 189 *see also* Indochina
Lavigerie, Charles, 51
Lawrence, T. E., 95
Laye, Camara *see* Camara Laye
League of Coloured Peoples, 125
League of Nations, 40, 103–104, 143, 182
  mandates, 102–104, 132, 148, 171, 177,
    188, 196
Lebanon, 95, 101, 170, 172–173, 190
Leichhardt, Ludwig, 54
Lenin, Vladimir, 49, 102, 124, 127
Leopold II, 39, 43, 44, 50, 55, 63, 71–72,
    73, 79, 81, 82, 84, 192, 217
Leroy–Beaulieu, Paul, 60
Les paysans noirs (1931), 117–118
Lever Brothers, 134
Liberia, 69
Libya, 6, 76, 89, 99, 115, 125, 147, 171, 209
Ligue de Défense de la Race Nègre, 126
Linlithgow (Victor Hope), 147
Livingstone, David, 53
Lloyd George, David, 101
Lobengula, 39
Locke, John, 57
loi-cadre of 1956, 165–166
Lomé Convention (1975), 211
London Missionary Society, 53
Lugard, Frederick, 37, 38, 74
Lumumba, Patrice, 181–182, 185, 193
Luxembourg, 144
Luytens, Edwin, 76

Macartney, George, 14
Macau, 3, 63, 203
Macaulay, Herbert, 127
MacMahon, Henry, 95
Macmillan, Harold, 187, 198
Madagascar, 62, 74, 76, 145, 155, 165
Madeira, 39
Magellan, Ferdinand, 26, 28
Mahan, Alfred Thayer, 37
Maharero, Samuel, 73
Mahdi *see* Ahmad, Muhammad
Mahdist State, 41, 47

230

Index

Mahfouz, Naguib, 172, 215
Maine (boat), 47
Maji Maji revolt, 73
Makana Nxele, 11, 15, 27
Malan, D. F., 169
Malaya (Malaysia), 62, 120, 133, 156, 158, 168
Mali empire, 7
Mandela, Nelson, 11, 194–195, *195*, 204–205, 206
Manduau, Édouard, 71–72, 73
Mangin, Charles, 98
Mansa Musa, 7–8
Mao Zedong, 142, 159
Maran, René, 141
Marchand, Jean-Baptiste, 40–41, 98
Marti, José, 47
Martinique, 61, 69, 165
Marxist socialism, 215
Mashinini, Emma, 204
Massu, Jacques, 186
Mathieu, Jules, 119
Mau Mau uprising, 155, 177
Mauritius, 84, 182–183
Max Havelaar (1860), 73
Maximilian I, 61
Mayotte, 183, 203
Mbop Mabiinc maMbeky, 153
McKinley, William, 88
medicine, 44, 55–56, 75–76, 120–121
Mehmed V, 68, 94
Melilla, 116, 183, 203
Menelik II, 40, 43, 68, 142
Mengistu, Haile Mariam, 210
Messali Hadj, Ahmed Ben, 127, 174
métissage, 58, 82, 113–114, 134–135, 173
see also race
The *Meursault Investigation* (2013), 215–216
Mexican–American War (1846–48), 61
Mexico, 17, 26
Mfecane, 12, 28
Mhlakaza, 11–12
Michelet, Jules, 214
migration, 18, 41–42, 58–59, 62, 79–80, 83–84, 96–99, 112–113, 116–117, 157, 168, 170, 194, 197–198, 208, 216–217

Mine Boy (1946), 170
Ming dynasty *see* China
miscegenation *see métissage*
missionaries, 34, 36, 37, 43, 51, 75, 77–78, 118, 121–122, 138, 162–163
mission civilisatrice see civilizing mission
Mobutu Sese Seko (Joseph-Désiré Mobutu), 182, 210, 217
Moctezuma I, 8
modernity, 24, 76, 139, 190
modernization *see* modernity
Mohammed V, 171, 185
Mongol empire, 7
Monroe Doctrine, 17, 61
Montenegro, 35, 90
Moody, Harold, 125
Morel, Edmund Dene, 60, 72, 103
Morocco, 68, 76, 91–92, 116, 145, 165, 171, 184, 185, 197
  first and second Moroccan crises, 91–92
Moshoeshoe, 42
Mossadegh, Mohammad, 171
Mouhot, Henri, 54
Mountbatten, Louis, 157
Mouvement National Congolais (MNC), 181
Mozambique, 1, 39, 63, 73, 99–100, 164, 196, 203, 207–208
Msiri, 44–47
Mugabe, Robert, 204, 208
Mughal Empire, 8–9, 14, 21–22, 202
Muhammad Ali (khedive of Egypt), 23–24
Mukhtar, Omar, 99, 125–126, *126*
Multatuli *see* Dekker, Eduard Douwes
Munza, 25
Murchison, Roderick, 52
Muscat, 25
Muslim League, 73, 111, 127, 156
Mussolini, Benito, 126–127, 142–143, 147
Mutesa I, 25, 37, 43

Naipaul, V. S., 135, 215
Namibia, 205 *see also* German South West Africa; South West Africa
Napoleon Bonaparte, 3, 9, 17, 61

Napoleon III, 4, 18, 27, 57, 61
Nasser, Gamal Abdel, 172, 190, 206
Natal, 35, 111
nationalism, 17, 19, 20, 40, 41, 51, 58,
　　59–60, 62, 69–70, 84, 89, 92, 101,
　　102, 111, 124, 126–128, 132, 150,
　　160, 185, 193, 214–215
Négritude, 141
Nehru, Jawaharlal, 111–112, *112*, 124,
　　127, 156–157, 182
neocolonialism, 183, 210–213
　　definition of, 5
Neo Destour party, 171, 185
Netherlands, 27, 50, 63, 75, 82, 83, 94, 128,
　　144, 154, 158–159, 164, 197, 217
New Caledonia, 42, 79, 100, 203
New Guinea, 197 *see also* Papua New
　　Guinea; Western New Guinea
New Imperialism, definition of, 5
Newton, Isaac, 57
New Zealand, 14, 27, 36, 62, 94, 99, 102,
　　146, 189
Ngũgĩ wa Thiong'o, 78, 122, 123, 201,
　　212, 213
Ngundeng, Guek, 116
Nicholas II, 68, 70, 89
Niger, 185
Nigeria, 6, 25, 38, 39, 62, 74, 78, 99, 121,
　　125, 127, 192, 194, 209, 212
　　Biafran War (1967–70), 194, 207, 209
Nixon, Richard, 189
Njango, Donga, 75
Nkrumah, Kwame, 162, 176–177, 184, 206
Non–Aligned Movement (NAM), 183
non-cooperation movement, 111, 125
Nongqawuse, 11–12, 27
Northern Nigeria *see* Nigeria
Northern Rhodesia, 39, 166 *see also*
　　Rhodesia; Zambia
North Korea *see* Korea
North Vietnam *see* Vietnam
Norway, 144
Ntaryamira, Cyprien, 206
Nwose, 99
Nyasaland, 74, 113, 166

oil (petroleum), 120, 171, 190, 194
Oman, 25, 170

On the Origin of Species (1859), 51, 58
"open door" policy, 40, 70
opium wars, 15, 19, 24
Orange Free State, 28, 48
Organisation Armée Secrète (OAS),
　　187, 198
Orientalism, 138–140
Orientalism (1979), 216
Orlando, Vittorio, 101
Orwell, George, 135–136, 151, 215
Ottoman empire, 2, 8, 13, 14, 18, 19–20,
　　23, 35, 62, 68–70, 88–90, 91, 94–95,
　　100, 101–102, 104, 209 *see also*
　　Turkey
"An Outpost of Progress," 79

Pakistan, 1, 157, 172, 182, 194, 210 *see also*
　　British India
Palace Walk (1956), 172, 215
Palestine, 9, 62, 95–96, 101, 131, 148, 171,
　　209 *see also* Israel
Pan–African Congress, 43
Pan–Africanist Congress (PAC), 170,
　　194, 205
Panda Farnana, Paul, 125
Papua New Guinea, 202
Park, Mungo, 52
parti colonial, 60
Parti Démocratique de Guinée
　　(PDG), 191
Parti Populaire Algérien (PPA), 127, 174
A Passage to India (1924), 118, 123,
　　134–135, 137, 215
Peace of Paris, 101–104, 141
Peace of Vereeniging, 48, 74
Peel Commission, 131–132
penal colonies, 42, 168
Pères Blancs *see* White Fathers
Perham, Margery, 119
Perry, Matthew, 16, 17
Pétain, Philippe, 145
Peters, Carl, 37, 52, 60
Peter the Great, 20
Pflimlin, Pierre, 186
Phan Đinh Phùng, 43
Philippines, 25–26, 27, 28, 47, 63, 69, 74,
　　146, 147, 149, 158, 185
Picasso, Pablo, 138

pieds noirs, 184, 186–188, 197, 198, 216
Pitcher, D. G., 80
Pizarro, Francisco, 25
plantations, 34, 77, 80, 82, 117, 133, 134, 167
Platt Amendment, 69
"Poème à Mon Frère Blanc," 141, 215
Poland, 7, 101, 144, 147, 207
Pompidou, Georges, 183
Pondicherry, 158
Portugal, 3, 13, 24, 39, 60, 73, 96, 101, 102, 124–125, 128, 154, 164, 167, 177, 186, 188, 196–197, 202, 203, 207–208, 209, 217, 220
    Estado Novo, 118, 124–125, 164, 220
Portuguese Guinea, 1, 39, 63, 164, 196, 208–209 *see also* Guinea–Bissau
postcolonialism, 202, 207–208, 210–220
    definition of, 6
Powell, Enoch, 197
Premchand, Munshi, 109–110, 111
Primrose League, 60
Protestantism *see* Christianity
Prussia, 18
Puerto Rico, 26, 47, 183

Qadiriyya brotherhood, 24
Qianlong emperor, 14
Qingdao, 70, 94
Qing dynasty *see* China
Qin Shihuangdi, 7
The Question (1958), 176, 186
Quit India movement, 146
quốc ngữ, 75

Raboisson, abbé, 60
race, 33, 56–58, 68, 81–82, 85, 92, 113, 114, 134–135, 148, 150, 166–167, 168–169, 170, 194, 198 *see also* racism
racism, 33, 56–58, 68, 136, 142, 150, 155, 166–167, 168–170 *see also* scientific racism
railroads, 19, 21, 22, 40, 43, 52, 69, 70, 71, 77, 83, 84, 111, 118, 119–120, 165, 191, 209
Rand Rebellion, 115

Rassemblement Démocratique Africain (RDA), 165, 191
Red Rubber (1906), 72
Remarque, Erich Maria, 117
Republic of Congo, 217 *see also* French Congo
Reshid Mustafa Pasha, 20
resistance, 42–43, 44–48, 72–73, 89, 99–100, 110–111, 115–116, 121, 125–128, 133, 143, 146, 148, 150, 155–162, 168, 170–178, 182, 184–193, 194–195, 196, 203–205
Resistência Nacional Moçambicana (RENAMO), 196
retornados, 197, 217
Réunion, 61, 80, 183
revolutions of 1848, 17
Reza Pahlavi, Mohammad, 171
Reza Shah Pahlavi, 171
Rhodes, Cecil, 28, 39, 48, 50, 60, 84, 218
Rhodesia, 28, 74, 166, 177, 185, 196, 197, 198–199, 203–204
Rif War (1920s), 116, 219
The River Between (1965), 78, 122
Rivonia Trial, 195
Robben Island, 11
Roman empire, 3, 7, 103, 149
Romania, 20, 35, 101, 207
Roman republic, 4
Roosevelt, Franklin, 127, 149
Ross, Ronald, 5
Roudaire, François Élie, 52
Royal Geographical Society, 52
Royal Netherlands East Indies Army, 158, 168
Royal Niger Company, 38
Ruanda–Urundi, 93, 104
rubber, 39, 42, 69, 71–72, 81, 82, 84, 85, 120, 131
Russia, 9, 13, 14, 17, 19, 20–21, 23, 30, 33, 36, 40, 49, 69–70, 78, 83, 84–85, 88–90, 91, 100, 101, 104, 106, 120, 124, 143–144, 149, 163, 171–172, 181, 188, 190, 207, 210
    Bolshevik revolution, 101, 120
    Civil War (1917–1922), 101, 105, 106, 124, 207

Index

Russo–Japanese War (1904–05), 70, 78, 88, 125
Russo–Polish War (1919–20), 104, 106
Russo–Turkish War (1877–78), 20, 35
Rwanda, 205–206, 211 *see also* Ruanda–Urundi

Safavid empire, 8
Sagar, G. S., 201
Said, Edward, 216
Saint–Domingue *see* Haiti
Saint Laurent, Yves, 173
Saint Martin, 69
Saint Pierre and Miquelon, 69, 183
Salazar, António, 118, 124–125, 164, 196
Salt March, 110, 111
São Tomé and Príncipe, 164
Sarhili, 12
Sarraut, Albert, 119, 124
sati, 23, 214
satyagraha, 112
Schnee, Heinrich, 93
Schumpeter, Joseph, 60
Schweinfurth, Georg, 25
science, 51–52, 56–58
scientific racism, 56–58, 82, 134
Scotland, 9, 52, 162
Second World War *see* World War II
Senegal, 27, 43, 52, 58, 61, 98, 120, 122, 145, 165
Senghor, Léopold Sédar, 141, 166, 193, 215
Sen, Surya, 112
sepoys, 21–22, 139, 202
Sepoy Uprising, 21–23, *22*, 36, 42, 61, 134, 202, 214
Serbia, 20, 35, 88, 90, 104
Serra, Junípero, 26
Sétif massacre, 155, 174
settler colonialism, 29, 72–73, 112–115, 131–132, 173
 definition of, 4–5
Seven Years' War (1756–63), 13
sex, 68, 80–83, 85, 114, 132, 137, 169
Seyyid Said, 25, 54
Shah Jahan, 9

Shaka Zulu, 12
Shantytown Kid (2007), 181
Sharpeville massacre, 194
"Shooting an Elephant," 135–136
Siam, 36
Sierra Leone, 62, 74, 120, 122, 133, 137
Sikhism, 201–202
Singapore, 146
Sino–French War (1884–85), 36
Sino–Japanese War, First (1894–95), 36, 70
Sino–Japanese War, Second (1931–45), 141–142
Sint Maarten, 69, 183
slavery, 8, 13, 14, 17, 42, 56–57, 80 *see also* forced labor
slave trade, 8, 13, 18, 24, 25, 40, 53, 85
Smith, Ian, 198–199, 203
Smuts, Jan, 114, 168
social Darwinism, 57–68, 92
Sociedade de Geografia de Lisboa, 60
Société de Géographie, 52
Society for German Colonization, 37, 60
Somalia, 6 *see also* French Somaliland; Italian Somaliland
Soustelle, Jacques, 174
 Soustelle Plan, 164, 174
South Africa, 11, 52, 61, 74, 84, 93, 102, 111, 114–115, 120, 146, 168–170, 177, 194–196, 197, 199, 203–205
 see also Cape Colony
South African Native National Congress (SANNC) *see* African National Congress
South African War *see* Boer War
Southern Nigeria *see* Nigeria
Southern Rhodesia, 39, 166, 177, 198–199 *see also* Rhodesia; Zimbabwe
South Korea *see* Korea
South Sudan, 40, 209 *see also* Sudan
South Vietnam *see* Vietnam
South West Africa, 102, 177, 196, 203–205 *see also* German South West Africa; Namibia
Soviet Union *see* Russia

spahis, 97, 139, 160
Spain, 19, 25–26, 27, 28, 47, 116, 117, 123, 128, 138, 164, 188, 197, 207, 209–210
Spanish–American War (1898), 26, 47, 138
Spanish empire, 8, 25–26
Speke, John Hanning, 52, 53, 54
Spencer, Herbert, 58, 92
Sri Lanka, 158
Stairs, William Grant, 44–47
Stalin, Joseph, 106, 124, 149
Stanley, Henry Morton, 37, 43, 50, 52, 53, 54, 71
Statute of Westminster (1931), 120, 166
Storm of Steel (1920), 87
Strikes Have Followed Me All My Life (1989), 204
Sturt, Charles, 53
Sudan, 37, 116, 119, 209 *see also* South Sudan
Suez Canal, 19, 24, 35, 37, 41, 83, 143, 172
Suez crisis, 171–173, 182, 190
Suharto, 197
Suhrawardy, Huseyn Shaheed, 147
Sujaria, 80
Sukarno, 150
Sundiata, 7
Sun Yat-sen, 70
Suriname, 63, 183, 197, 216–217 *see also* Dutch Guiana
Sykes–Picot Agreement, 95–96, 101, 209
Syria, 6, 95, 101, 116, 127, 145, 170, 172, 190, 209

Tabora (Tabor), 25, 54, 55, 93
Taiping Rebellion, 13, 15, 30
Taiwan, 70, 159, 188
Tamerlane, 7, 8
Tanganyika, 117 *see also* German East Africa; Tanzania
Tanzania, 211 *see also* German East Africa; Tanganyika
Tanzimat, 20, 30
technology, 12, 19, 43–44, 62, 139, 164
Teitgen, Paul, 176
Tenochtitlan, 26

Thatcher, Margaret, 219
Things Fall Apart (1958), 78, 215
Tijaniyya brotherhood, 24
Timor–Leste, 164, 203
Tintin in the Congo (1930–31), 122–123
Tippu Tip, 43, 54, 84
tirailleurs sénégalais, 27, 98, 100, 104, 105
Togoland, 39, 93, 102
Tombeur, Charles, 93
Tonkin, 36, 43, 160 *see also* Vietnam
Touré, Ahmed Sékou, 191, 193, 213–214
Touré, Samori, 38, 43, 47
Toyotomi Hideyoshi, 16
Transvaal, 28, 35, 48, 49
Treaty of Bardo (1881), 35, 44
Treaty of Berlin (1878), 35
Treaty of Brest–Litovsk (1918), 106
Treaty of Lausanne (1923), 102
Treaty of Sèvres (1920), 101
Treaty of Shimonoseki (1895), 40
Treaty of Tianjin (1885), 36
Treaty of Ucciali (Wuchale) (1889), 40
Treaty of Versailles (1919), 90, 102, 103–104, 106, 118, 124, 144, 148, 219
Trial, Georges, 118
Trinidad and Tobago, 69, 120
Triple Alliance, 88–89, 91–92, 93
Triple Entente, 88–89, 91–92
Truman Doctrine, 124, 156
Truman, Harry, 156, 159
Tshibumba Kanda–Matulu, 72
Tucholsky, Kurt, 117
Tunisia, 35, 44, 52, 62, 91, 127, 147, 165, 171, 197
Turkey, 101–103, 105, 172 *see also* Ottoman Empire

Uganda, 74, 93, 205, 208 *see also* Buganda
uitlanders, 48
Ujiji, 25, 53, 54
Ukraine, 210
Umar Tal, 24, 38, 214
Umayyad caliphate, 7
Umkhonto we Sizwe, 194–195

Uncle Tom's Cabin (1852), 17
Unilateral Declaration of Independence, 177, 198–199, 203
Union Coloniale Française, 60
Union of South Africa *see* South Africa
United Arab Republic (UAR), 172
United Gold Coast Convention (UGCC), 176
United Kingdom *see* Britain
United Nations, 1, 6, 104, 145, 148, 164, 171, 175, 203, 213
   and decolonization, 148–149, 159, 181–182, 188, 191
   Special Committee on Non-Self-Governing Territories, 188, 203
   trust territories, 104, 167, 185, 188
United States, 3, 13, 17, 18, 19, 20, 26, 30, 40, 41, 43, 47, 49, 58, 59, 61, 62, 63, 69, 74, 84, 99, 100, 105–106, 113, 116, 128, 138, 145, 147, 149–150, 155, 158, 160–162, 163, 166, 171–173, 175, 176, 181, 183, 185, 188, 189–190, 209, 210
   civil war (1861–65), 13, 15, 17, 21, 24, 56
   war in Vietnam, 161–162, 189–190, 206

Vacher de Lapouge, Georges, 57
van Gogh, Vincent, 138
van Heutsz, J. B., 69
Vereenigde Oostindische Compagnie (VOC), 18, 27
Verlaine, Paul, 75
Vernichtungsbefehl, 73, 148
Victoria (British queen and empress), 3, 22
Victoria League, 60
Viet Minh, 188, 206
Vietnam, 27, 36, 43, 75, 78, 116, 120, 121, 127, 138, 150, 159–162, 168, 173, 175, 177, 188, 208, 210, 213 *see also* Indochina
   American war in, 189–190
   North Vietnam, 161, 168, 189–190, 198
   South Vietnam, 161, 189–190, 198, 206
Vietnamese Workers' Party, 125, 162
villages indigènes see human zoos

Virginia (U.S. state), 4
Virgin Islands, 183
Völkerschauen see human zoos
von Bismarck, Otto, 18, 36, 60
von Lettow-Vorbeck, Paul, 93, 101, 104
von Metternich, Klemens, 17
von Trotha, Lothar, 73, 148
Vorster, B. J., 204

Wadström, C. B., 55
Wafd Party, 102, 115
Wales, 9
Wavell, Archibald, 157
Western New Guinea, 183, 189 *see also* New Guinea
White Fathers, 37, 51
"The White Man's Burden," 33, 215
Wilhelm II, 37, 47, 68, 78, 91
Williams, George Washington, 72
Wilson, Woodrow, 101, 102, 103, 106, 124, 127
Wissman, Hermann, 52
World War I, 40, 44, 84, 87–100, 104–106, 110, 112, 113, 117, 119, 124, 125, 141, 144, 150, 207, 209
World War II, 3, 85, 121, 122, 144–151, 155, 169, 171, 173–174, 184, 186, 189, 210, 219
The Wretched of the Earth (1961), 175, 208
Wylie, 54

Yaa Asantewaa, 38
Yaoundé Conference, 211
Yen Bay Mutiny, 116, 126
Young Turk revolt, 70, 89
Yugoslavia, 210

Zaghloul, Sa'd, 115
Zambia, 166
Zanzibar, 25
Zimbabwe, 166, 204, 208, 209 *see also* Rhodesia; Southern Rhodesia
Zimbabwe African National Union, 204
Zionism, 96
Zululand, 35